Sailing
Ships

Valley
July 6, 2002

DANIEL ESCHEN
41 VERNON DRIVE
SCARSDALE, N. Y.

W9-CCY-475

Sailing Ships

BY
ATTILIO CUCARI

FULL-COLOR ILLUSTRATIONS
Guido Canestrari

SIENA COLLEGE LIBRARY

RAND McNALLY & COMPANY
CHICAGO
NEW YORK
SAN FRANCISCO

Copyright © 1976
by Europa Verlag

Copyright © 1976
by Arnoldo Mondadori Editore S.p.A., Milano

English translation copyright © 1977
by Arnoldo Mondadori Editore S.p.A., Milano

All rights reserved
including the right of reproduction in whole or in part in any form

Printed in Italy
by Officine Grafiche di Arnoldo Mondadori Editore, Verona

Published in U.S.A., 1978
by Rand McNally & Company, Chicago, Ill.

Library of Congress Catalog Card No. 77-88443
ISBN: 0-528-88172-8

Contents

Introduction

For thousands of years the ship has been one of man's tools for mastering the world about him, a vehicle of exploration and discovery and a means of transport. But the ship has also been a testimony to man's faith in his ability to meet and conquer the challenges of the sea, and for many it has been a declaration of love for the sea. One could write endlessly about ships by citing statistics from innumerable sources, but the world of sailing should not be summed up in a dry and schematic outline of names and dates and events. Writing about sailing ships and the sea is more like an exploration, breathtaking at times, of a world that has been intimately connected with the evolution and development of our civilization.

One obstacle to a systematic study of the sailing ship is the lack of early source materials and detailed information. Almost until the end of the 18th century, there were no rules or regulations for shipbuilding. The art was in the hands of master craftsmen who handed on their tradition orally and by example, so that much of our knowledge of earlier techniques is inferential. Despite the wealth of material in naval museums around the world, there is a dearth of written evidence from before the middle of the 17th century.

The sailing ship is perhaps the most exciting ship of all. For at least ten centuries, if not more, the sailing vessel was synonymous with the idea of the sea. And the great sailing ships have a fascination all their own—the ships that first set out against the open sea, challenging unknown dangers in an uncharted world. These were the first ships in which men learned to sail against the wind, anticipating by some centuries the same principle that would later make air flight possible.

The cog was the first sailboat to be used both for merchant transport and for combat. The subsequent development of sailing craft, with successive improvements and technical changes in the hull, armament, and navigational instruments; the changing life of the crews; as well as the shifts in the functions of ships, reflect some of the major developments in man's history over the past millennium. The story of sail takes us along the routes of Columbus and Magellan, in the wake of the galleons of the Spanish Armada, toward the exotic lands of Polynesia in the track of Captain Cook, and to Cape Horn, the guardian of the southern seas. By the time the steamship arrived, the sailing vessel had already achieved all it was called upon to do.

The present volume, which covers almost seven centuries of naval history, is an attempt to outline the great adventure of sail. Because of the vastness of the material, not all of the ships are considered in the same detail. Four sectional drawings are given of only those ships that seem especially important for technical or historical reasons. These drawings are intended to give an idea of the main lines of the vessel's structure and are not meant for model builders. When it has been impossible to establish the launching date of a particular ship reference is made to a specific event, its presence in a particular battle, for example. Otherwise the dating is based on construction technique, materials employed, and other inferential data.

The evolution of the sailing ship reflects the evolution of man's relationship to the open sea. For those who love sailing, it is worthwhile to try to visit any of the surviving great sailing ships that are still used in naval training academies or the few that have been rebuilt and restored and are maintained as floating maritime museums.

Sailing
Ships

Anchors

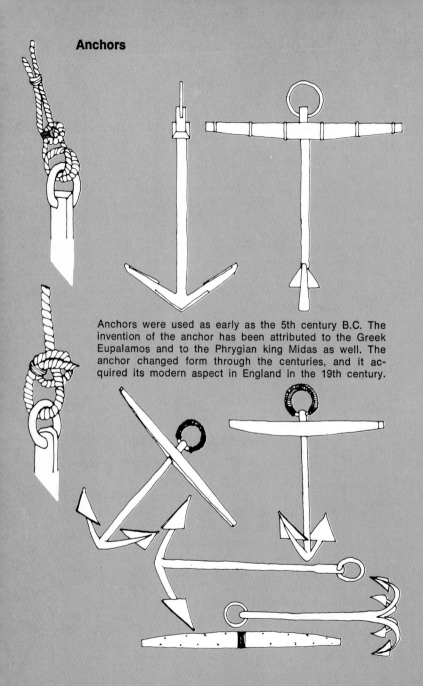

Anchors were used as early as the 5th century B.C. The invention of the anchor has been attributed to the Greek Eupalamos and to the Phrygian king Midas as well. The anchor changed form through the centuries, and it acquired its modern aspect in England in the 19th century.

The Wind as an Engine

We shall probably never know when man first discovered that he could move on the surface of the water with the most economical and most readily available means of propulsion offered by nature—wind. It was wind power that freed man from his age-old slavery to the oar, but man had to learn to harness that power. The first sailors simply tried to "catch" the wind, and the first sailing boats were simply given a push by the wind. But gradually it was discovered that the arrangement of masts, the use of wind-resistant materials for sails, and the use of cables and cords for moving the sails could make it possible to move in directions other than the one in which the wind was blowing.

First it is helpful to recall that the direction of the wind can be indicated by a Wind Rose. This is a geometric figure in the shape of a star with 16 points, each one corresponding to one of the directions from which the wind blows.

Wind direction can vary from the prevailing direction for a host of reasons, such as storms, sudden gusts, natural obstacles (mountains, for example). But what is important for the sailor is to distinguish between the real wind, in relation to the sea's surface and the apparent wind, i.e., that involving the movement of the ship itself. The apparent wind can be measured by the difference between the real wind and the vessel's speed. If one knows the direction and speed of the wind and the ship, it is easy to establish the actual wind direction. If one looks around the marine horizon one sees a circle with the observer always at the center. Dividing that circle into 360° and setting the ship in the center with the bow facing north, we can establish the source of the different winds according to the angle formed between the ship and the horizon. Hence it follows that a straight head wind is blowing from 360°. From 0° to 44°: wind blowing on the bow ·sides. From 45°: narrow bowline wind. From 56°: full bowline wind. From 67°: wide bowline wind. From 90°: wind on the beam. From 112°: wide or slack wind. From 135°: very wide wind. From 175°: buttock wind. From 180°: aft wind. Of course this division covers only half of the circle, because the other half is exactly the same.

In respect to the sail and to the ship, there is a *windward side,* the one from which the wind is blowing; and the *lee side,* or protected side, that corresponds to the direction of the wind. *Downwind* is the direction toward which the wind is blowing, while *upwind* is the direction from which the wind is blowing.

It is clear that man's mastery of the art of sailing was a slow process. The first step was to exploit the

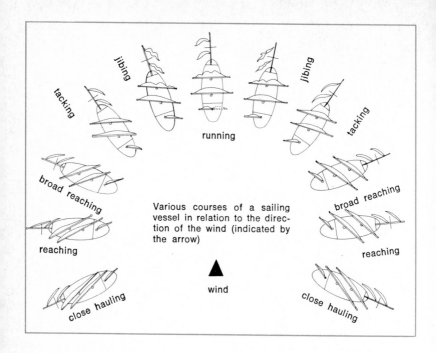

Various courses of a sailing vessel in relation to the direction of the wind (indicated by the arrow)

wind

wind's propulsive power in order to move in the same direction as the wind. The first sails, the square sails, were used solely to receive the wind from one direction and to give the wind a *running* course, that is, to move along with the wind and in the same direction as the wind.

Thus the ancient sailing vessels were not particularly maneuverable, and it took centuries before man learned to sail against the wind.

As time went by, it became clear to navigators that no matter how they improved their sails, it was impossible to go beyond a certain point established by two angles. That is to say,

there was a point beyond which the ship could no longer move because its sails no longer received any propulsive force from the wind. Thus, to sail upwind a ship had to tack. It had to follow a zig-zag course if it were to proceed against the wind, taking the wind first on one side and then on the other side of the sail.

The introduction of the lateen sail was a partial solution to this problem, for the lateen sail could receive the wind on both sides. The ability to sail against the wind was also influenced by the shape of the hull of a vessel. Thus the hull was also improved, and in the 19th-century clipper it reached its peak of perfection. A sailing ship's ability to sail against the wind is influenced by three factors: the force of the wind on the sail surface, the suction force that develops on the downwind side of the sail, and the lateral resistance of the vessel's keel.

What is of fundamental importance in changing a vessel's route is tacking. When a vessel reaches the point beyond which it can no longer take advantage of the wind's propulsive force, it must tack in the opposite direction. This maneuver, when the vessel has gone beyond the angle at which it receives propulsive force and the sails begin to flap, is called close hauling.

On old sailing vessels equipped exclusively with square sail, changing direction with the wind from behind was extremely difficult and required careful coordination of the various riggings of the sails. It should be pointed out that these sailing vessels, especially those that made ocean voyages, generally followed the trade winds, those regular winds of the tropics that blow in the direction of the equator. Thus in crossing the Atlantic from east to west they would have the wind behind them out of the northeast.

The ship could also rotate on its vertical axis to change direction without having the sails flap. This was a faster maneuver.

In any case, whether one sails in the direction of the wind or at an

The forces acting on a child on a slide are similar to those acting on a sailing ship going against the wind. The boy follows the direction of the slide, overcoming the resistance of the slide surface and being propelled by the force of gravity. A ship advances in a certain direction overcoming the lateral resistance of the keel in the water, while the force of the wind on the sails comes from a different direction than that in which the ship is sailing.

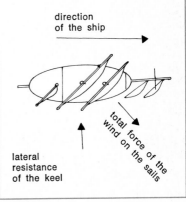

direction of the ship

lateral resistance of the keel

total force of the wind on the sails

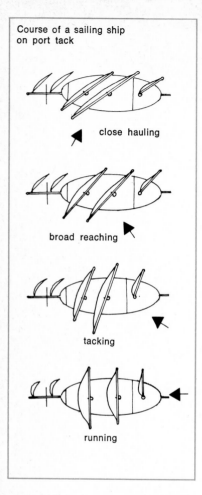

Course of a sailing ship
on port tack

close hauling

broad reaching

tacking

running

the wind are in the same direction, the ship is running. A ship is reaching when the wind comes from one side of the ship. When the ship is sailing against the wind it is hauling.

When a ship is close hauling, it is sailing as close to the wind as possible. But it reaches its greatest speed when it is broad reaching. There are two forces at work on the sails. One is a driving force that is impressed on the sail surface by the wind itself. At the same time a suction force is created on the downwind side of the sail.

The overall organization of the sails is referred to as the ship's rigging. The sail surface can be reduced by reefing or by lowering sails.

As early as the 17th century sails were reefed, which is to say, they were divided into zones that could be folded down to reduce sail surface. These sewn bands also prevented tears from continuing the full length of the sail. The side of the square sail rigged to the yard used to be called "head," whereas the lower side used to be called foot or bottom. The two vertical sides of the square sails or the stern side of the lateen sail used to be called forward leeches, while the fortresses used to be, and are even now, pieces of material sewn into areas of sail most subject to stress or rubbing.

The running rigging of the sails include halyards used to raise and lower the yards, braces to turn the yards to catch the wind, and sheets

angle to it, a sailing vessel is driven by the force of the wind on the windward side of the sail.

The wind direction, of course, determines the orientation of the sails and the route that a vessel can follow. Thus a sailing vessel can follow three general courses: running, reaching, and hauling. When the ship and

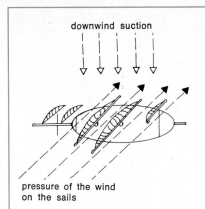

downwind suction

pressure of the wind
on the sails

The flow of air on the surface of
the sails creates a kind of negative
pressure on the downwind side,
which develops a veritable suction
force.

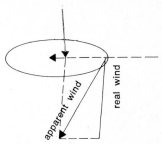

wind produced
by the forward motion
of the vessel

apparent wind

real wind

The apparent wind is the wind
caused by the forward motion of
the vessel. Depending on the
speed, the real wind seems to blow
further to the bow.

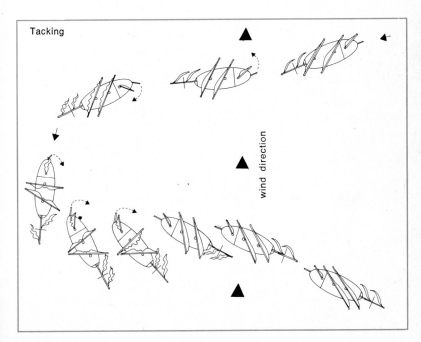

Tacking

wind direction

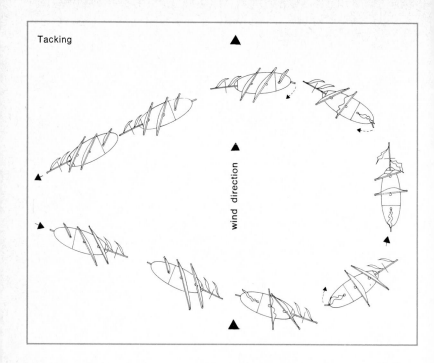

Tacking

wind direction

to control the bottom of the sail, as well as buntlines, bowlines, and martnets. The standing rigging supports the masts and comprises the shrouds, which give lateral support, and the stays, which provide longitudinal support. The latter also supported the stay-sails which first appeared on sailing ships in the 18th century. The foremast stays support the jib-sails, triangular sails which provided greater maneuverability.

The choice of a route to follow was and is an extremely important part of sailing. Centuries ago navigators were obliged to adjust their routes to the prevailing winds in various areas of the world. This sort of consideration helps to explain the expansion of Polynesian civilization, the expansion of the Arabian empire as far as Spain, the Venetian penetration of the Far East, and even the routes followed by 19th-century clipper ships.

From the earliest times navigation required a good knowledge of weather and meteorology. With the development of scientific weather forecasting sailing became safer.

In zones where the wind is constant, the best route may not be the direct and shortest route. Longer routes may actually be faster. Thus meteorology is of prime importance to sailing. Currents and tides also play an important role and may have a decisive effect on the speed of a ship. Bad weather has also presented serious difficulties for sailing, although improved structures and the development of scientific instruments have in part overcome this obstacle. In high winds the first thing to do was to reduce the area of sail exposed to the wind. On large sailing ships, three- and four-masters, the sails were reefed. The technique was to lower some of the sails, and this custom must be very old if we consider it was a suitable means for reducing the sail area of the large woolen or canvas nets employed by the Vikings on their ships. In bad weather sailing against the wind became extremely difficult, if not impossible, and if the sail surface could not be reduced sufficiently the sails might be lowered altogether. In some cases the only thing to do was to fly before the storm, or entirely without sails, with a dry companion, or with just a small sail surface exposed to the wind, just enough to avoid being pulled too far away from the course.

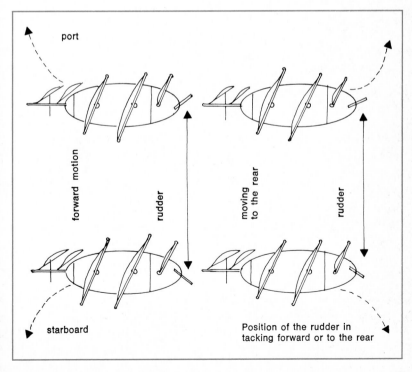

Old Nautical Instruments

Nocturnal (or nocturnlabe), 1580

Spanish astrolabe, 16th century

Provençal compass (showing Chinese influence), 16th century

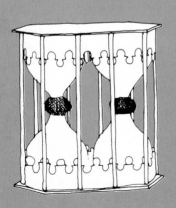

Hourglass, showing the hour and half-hour

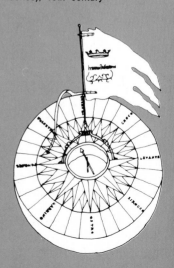

The Cog

The remains of a ship about 80 feet long and some 25 feet in beam were found in 1962 near Bremen. Careful comparative studies suggest that it is the fairly well-preserved hull of a cog, the medieval sailing ship that dominated the North Sea and the Mediterranean for about four centuries. The cog was used for both military and commercial service, since ships were not clearly distinguished by function. The stern and the bow both came to a point, perhaps a survival from the Viking long boats. In addition the ship carried a castle at bow and stern, but these two structures were added to the ship, not a part of the original construction. They were installed for military purposes, to facilitate defense and attack. The sterncastle was prac-tically a quarterdeck, while the for-ward one was rather a forecastle. They consisted of two platforms pro-jecting beyond the flanks of the ship and surrounded by a sturdy railing. The railing was often turreted like a medieval castle, though sometimes shields were hung over the sides as protection. Naval encounters of the time consisted in drawing ships abreast and trying to force one's way onto the enemy ship.

Throughout the 13th century the cog carried a single mast in the center of the ship with a large square sail. (The mast was built in a single piece.) The rudder consisted of one or two long oars fixed to the sides of the stern, so that the helmsman could steer the ship by putting down the oar on the side he wished the ship to turn. An innovation at the beginning of the 13th century made the cog much easier to handle and easier to steer: the rudder was suspended over the center of the stern. The stern of the ship was gradually modified as a result and took on a squarish shape. This was to be the usual form of a ship's stern until the end of the 18th century.

At first the new rudder was held by a bar that curved around the stern, but later this bar became straight and passed through the quarterdeck. A vertical handle was attached to the bar so that the helmsman could see the forward part of the ship as he steered. This system, which is still used on some Norwegian boats, is not especially functional. Finally a hole was made in the stern to accommodate the axis of the rudder, making it possible to steer with a horizontal bar, the tiller, protruding into the quarterdeck. Thus the cog's suspended rudder was finally installed within the hull.

The planking of the cog was applied with overlapping edges, clinker planking. The decks were supported by crossbeams that protruded from the sides of the ship.

It was sometime about 1300 that northern European and Mediterranean building techniques were amalgamated.

In a passage of the *Cronica* of Giovanni Villani (1276 ca.–1348), quoted by M. Jal in the *Glossaire Nautique* (1847), there is mention of some *cogge*

that were manned by Bayonne pirates making their appearance in the Mediterranean. This may have been why merchants of Barcelona, Genoa, and Venice became interested in the ship.

Shipbuilding thrived in the Mediterranean in this period, and firearms began to appear as part of a ship's equipment. The cog's mast, hull, and superstructure were reinforced. A second mast, the foremast, was added, and later, a third and smaller mast, the mizzenmast, was added at the stern. Thus the three-master made its appearance. This ship was more maneuverable because of the additional sails, while the mainmast maintained its eminently propulsive function.

The masts were equipped with tops, round turreted platforms (crow's nests), that could accommodate archers or crossbowmen and later harquebus gunners. The rigging was also improved. And the shrouds were strung with ratlines so that the crew could reach the yards and tops more easily. By the 14th century the improved cog might have as many as four masts with square and lateen sails together.

It is likely that the maximum length of a cog was about 100 feet overall, and about 70 feet at the waterline. Its depth was about 10 feet, and the sail surface must have been about 2,044 square feet. The cog could carry about 150 tons of cargo and required a crew of 20-30 men.

The cog could carry heavy artillery, although the weapons were simple

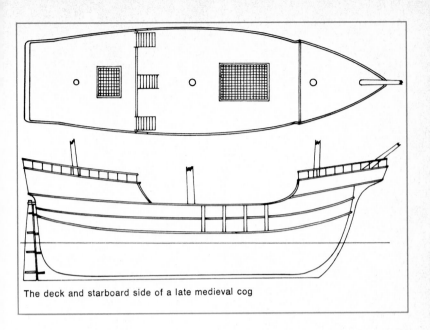

The deck and starboard side of a late medieval cog

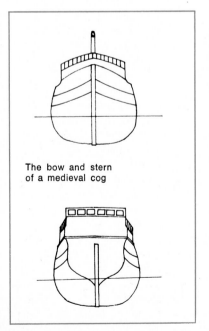

The bow and stern of a medieval cog

land guns and not weapons specially designed for shipboard. The first guns appeared on board about 1200 on Aragonese cogs. The bombard and the spingard were adopted in 1304 by the Genoese admiral Raniero Grimaldi, who was in the service of the French crown. These early guns were mounted on forked supports. But the bombard became the typical cog artillery. It had two basic parts. One carried the explosive charge, and this was inserted into the barrel containing a large stone ball. The *Statuto genovese di Gazzeria* of 1316 specified that a 600-ton cog should carry 5 bombards, 120 projectiles, and 13 barrels of powder, while the *Statuto marittimo di Venezia* of 1255 established the number of bombards at 4 or 8 depending on the size of the ship. At first the bombards were made of soldered iron staves reinforced with iron hoops. Later bombards were cast in bronze using the same system that was employed for casting church bells.

The gun mounts were carved out of oak trunks and had two wheels. The spingards were installed with forked mounts along the sides of the ship. They were front-loading weapons, operating on the principle of a catapult.

The rigging of the cog marked another step on the road to the highly maneuverable ship. The cog usually carried what are called square sails, although they were actually rectangular and then trapezoidal in shape. It was certainly the best rigging that the age could produce. The cog's sails did exactly what was required of them. They provided propulsion when the wind came from the stern, but they were ill-equipped for close-hauling, sailing against the wind. The cog's sails were reefed so that the sail surface could be reduced almost in half. Thus without lowering the whole sail, the sail surface could be reduced in case of high winds.

Reefing is still used in sailing ships, and it seems clear that this was an innovation in the medieval cog, equally as important as the installation of a central rudder.

For almost four centuries the cog was the merchant vessel par excellence. Larger and larger cogs were built, and by the end of the 15th century there were cogs with a cargo capacity of 1,000 tons. The forecastle was lowered so that the helmsman had greater visibility. The quarterdeck was raised to accommodate the captain and passengers.

The final development of the cog was to lead directly to the birth of the carrack.

The cog played an important role in the development of Venice's international trade. Ships like the one illustrated here (reconstructed inferentially) must have carried such important merchants as Niccolò and Matteo Polo, father and uncle respectively of the famous Marco Polo.

Venetian merchants carried goods between the West and the Far East in cogs. Venice was an *entrepôt* for French and Flemish merchandise to be exported to the East. Transport from France and Flanders was overland to Venice, where goods were loaded on ships for Constantinople and points east. The luxury goods of the East—sugar, spices, dyes, precious stones—were purchased by the Venetians and brought back to Venice for transport to Europe.

It was due to the enterprise of its merchants that the small republic became one of the richest and most prosperous mercantile centers of its time.

Type: **Mediterranean cog, two masts, lateen sails**
Launching: **about 1207**
Length: **90 ft.**
Beam: **22 ft.**
Depth: **10 ft.**
Displacement: **140 tons**
Sail surface: **2,000 sq. ft.**
Crew: **28**

It is hard to establish when the first all-sail vessel was built. The early mariners who traveled the Atlantic coast were quick to learn from each other and toward the end of the 13th century Mediterranean and northern shipbuilding techniques began to mix. From this mix was born the round boat, large enough to carry substantial cargoes and strong enough to stand up to enemy firepower. *Nuestra Señora* was a Spanish cog driven by oars but equipped with simple and functional sails. The foremast carried a square sail, while the mainmast, slightly off-center to the stern, had a

Type: **Mediterranean cog**
Launching: **about 1275**
Length: **87 ft.**
Beam: **15 ft.**
Depth: **10 ft.**
Displacement: **196 tons**
Crew: **80 oarsmen; 120 soldiers; 24 seamen**

yard and carried a triangular lateen sail. There were 20 oars on each side of the ship. The ship was driven by oars when the sea was becalmed, and oars provided greater maneuverability during combat. The *Nuestra Señora*'s rudder was of the northern type, with two long oars, one on each side of the stern.

This cog was launched for John Plantagenet, Duke of Bedford, the son of Henry IV. The single sail carried John's coat of arms. It is an example of the classic "large ship" of the Middle Ages in Europe. The ship, used for transporting goods and for military purposes, was equipped with the weapons of the time.

There was a crow's nest at the top of the mast. Archers, crossbowmen, and launchers of "Greek fire" could take up positions in the crow's nest. "Greek fire" was a mixture of naphtha, sulphur, and saltpeter. Highly combustible, it could be launched in

Type: **northern cog**
Launching: **about 1300**
Length: **86 ft.**
Beam: **22 ft.**
Depth: **10 ft.**
Displacement: **132 tons**
Crew: **28**

thin rockets or catapulted in clay jars. During combat tallow or soap might be spread over the deck to make the enemy slip and fall. Arrows were tipped with wide heads to tear enemy sails, and large scythes were used to cut the riggings. Underwater warfare already existed. Divers drilled holes in the hulls and keels of enemy ships.

This ship was built for the king of England and captured by the French on September 23, 1338. Two years later, in 1340, this large northern cog was attacked and sunk by English sailors and archers during the battle of Sluys, when Edward III won a decisive victory over the French.

Both the bow and the stern of this large cog were pointed. The ship was built with clinker planking. The single deck had two large hatches that could even accommodate horses for mounted warriors.

At the bow there was a small bowsprit, but it was not used for the

Type: **northern cog**
Launching: **about 1336**
Length: **95 ft.**
Beam: **16 ft.**
Depth: **11 ft.**
Displacement: **186 tons**
Armament: **5 bombards**
Crew: **60 seamen; 135 soldiers**

triangular sail known as a jib. Lines to the rigging of the sails were attached to it. This is evidence that the sailing qualities of the cog were continually in the process of being modified and improved as the ship was used for warfare as well as mercantile purposes.

Although the square sail did not disappear completely, it was the lateen sail that was to reign supreme in the Mediterranean for about one thousand years. This is confirmed by various contemporary illustrations throughout the centuries. In the *Atlas Catalàn* of 1370, there is an illustration of a cog (whether military or mercantile is not known) equipped with two lateen sails. The forward mast is inclined toward the bow, evidently an attempt to give the ship greater stability and to achieve the best balance between tractor and pusher force. The 14th century Portuguese cog (and Mediter-

Type: **Mediterranean cog, two masts, lateen sails**
Launching: **14th century**
Length: **86 ft.**
Beam: **26 ft.**
Depth: **13 ft.**
Displacement: **164 tons**
Crew: **34**

ranean cogs generally) did not have a forward castle, and the general structure of the hull was reminiscent of Roman ships. The ship was steered by a lateral rudder. It is mere hypothesis that the rudder was moved to the center of the stern of Mediterranean ships toward the end of the 14th century.

The Round Boat

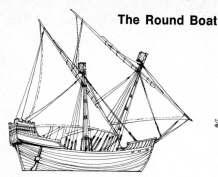

Venetian cog of the 13th century

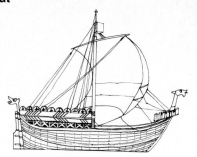

Danish cog, Skamtrup, 14th century

This is a reconstruction of a Venetian cog of the 13th century, of the type that was probably used during Louis IX's crusade in 1270. The length from stem to stern was about 85 feet, and the beam was about 20 feet. Two partial stern decks accommodated the cabins. The rudder system consisted of two long oars at the stern. The crow's nests are on the stern side of the masts.

The 15th-century seal of the city of Danzig, a member of the Hanseatic League, bears a depiction of a relatively advanced northern cog. There is a single improved mast, and a crow's nest, a feature that had been

Hanseatic cog, Danzig, 15th century

used in Phoenician and Egyptian boats many centuries before.

This reconstruction of a Danish cog is based on a 14th-century fresco in the church of Skamtrup. The structure is similar to that of Viking ships, and the decorations of the quarterdeck suggest that it was probably a warship. The quarterdeck occupies the whole area to the rear of the mast, but it is not an integral part of the hull.

Details for creating this reconstruction are based on 15th-century French miniatures. The mast is made of several poles bound together, a clear

French cog, 15th century

Venetian cog, 15th century

Venetian cog, 15th century, with lateen sails

indication that this is a larger ship. Quarterdeck and sterncastle are integral parts of the hull, which is a departure from earlier cog construction, and ratlines are by now a common feature.

In the 15th century the Venetian Republic discovered a new source of income: pilgrimages to the Holy Land. The Venetian cog became the most important passenger carrier of the time, and perhaps the largest pilgrim travel agency was born.

Everything was done to make the passengers' accommodations as comfortable as possible, but once on

board, the pilgrim was confronted with the worst possible conditions. The holds were filthy, the food poor, and water polluted. The animals on board were in a constant state of agitation.

The crossing lasted two months. Every pilgrim cog had to carry a doctor, the captain could enter certain ports only, and the crew had to swear not to rob the passengers of more than five *soldi* each during the voyage.

Every time the sails were rigged the passengers had to move to the windward side of the ship to keep it balanced. The return journey was no less difficult.

Venetian usher, 15th century, modified for horse transport

Venetian cog, 15th century, with lateral rudder

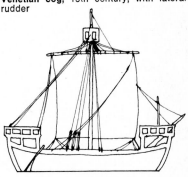

Knots

Overhand

Bowline

Figure-of-eight

Sheepshank

Half hitch

Round turn with
two half hitches

Double turn with
half hitch

Double clove hitch

Double
sheet bend

Sheet bend

Square knot

The Caravel

We actually know very little about this remarkable ship, which played such an important role in the history of navigation. In the 14th century the term was applied to small boats equipped with oars and sail that plied the waters of the western Mediterranean area and, beyond the Strait of Gibraltar, frequented the Atlantic ports of Portugal. These vessels were used for fishing and for coastal transport. The transformation of the simple fishing boat into the first sailing ship to face the dangers and mysteries of ocean sailing was a gradual one. By the beginning of the 15th century the caravel was a round-hulled vessel with a square stern and a rounded bow. Larger caravels had a covered deck, while the smaller ones were open vessels. Its displacement varied

from 25 to 60 tons. Generally this caravel had two or three masts, with lateen sails. The mainmast stood in the center of the ship. Larger caravels had a fourth mast, the foremast, carrying square sail. The planking was typically Mediterranean. The planks were juxtaposed one to the other.

For a long time scholars puzzled over one of the few known facts about the caravel's construction: the rule of *tres, dos, y as* (3:2:1). The interpretation of this rule is still subject to discussion. Some maintain that the ratio 3:2:1 refers to the ratio between length, width, and depth. Others believe that it refers to the ratio between length from bow to stern, length at the waterline, and beam. In any case, drawings, engravings, and paintings of the period, as well as nautical charts, do not depict two caravels alike.

The caravel of the middle of the 15th century was a larger vessel, thanks especially to the Portuguese, who improved the ship for oceanic explorations. These ships reached 150-200 tons. This was the small, efficient ship's golden age. At this time the ship often had a quarterdeck and a forecastle. That is to say, the caravel was equipped with structural elements typical of the larger vessels of the time, such as the carrack. Notwithstanding the addition of these superstructures, the caravel did not lose its great maneuverability and its capacity for sailing against the wind. In this it outdid the round ships of the era, which generally carried square sail, and it surpassed the galleys, which were hard to row in bad weather. Unlike the round ships, the caravel could easily move away from the coast in violent landward winds, and it was more adaptable than the galleys because it carried sail as well as oars.

Thus the caravel had an important role to play alongside these other two types of vessel. The Portuguese were the first to understand and exploit to the utmost the natural advantages of the caravel. Indeed, they took pains to keep construction details secret. The Portuguese caravel was originally a coastal and fishing vessel, but it eventually became the ocean-going ship par excellence. Light artillery could be carried on the deck. It has already been noted that for the most part caravels carried lateen sail.

The lateen sail was especially suited for sailing against the wind, but the appearance in the Mediterranean of the square sail together with the lateen sail resulted in the development of a larger, safer, and faster ship, more suited for oceanic sailing. This event, toward the end of the 15th century, was the beginning of the decline of the caravel. It survived for some time, however, thanks to some modifications: the foremast was rigged with square sail, while the main and mizzenmast were rigged with lateen sail. This larger caravel was called a *redunda,* to distinguish it from the *latina,* the caravel equipped with lateen sail only.

An interesting hypothesis is that the caravel was an invention of the naval architects that Prince Henry the Navigator assembled in 1438, together with cartographers, astronomers, and navigators, in what may be considered the first authentic oceanic navigation school. (This formidable assembly of talent gathered at Sagres, near Cape St. Vincent on the Atlantic coast of Portugal.) But this is only a hypothesis. For the caravel had long been in use. Caravels were used as early as 1420 in circumnavigating the continent of Africa, and it was in caravels that Vasco da Gama's expedition reached the coast of India. The most, then, with which Henry the Navigator's colleagues can be cred-

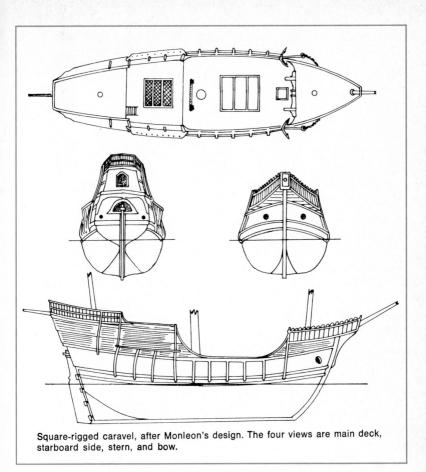

Square-rigged caravel, after Monleon's design. The four views are main deck, starboard side, stern, and bow.

ited is the improvement of an already existing type of vessel.

The caravel had a long career, although the need to take the greatest advantage of strong and constant ocean winds on the Atlantic made carracks and, later, galleons preferable. There is evidence, however, that the caravel survived well into the 17th century in the military and mercantile fleets of Portugal and Spain.

This later caravel generally had four masts, with square sail on the foremast and lateen sail on the other masts. It had a tall quarterdeck and forecastle, and the form of the hull was not much different from that of the galleon of the time. Or so it appears from contemporary paintings and nautical documents. It was not until about the middle of the 17th century that the caravel made its appearance in the northern seas. It still had its original hull shape and much of its original rigging, which made it particularly suitable for shallow-water navigation. Northern winds are quite different from those of the Mediterranean, and in stronger winds the lateen sails were lowered and only the foremast's square sails hoisted. At the same time this northern caravel had improved standing and running rigging.

As the caravel grew in size the first artillery began to be carried. These early weapons had such exotic names as serpentine and falconet. Early cannons were not unlike barrels in construction, with staves and hoops in iron, brass, or bronze. These weapons were mounted at the bow and at the stern and along the sides of the ship. In the 16th century cannons appeared that were cast in single pieces. These front-loading pieces were stronger and had a greater range than the earlier cannons. They could be fired almost every minute. The primary ammunition was small iron balls. Some late 16th-century caravels carried a few of these cannons in battery below deck.

Toward the middle of the 16th century the cannons were placed on forked mounts with wheels.

It is rare to find heavy-caliber artillery on late 17th-century caravels. Cannons between three and eight pounds were the rule.

One might say that the real art of navigation was born with the great explorations of the oceans, voyages carried out on board the caravel and later the carrack, the two "major" vessels of the time. But it was an art that relied chiefly on the intuition and skill of its practitioners. The fairly delicate structure of the caravel, notwithstanding notable improvements in shipbuilding made by the Spanish and the Portuguese, was subject to constant damage. Especially vulnerable were masts and spars, which snapped in high winds. The seams of the hull sprang leaks, and a ship could be reduced to a pitiable state in a matter of weeks. It was probably not infrequent that a caravel limped into a port and had to be scrapped on the spot.

Nevertheless it was such small and fragile ships as the caravel that carried out voyages of discovery for some two centuries, voyages that introduced Europeans to new and hitherto unknown lands and first opened those ocean routes that are still traveled today. There is a Majorcan map of 1375 with a legend at the position of Cape Noun reading: "Here ends the known world." It was the caravel that erased that legend from the map of the world and dismissed the Ptolemaic cartography that had reigned undisputed for centuries.

The small caravel was the first oceanic sailing ship. It was the sailing ship on which Renaissance man emerged from the nautical obscuran-

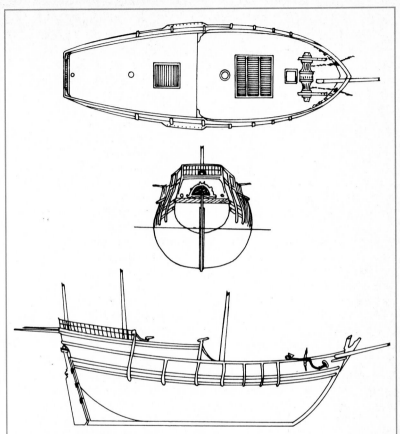

The deck, stern, and starboard side of a caravel with lateen sail. The historian Monleon gives the overall length as about 50 feet.

tism of the Middle Ages, overcame his fear of the unknown, and set out with a new faith in progress. Patiently the little caravel carved out its path on the sea, overcoming the violence of nature and the prejudices of man. According to Alvise da Ca' da Mosto, writing in 1455, it was the finest ship that sailed the seas and well-equipped for any eventuality. The caravel disappeared from the scene about the middle of the 17th century. Reminiscences of its structure were to reappear in the 19th-century merchant schooner and in the 20th-century xebecs that sail the Red Sea.

Santa Maria

The *Santa Maria,* the ship that Columbus sailed across the Atlantic, has received a great deal of attention from scholars. The *Santa Maria* was a three-masted carrack with square sails. It was built in Santander and belonged to Juan de la Cosa. Columbus rented the ship for his first crossing. The ship's stowage was 105.9 Sevillian *tonels.* A *tonel* was equivalent to a wine barrel of 1.37 cubic meters. So its tonnage in modern measurements would be about 51 tons. This tough ship was built by able craftsmen without the aid of plans or drawings. There were five sails. The mainmast, about 90 feet tall, carried the large cotton *trevo* (lower square sail) with the Castilian red cross and a small topsail. The foremast carried the foresail. The mizzenmast carried a triangular lateen

sail. The bowsprit, the horizontal mast at the bow, carried a small square sail. The mainsail could be augmented with two small square sails to the sides, studding sails.

The raised quarterdeck at the stern accommodated the captain's simply appointed cabin. The rest of the crew slept below the main deck on wooden bunks.

The defensive armament of the *Santa Maria* comprised bombards and culverins and a few portable springals. The masts were topped by the standards of Castille and Leon, red and white with castles and lions. The mizzenmast carried the insignia of the fleet, a green cross on a white ground framed by an F and a J, the initials of Ferdinand and Isabella, the king and queen. Columbus' insignia was blue with five golden anchors.

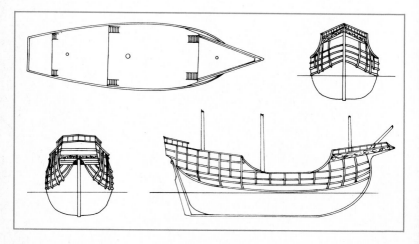

Type: **three-masted carrack**
Launching: **about 1480**
Length: **approx. 78 ft.**
Beam: **26 ft.**
Depth: **7 ft.**
Tonnage: **51.3 tons**
Armament: **four 90-mm. bombards; several 50-mm. culverins; portable crossbows and springals**
Crew: **39**

Niña

Maritime literature in general, and Spanish maritime literature in particular, do not provide precise information about Columbus' ships. All we know comes from Columbus' log, and that is only approximate information. The *Niña* carried lateen sails, and this is reflected in various depictions and reconstructions. The name "Niña" means "young girl," rather than "little one." This latter translation led some people to think that the *Niña* was the smallest of the three ships.

This caravel belonged to the Pinzòn brothers before it took part in Columbus' voyage, and it was they who named the ship. An Italian reconstruction of the *Niña* represents a classic caravel with lateen sails hung in the middle of the yards. The sails do not have reefs for reducing the sail surface during heavy winds, and the shrouds are attached to the sides of the ship. The *Niña* did not have a forecastle, so one may assume that the capstan was on the open deck. The small sterncastle was not high enough for a man to pass. Most likely the helmsman stood in a sort of well beneath the quarterdeck, with the upper part of his body above the level of the deck. Thus he would not have been able to see the movement of the ship.

The *Niña* had three anchors. We know from Columbus' diary that two were lost in the Azores. After losing the *Santa Maria,* he went on board the *Niña* for the return voyage. During a storm that broke near the Azores on February 14, 1493, he had to maneuver with the trysails, the sails that were raised against a high

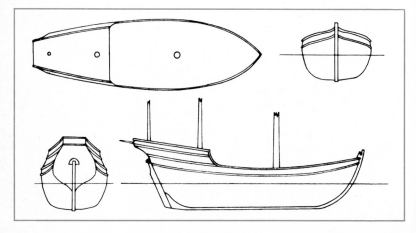

wind to prevent the ship from being flooded. This detail suggests that the *Niña* had boat decks. This caravel was almost certainly modified during its stay in the Canaries and transformed from a *carabela latina* into a *carabela redunda*.

Thus its triangular sails were replaced by square sails, which were more suitable for the prevailing winds the ship would encounter. Columbus sailed aboard the *Niña* on his second voyage and returned to Spain in 1496.

Type: **caravel, lateen sails**
Launching: **unknown**
Length: **71 ft.**
Beam: **21 ft.**
Depth: **6 ft.**
Displacement: **52.72 tons**
Crew: **20**

Later the *Niña* was captured by Barbary pirates and then recaptured by its crew. It returned to Cadiz, and it took part in Columbus' third voyage in 1498. Under Columbus' command this sturdy caravel covered no less than 25,000 nautical miles.

SIENA COLLEGE LIBRARY

Pinta

There is very little certain information about Columbus' third ship, the *Pinta*. All that is certain is that it was a square-sailed caravel. The various reconstructions that have been attempted show a large square foresail and mainsail, while the mizzenmast carried the long yard of the triangular lateen sail. It is possible that this sail was Arabic in origin, but it may be that the Arabs brought it to the Mediterranean from the East.

The *Pinta* ("Painted") was hired by Columbus from Gomez Rascòn and Cristobal Quintero, who also commanded the ship, together with Martin Alonso Pinzòn. The ship's pilot was Francisco Martin Pinzòn, the brother of Martin Alonso.

An Italian reconstruction of the ship has a forecastle, a quarterdeck, and a poop deck. There is no information about the staircases that connected these decks. If one even knew the number of steps between decks, one could make an estimate of the size of the decks themselves.

One can infer, however, that the quarterdeck was above the tiller. Otherwise it would have struck against the mizzenmast. The quarterdeck must have been a little over three feet high, just enough space for sleeping quarters for the crew.

The forecastle must have been almost five feet high so that the capstan could be handled comfortably.

Columbus' log entry for October 8, 1492, says that they sailed 15 miles per hour. The nautical mile of the period corresponds to 4/5 of the modern nautical mile. During the return voyage, according to the ship's log, a speed of 14 miles was main-

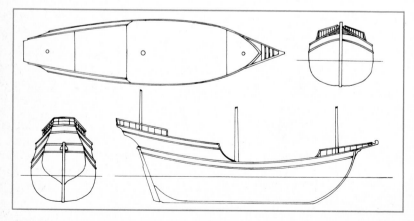

tained for 11 hours on February 6, 1493, equal to 11.2 modern nautical miles per hour. This is the average speed of a modern medium-size cargo ship. The *Pinta* must have been a fast ship. According to the log of Juan de la Cosa, the owner and pilot of the *Santa Maria*, this caravel was often far ahead of the other two ships. There are various theories about the structure of the *Pinta* and of Colum-

Type: **caravel, square sails**
Launching: **unknown**
Length: **60–78 ft.**
Beam: **19–21 ft.**
Depth: **5–6 ft.**
Displacement: **approx. 50 tons**
Crew: **25**

bus' other two ships as well. In any case, these three ships will long be remembered in the annals of maritime exploration.

The *Estremadura* was one of the caravels in the great fleet assembled by Charles V, emperor of the Holy Roman Empire, against Khair ed-Din, the formidable Barbarossa, leader of powerful Barbary states on the North African coast. The *Estremadura* represents a transition from the caravel to the carrack, the ship that was to play a leading role in the great ocean voyages. This heavily armed ship was one of the 400 transports that gathered in the Bay of Algiers October 1541, together with the 50 galleys of the Knights of Malta, the Kingdom of Naples, Genoa, and the Papal States. The *Estremadura* had disem-

Type: caravel, four masts
Launching: **about 1511**
Length: **115 ft.**
Beam: **14 ft.**
Depth: **13 ft.**
Displacement: **228 tons**
Armament: **twenty-four 9-pound culverins**
Crew: **86 seamen; 120 soldiers**

barked its troops when a storm broke, sinking 20 ships and drowning hundreds of soldiers and sailors. The *Estremadura* went down, but its crew was saved, thanks in part to the assistance of their enemy, the Turks.

Charles V's hopes of destroying Barbarossa and the Turks were dashed by bad weather.

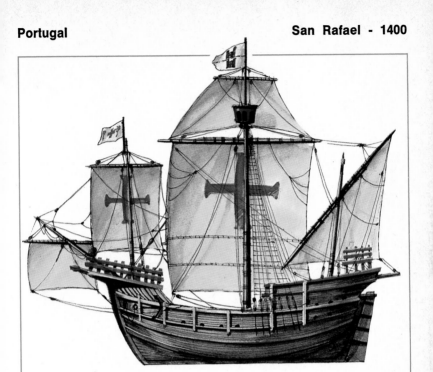

Some scholars maintain that the caravel was "invented" by the architects of Prince Henry the Navigator, the great Portuguese promoter of naval exploration. But it is more likely that the caravel was simply the development of the coasting vessels of the time.

The *San Rafael* was a typical *redunda* caravel, that is to say, it was equipped with two square-sailed masts and one lateen-sail mast. It was fairly light and had a limited depth. The heavier carracks with square sails and the contemporary galleys could not withstand bad weather without serious damage, but the hull of ships

Type: **redunda caravel**
Launching: **1400**
Length: **71 ft.**
Beam: **21 ft.**
Depth: **6 ft.**
Displacement: **53 tons**
Crew: **30**

like the *San Rafael* was designed to stand up to bad weather with greater safety. In 1434 the *San Rafael* took part in the expedition of Alfonso Gonçalves, the first Portuguese navigator to go beyond Cape Bojador on the South African coast. He was also the first in the history of Portuguese naval exploration to encounter the natives of the Bay of Horses.

The *Vijia* represents the final development of the caravel before its disappearance. The ship was built about the beginning of the 17th century and sailed for almost 50 years.

The *Vijia* may be considered the last caravel to have made a long ocean voyage. In 1618, together with a sister ship, the *Vijia* sailed from Lisbon to the Strait of Magellan under the command of Bartolomeu Nodal. It was almost a routine crossing. The two ships never lost sight of each other, and only one member of the 40-man crew died. The *Vijia*'s hull was not much different from those of the larger contemporary vessels, but

Type: **caravel, lateen sails**
Launching: **about 1600**
Length: **106 ft.**
Beam: **22 ft.**
Depth: **12 ft.**
Displacement: **126 tons**
Crew: **40**

its riggings were. There were three masts with lateen sails and a fourth mast, the foremast, with square sails. The hold could preserve perishables for up to ten months.

The constructional tradition of the caravel may be recognized in the 19th-century schooner and in the still-surviving Arab sambuk that plies the eastern coast of Africa and Arabia.

Spanish lateen caravel, 15th century

Spanish *carabela redunda*, 15th century

The swelling sides of the caravel (both the *redunda*, with square sails, and the lateen caravel) made the ship stronger and made it possible to sail against the wind. One distinctive structural feature of the small ocean-going vessel was the square stern on which the central rudder was installed.

Small ships, like the *Tagus*, were known as frigates, but these Portuguese vessels that plied the coastal

Portuguese coastal caravel, 15th century

waters were similar to the caravels in their lines.

The drawings in the atlas of Juan de la Cosa, owner and pilot of Columbus' *Santa Maria*, and the drawings in the 1520 nautical map of the Portuguese Lopo Homen show some types of caravel with long hulls lying quite deep in the water and large quarter-decks at the stern. In the earliest surviving illustrations the term caravel is generally applied to a large coastal fishing vessel with lateen sails.

The term caravel appears for the first time in a "Chart" of King Alfonso II of Portugal, from the year 1255. In 1459 and 1460, in the Dutch provinces of Seeland and Okanda, three *cravel-schepen* were built. These were caravels built with the typical Mediterranean feature of the smooth hull, with the planking arranged side by side. Thus heavier planking could be used than in the clinker-built ships of northern Europe which were made with overlapping planks. This innovation from the south was one of the preconditions of building larger and larger ships.

Development of Superstructures

From the 13th to the 18th century sailing ships carried superstructures that rose above the main deck but did not run the full length of the ship. The forecastle at the bow served originally as a combat deck. As the sailing ship evolved toward the galleon and the man-of-war, the forecastle accommodated light cannons.

The quarterdeck at the stern also carried light cannons. The poop deck was above the quarterdeck and ran forward beyond the mizzenmast. Drawings 1–5 show the evolution of the quarterdeck and forecastle of the carrack until the end of the 15th century. Drawings 6 and 7 show the first galleons; the quarterdeck and forecastle are clearly reminiscent of those of the carrack. Drawing 8 shows the fully-developed 17th-century galleon.

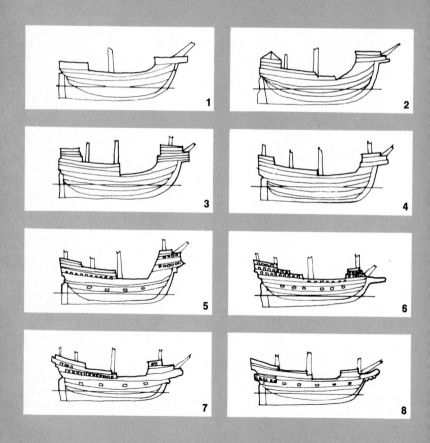

The Carrack

The carrack made its first appearance in southwestern Europe, during the second half of the 15th century. It was probably a development of the northern cog. It seems fairly certain that the northern cog was imitated by the Spanish and the Portuguese, who would have become familiar with the ship through contact with the people of the Atlantic coast of France. Nevertheless the northern cog would not have met the needs of such countries as Spain and Portugal, which were in a phase of naval expansion at that time. Thus a new type of vessel was developed.

The term carrack comes from the Arabic *qarāqīr,* the plural of *qurqūr,* "merchant ship." The Spanish called it a *nao.* The carrack incorporated structural features of the northern cog, especially the Hanseatic cog. At the same time it represented a marked advance over that ship. The carrack had a triangular forecastle that was integrated into the structure of the hull and did not project over the sides of the ship. It was taller than the forecastle of the cog and could carry several decks.

The sterncastle also carried more than one deck. It, too, was integrated into the structure of the hull and might carry more than one gundeck. Thus the carrack was longer and taller than the cog. Generally the structure of the carrack was roundish and this, plus the nature of its rigging, made the ship unsuitable for sailing against the wind. Yet it was ideally

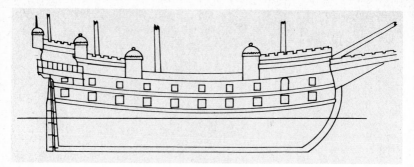

Gunports along the side of a carrack. The carrack was the first sailing ship so equipped for naval combat.

suited for sailing with the wind. It was with the development of the carrack that the three-masted system of rigging was born and improved. The foremast and the mainmast were rigged with square sail. At first they carried only large lower sails, but later, smaller topsails were added. The mizzenmast carried a triangular lateen sail. Subsequently the carrack acquired a fourth mast, the bonaventure, and this was also rigged with lateen sail. A long cable, known as a stay, joined the bowsprit and the foremast, providing greater resistance to the wind. A small square sail was carried by the bowsprit to increase the ship's maneuverability. For the first time the standing rigging was fixed by chains to a small platform projecting outside the ship. Until then

the shrouds that propped the masts had been connected to a winch inside the hull. The typical rigging of a carrack consisted of six elements, thus providing a larger sail surface than the caravel. Another important innovation of the carrack was the gunport. Gunports were opened along the lower deck.

It was on the carrack that the first cannons were arranged in battery along the sides of the ship.

Thanks to its technical innovations and to its adaptability as a military or a merchant vessel, the carrack became extremely popular in the Mediterranean and in the northern seas. Alongside the caravel it took part in the great voyages of exploration that were undertaken in the 15th and 16th centuries.

The *Galicia* was one of the first Spanish commercial carracks, sailing between Spanish and Flemish ports. It is clear that the carrack was influenced by the northern cogs when they made their appearance in the Mediterranean.

Type: **transport carrack**
Launching: **1400**
Length: **88 ft.**
Beam: **13 ft.**
Depth: **10 ft.**
Displacement: **258 tons**
Armament: **8 bronze stone-launchers**
Crew: **52**

The *Galicia* was one of the first carracks to have fixed artillery pieces along the sides. The cannons of the day were built in iron, brass, and bronze and were given bizarre names, like serpentine, bombardella, and falconet. In the 16th century technical advances made it possible to cast cannon barrels in a single piece. These guns fired balls weighing 6, 8, 12, and up to 68 pounds. The cannons on the *Galicia* had moveable mounts, but they were fixed to the sides of the ship with a system of pulleys and cables so that the recoil would not send them rolling across the deck.

Unfortunately the most careful research has failed to provide exact information about the precise dimensions of the typical Mediterranean carrack.

Type: **Mediterranean carrack**
Launching: **about 1470**
Length: **102 ft.**
Beam: **16 ft.**
Depth: **12 ft.**
Displacement: **500–600 tons**
Crew: **67**

All that we have is general information, and modern reconstructions are based on approximate calculations. Thus we know that the *San Matteo,* a Genoese transport carrack, had a tonnage somewhere between 500 and 600 tons. This inference is based on the number of barrels of wine it is known to have carried.

The *San Matteo* was certainly one of those hardy ships that sailed from Italy across the Mediterranean to Portugal and on to Flanders and England. They did not go farther north, because those areas were under the control of the Hanseatic League of German mercantile cities.

The mariners who sailed the Genoese carracks brought back detailed knowledge of the western coasts of Europe.

This Hanseatic carrack served both military and mercantile purposes. The Hanseatic League, one of the oldest and longest-lived commercial associations, was founded during the first half of the 13th century and lived, one might say, on a permanent war basis, ever ready to strike at anyone who interfered with its commerce.

The last meeting of the league councillors took place in 1669, after some four centuries of commercial activity, during which the league fought English and Dutch corsairs and resisted attempts by the Danish kings to break its trading monopoly in the

Type: **Hanseatic carrack**
Launching: **about 1500**
Length: **122 ft.**
Beam: **19 ft.**
Depth: **15 ft.**
Displacement: **527 tons**
Armament: **twelve 9-pound culverins**
Crew: **78**

north. But the league's importance had already begun to decline by the time of the great Spanish and Portuguese exploration voyages.

The *Seylagien* was attacked in October 1528 by three English pirate carracks. The Lubeck seamen on board the large Hanseatic carrack sank one of the attackers and drove off the other two.

Type: **northern carrack**
Launching: **about 1500**
Length: **118 ft.**
Beam: **19 ft.**
Depth: **13 ft.**
Displacement: **537 tons**
Crew: **86**

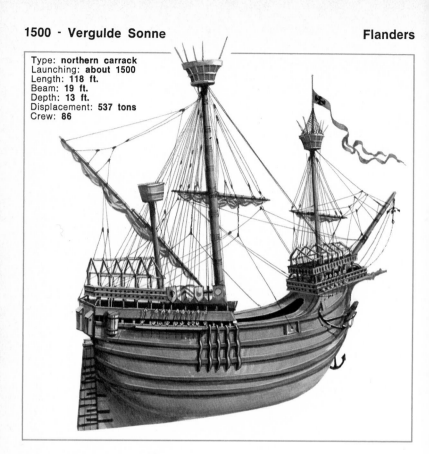

Holland was the home of great navigators and navigation scientists. In 1545 Gemma Frisius tested a "nautical quadrant" for the first time on board the *Vergulde Sonne.* This instrument made it possible to calculate with reasonable accuracy the number of miles sailed in a given direction in a fixed period of time. It consisted of a compass card carved on a wood tablet. The 32 rhombs of the card had 8 holes, each representing a half hour. After a half hour a wooden peg was inserted in the holes corresponding to the direction of the ship and indicated by the compass. Every hour a second peg was inserted in one of the areas of the square beneath the card, consisting of 50-60 holes in four rows. This indicated, from left to right, the speed in knots as registered by the log. Every four hours the route could be plotted in number of miles traveled and in direction.

Type: **four-masted carrack**
Launching: **1515**
Length: **125 ft.**
Beam: **22 ft.**
Depth: **17 ft.**
Displacement: **560 tons**
Armament: **140 bronze cannons**
Crew: **240 seamen; 300 soldiers**

The *Santa Catalina* was the flagship of the Portuguese fleet. Together with the English *Henry Grace à Dieu* and the French *Grande Françoise* it formed the trio of the last large 16th-century carracks. The hull, setting aside the high quarterdecks and forecastle, is structurally close to that of the galleon. The *Santa Catalina* (or *Catarina*) had six decks, five at the stern. According to contemporary usage, the cannons were lined up on the upper deck, the quarterdeck, and the forecastle. The ship had the four masts of the carrack, but the dimensions of the sails were different.

The ship incorporated an innovation in handling the rudder. The helmsman had a system of cables and pulley to lighten his task. Later the same system was used aboard the large sailing vessels of the 19th century, with metal instead of hemp cables.

Madre di Dio

The Venetian merchant ship, a model of which is preserved in the Arsenale Museum in Venice, was called the *nave pantofola* ("the slipper ship") because of its unusual shape. It long dominated the great commercial routes that the Venetian Republic kept open to the markets of the East and the rest of the Mediterranean. The historian Charles Diehl has described the commercial wealth of Venice in the 16th century. "The population numbered 190,000 souls, of which 3,000 were employed in the silk industry, 16,000 in the wool industry, 17,000 at the Arsenale with its naval constructions, while 25,000 served as crews in the fleet. The Venetian navy counted 3,000 merchant ships and 300 warships.

"The total value of the Venetian houses reached seven million ducats, and the republic's mint put in circulation every year about one million gold ducats and another million silver pieces . . . Trade with the East was highly remunerative . . . ."

The Venetian merchant ship was the commercial vessel par excellence, and it was often rented out to countries with little or no maritime facilities. The commercial routes of the Venetian Republic were so safe that insurance rates were extremely low. Venetian galleys served as escorts, and the carrack itself was well-armed with cannons and well-trained crews. The big ship made its voyage with the same sense of routine that modern oil tankers have. The ship set out for the island of Euboea in the Greek archipelago. From there it might sail to the Black Sea for grain, or to Constantinople and Alexandria, where spice

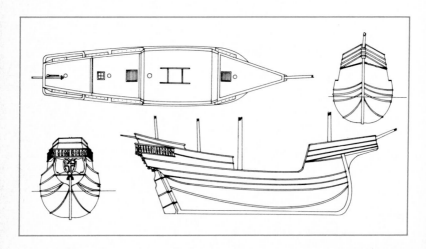

Type: **Venetian merchant
    ship**
Launching: **about 1500**
Length: **132 ft.**
Beam: **22 ft.**
Depth: **16 ft.**
Displacement: **580 tons**
Crew: **94**

caravans arrived. It might head for
Crete and then to Tunis or the ports of
Egypt and Syria. Later the Venetian
carrack was also to venture beyond
the Strait of Gibraltar and sail to
Spain, France, England, and Flanders.

But at the end of the 15th century
an event occurred which was to mark
the eventual end of Venetian commercial hegemony in the Mediterranean.
In 1498 Vasco da Gama landed at
Calicut on the Malabar coast of India.

The Portuguese discovery of the route
to the Indies sealed Venice's mercantile fate. Spices carried around the
Cape of Good Hope cost less.

A few more centuries of apparent
splendor, and then the Venetian Republic, its structure undermined by
spreading corruption, collapsed without resistance the day a young general named Napoleon Bonaparte decided at Campo Formio to sell Venice
to Austria.

Type: **English carrack**
Launching: **about 1470**
Length: **116 ft.**
Beam: **20 ft.**
Depth: **15 ft.**
Displacement: **500 tons**
Crew: **70**

Sometime after 1470 the English built their first carrack, the new kind of ship that rapidly took the place of the cog in the northern seas. The *Sparrow* was originally built as a mercantile vessel, but it was later equipped with artillery. Because of its large size —large for its time, that is—the *Sparrow* could easily accommodate cannons.

The *Sparrow* was the first north-ern carrack in which clinker planking was replaced by carvel planking. This method of construction came from the Mediterranean caravel, which must already have made its appearance in the northern seas, thanks to the commercial routes established by Mediterranean fleets. Because of its sturdiness, the carrack soon became the warship par excellence of the north.

Henry VIII had this large carrack built. Its four masts carried gilded sails, and there were high and elaborate superstructures and a host of guns. It was the naval marvel of the century. The *Henry* was the first English ship to have masts constructed in more than one section, providing greater height. The mizzenmast had three lateen sails, while the bonaventure (horizontal mast) at the

Type: **four-masted carrack**
Launching: **1514**
Length: **132 ft.**
Beam: **23 ft.**
Depth: **20 ft.**
Displacement: **1,000 tons**
Armament: **21 bronze cannons; 130 iron culverins**
Crew: **400 seamen; 600 soldiers**

stern carried a second lateen sail above the principal one. Rebuilt in 1536 and freed of its cannons, the ship was rebaptized the *Great Harry.*

Type: **four-masted carrack**
Launching: **1535**
Length: **135 ft.**
Beam: **24 ft.**
Depth: **20 ft.**
Displacement: **1,124 tons**
Armament: **120 bronze cannons**
Crew: **278 seamen; 320 soldiers**

The *Grande Françoise* was the French answer to the British *Henry Grace à Dieu.* This gigantic carrack was built in Le Havre and, as it happened, never left port. The ship was so large that even at high tide it could not pass through the entrance to the port of Le Havre.

The *Grande Françoise* was the first French ship to carry a fourth mast in the stern with a lateen sail in addition to the one on the mizzenmast. To offset the weight of this fourth mast, the bonaventure, a horizontal mast, projected from the stern.

The *Grande Françoise* was very heavily armed for its time. In the early part of the 16th century cannons designed especially for naval use had not yet been developed, and the French ship carried ordinary land artillery.

On the Route to the Indies

French carrack, late 15th century

Flemish armed carrack, late 15th century

The carrack represented the final transition from the single-masted to the three-masted ship. Perhaps as early as the beginning of the 15th century, there were three-masted carracks, but the earliest documentary evidence we have is a seal depiction of a carrack dating from 1466—a document with Louis Bourbon's seal.

Another step forward in the development of the carrack was the introduction of the foremast. The foremast and mainmast carried square sails, the mizzenmast carried a lateen sail. The deck beams, which reinforced the ship transversely, projected beyond the rails.

The *kraeck,* the Flemish carrack, made its appearance about 1470 in the form of an armed merchant ship. The stern-castle has two decks. A protective framework could be laid across the upper part during combat. Both the foresail and the mizzensail are relatively large.

The Spanish term *nao* means "ship." It is probable that any large ship of the time with a round stern and square sails was called a *nao* in Spain, while elsewhere it was called the equivalent of carrack. It is difficult today to know whether the two terms were applied to the same type of ship.

German carrack, 15th century

Spanish carrack, about 1517

On the Route to the Indies

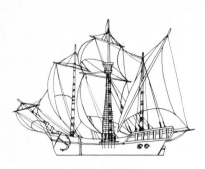

Portuguese carrack, 1544

The square sail and the lateen sail both have their advantages. The square sail is suited to the open seas with the wind from the stern. The lateen sail is better adapted to coastal sailing. The two sails were combined for the first time in the carrack. Thus sailing against the wind became easier, and combinations of rigging added to the carrack's maneuverability.

The sides of the carrack were curved and rounded, not only for technical reasons but also to make it more difficult for raiders and enemies to board the ship by force. Naval encounters of the early 16th century were more often resolved by hand-to-hand combat than by artillery fire.

English carrack, 1536

Spanish carrack, about 1534

The main armament of the time was provided by archers and warriors. One cannot set a date to the birth of the carrack, nor is it easy to trace its early development. It probably emerged gradually as a result of contacts between the vessels of the Mediterranean and those of the north, as did the cog no doubt.

Early in the 15th century, the maximum cargo load of a carrack must have been about 400 tons. By the beginning of the next century, it was more than 1,000 tons. The largest carracks reached a length of more than 120 feet overall, about 90 feet at the waterline, and a beam of more than 30 feet.

Mediterranean carrack, about 1526

The Discovery Vessels

The caravel and the carrack, the two typical sailing vessels of the 15th century, can stake a fair claim to being the first ocean-going sailing ships.

Two of Columbus' ships, the *Niña* and the *Pinta,* were caravels, and his flagship, the *Santa Maria,* was almost certainly a carrack.

The ships that carried Vasco da Gama's expedition to the coasts of India were carracks, as was the ship that Vespucci sailed along the coast of South America. The ships that Magellan led through the strait that was later named after him were carracks.

The introduction of the vertical rudder at the stern and the use of the compass, together with the technical developments represented by the caravel and the carrack, contributed in large measure to the development of new shipping routes. The great voyages of exploration and the discovery of new lands beyond the oceans led to the development of new and increased trade across the Atlantic. At the same time, the Mediterranean began to lose its central place in navigation.

Portuguese navigators of the time followed the longer route toward the east, sailing their carracks down the coast of Africa, doubling the Cape of Good Hope, and then heading toward Goa and Macao, before pushing on to Manila. Then they crossed the Pacific at the fourth parallel to reach Acapulco. From that point they turned around and headed back to Europe. The Spaniards instead sailed from Cadiz to Vera Cruz, passing to the south of Cuba. Jacques Cartier, at the service of Francis I of France, made three exploratory trips to Canada between 1534 and 1541, claiming the territories around the St. Lawrence River for the French crown. French carracks went as far as Senegal, where commercial bases were established. John and Sebastian Cabot sailed along the North American coast for the English, and soon after the Dutch were also heading for America.

As the carrack had opened the route to the Indies, so it later came to carry gold and silver, as well as spices, from the Americas. Atlantic seaports flourished; Bilbao and Bayonne, La Rochelle and Nantes, Le Havre, Bristol, and Southampton. Merchants from Germany, the Low Countries, and France carried their goods to Lisbon, Cadiz, and Seville. The discovery vessels carried a wealth of goods, yes, but they also carried ideas and new possibilities across the oceans.

Vasco da Gama's Ships

São Rafael

Columbus' voyages not only opened a new route for man's spirit of adventure but also paved the way for the remarkable development of navigation in Portugal as well as in Spain that was to place these countries in the forefront of 15th- and early 16th-century explorations across the oceans of the world.

Vasco da Gama's expedition set sail from Lisbon for India on July 8, 1497. There were four ships, including the *São Rafael,* a 100-ton carrack commanded by Paulo da Gama, Vasco's brother. The small fleet was equipped with the best that nautical science could offer at the time. The results of this expedition were of the greatest importance in the history of navigation. On the return voyage, in 1499, the *São Rafael* was set afire. Its crew had been reduced by half by the strains of the voyage and by scurvy.

Vasco da Gama's voyage radically modified the trade routes of the world, and the long route of caravans carrying spices to Alexandria from the East lost its importance.

Berrio

The *Berrio,* commanded by Nicolau Coelho—together with the *São Gab-riel* and the *São Rafael* and a supply ship—was one of the four vessels that set off with Vasco da Gama for the coasts of India. It was a *redunda* caravel, that is to say, it carried square sails on the foremast and the mainmast and a lateen sail on the mizzenmast. Because of the length and difficulty of the voyage two decks were installed at bow and stern for the crew, and the hull and frame were reinforced.

The *Berrio* was particularly well adapted for shallow waters and explored the mouth of the Limpopo River in the African territory of the Bantus. The *Berrio* demonstrated the particular seaworthy features of the caravel by reaching the mouth of the Tagus (July 10, 1499) a good two months before the *São Gabriel,* the carrack sailed by Vasco da Gama.

São Gabriel

The *São Gabriel* was the first carrack to double the Cape of Good Hope, the southernmost point of the continent of Africa, when Vasco da Gama set out to find the route to the Indies.

The expedition left Lisbon July 8, 1497. On May 20, 1498, the anchors were dropped in the port of Calicut (modern Kozhikode) on the Malabar coast—the west coast of India. Vasco da Gama's ships had followed a direct

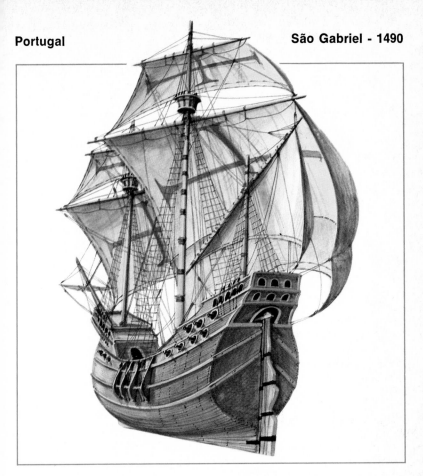

route to the Indies, the one that was to be followed for centuries by other navigators.

The *São Gabriel* was a carrack. It was a three-masted ship with a well-balanced rigging. The mainsail was much larger than the other sails and was hoisted on a yard longer than the keel of the ship. The lateen sail on the mizzenmast was useful for sailing

Type: **three-masted merchant carrack**
Launching: **about 1490**
Length: **106 ft.**
Beam: **16 ft.**
Depth: **13 ft.**
Displacement: **approx. 250 tons**
Armament: **10 iron culverins**
Crew: **46**

against the wind. The skillful combination of the lateen and square sails gave the carrack a great deal of flexibility.

Ferdinand Magellan's Ships

Trinidad

Ferdinand Magellan's flagship, the *Trinidad,* was a 110-ton carrack. After the great navigator's violent death while defending the retreat of a landing party of his men, two surviving ships, the *Trinidad* and the *Victoria,* turned back to Spain.

A leak in the *Trinidad*'s hull made it impossible for it to keep pace with the *Victoria,* and the two ships traveled at several days' distance from each other. A storm drove the *Trinidad* back to the Moluccas, where the ship was captured by the natives and the crew taken prisoner.

San Antonio

This 120-ton carrack was commanded by Juan de Cartagena. During the long sail along the coast of Africa he fought with Magellan and was replaced at the command of the ship.

The *San Antonio* was the first ship to enter the strait joining the Atlantic and the Pacific oceans that was later to be known as the Strait of Magellan. In the face of the perils and uncertainties of the Pacific Ocean the new captain of the *San Antonio* preferred to desert the expedition and head back to Spain, where he accused Magellan of treachery and murder.

Concepción

The *Concepción* was a 90-ton carrack. When it joined Magellan's expedition in 1519, its captain was Gaspar de Quesada.

On October 21, 1520, the *Concepción* began exploring the broad bay leading to the strait that Magellan was to call *"Todos los santos"* ("All Saints") and was later to be named for the great navigator. A polar tempest drove it into the hidden entrance of the narrow opening.

This carrack did not return to Spain because there were too few crew members left to man the ship, and the survivors set the *Concepción* afire.

Santiago

The *Santiago* was the smallest (75 tons) of the five carracks that took part in Magellan's oceanic expedition. The captain of the *Santiago,* Joâo Serrâo, was among those who supported Magellan's decision, taken during the stop at Puerto San Julián (south of the Rio de la Plata), to continue the search for a passage to the Pacific. While the other ships waited for the end of the southern winter, the *Santiago* scouted along the coast. It was the most maneuverable carrack in the expedition. While exploring the mouth of the Rio Santa Cruz the ship sank, and its crew made the arduous return to camp on foot.

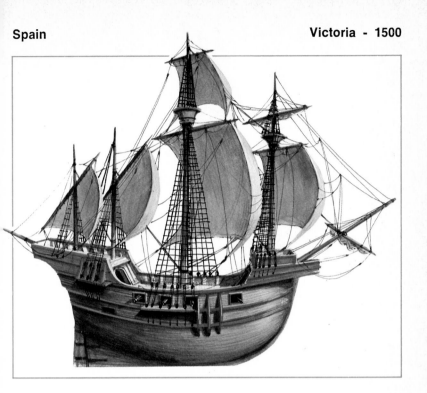

Victoria

The five ships that took part in Magellan's expedition set sail from the port of Sanlucar de Barrameda on September 20, 1519. This was to be one of the most dramatic and adventurous naval explorations in history. The *Victoria,* an 85-ton carrack, was the only one of the five ships to go through the Strait of Magellan and return to Spain safely. Thus the *Victoria* was the first ship to circumnavigate the earth.

The *Victoria* had ten culverins

Type: **four-masted merchant carrack**
Launching: **about 1500**
Length: **92 ft.**
Beam: **12 ft.**
Depth: **7 ft.**
Displacement: **85 tons**
Armament: **10 culverins**
Crew: **43**

aboard, but they were never fired, not even during the episode when the natives of Mactan, in the Philippines, attacked and killed Magellan. Of the 260 crew members who set out, only 18 returned, together with four Indians. They reached Spain in September 1522. One survivor, Antonio Pigafetta, left a full account of the journey.

It must have been a large caravel like the one illustrated here that carried Amerigo Matteo Vespucci on his two voyages to America. Because of its particular characteristics this caravel can be classed among the carracks.

Type: **three-masted carrack**
Launching: **about 1480**
Length: **115 ft.**
Beam: **19 ft.**
Depth: **15 ft.**
Displacement: **468 tons**
Crew: **86**

Vespucci's first voyage for the King of Spain lasted from May 16, 1499, until June 1500. After touching the coast of Guiana, the Florentine navigator went up the Amazon a short distance, and continued along the coast as far as 6° 30′ south latitude. The second voyage, this time for Portugal, lasted from May 13, 1501, until July 22, 1502. Vespucci was looking for a southern passage to the rich lands of the East. On this voyage Vespucci's ships went beyond 50° south latitude along the South American coast. There are serious doubts about a third voyage supposedly made between May 1503 and June 1504.

Type: **three-masted merchant carrack**
Launching: **about 1490**
Length: **112 ft.**
Beam: **15 ft.**
Depth: **13 ft.**
Displacement: **approx. 160 tons**
Armament: **6 iron culverins**
Crew: **40**

The *Matthew* was a typical English small merchant ship. John Cabot, a Venetian living in Bristol, set sail in the *Matthew* on May 2, 1497. Fifty-two days later, June 24, he set foot on Cape Breton Island and claimed it for the crown of England. He planted the royal insignia of England and the Venetian flag as well.

Cabot had rented the *Matthew* for his voyage. Afterward the *Matthew*, like most carracks of the period, saw merchant service between England and Ireland. On December 20, 1503, the *Matthew* sailed from Bristol for Ireland and returned on May 5, 1504.

On June 13 it set off for Bordeaux, returning on August 12. Two weeks later, with a fresh cargo, it set off for Spain. In a few monotonous commercial voyages the small carrack covered a great many miles. Because of the number and variety of its sails, the carrack was a highly maneuverable and reliable ship.

Type: **redunda caravel**
Launching: **about 1500**
Length: **109 ft.**
Beam: **20 ft.**
Depth: **10 ft.**
Displacement: **200 tons**
Crew: **50**

"The most beautiful region you could hope to find anywhere in the world. The river kept flowing as far as the eye could see." These were the words of Jacques Cartier (1491-1557), the French navigator, on his return from a second voyage to Canada, when he had discovered the St. Lawrence River. The expedition, backed by Francis I of France, consisted of three caravels, the *Ermillon,* the *Petite Hermine,* and Cartier's flagship, the *Grande Hermine.* Cartier's first voyage to Canada had taken place in 1534. He made that voyage, too, aboard the *Grande Hermine* but with ten other ships as well. In 1541 Cartier and the Seigneur de Roberval were sent to establish a permanent settlement in Canada, but failed. Cartier returned to France in 1542; Roberval and the colonizers left a year later.

Type: **merchant flute**
Launching: **1612**
Length: **128 ft.**
Beam: **15 ft.**
Depth: **10 ft.**
Displacement: **360 tons**
Armament: **19 bronze cannons;
12 stone launchers**
Crew: **65**

It was aboard the *Concorde* on January 31, 1616, that two adventurous Dutchmen, Schouten and Lemaire, opened a new trade route between Europe and the Indies by going beyond the Strait of Magellan and doubling Cape Horn for the first time. Among other things, they were the first Europeans to sight the albatross.

At the time, the achievement of doubling Cape Horn was not sufficiently appreciated. When the two men arrived in Java, the local authorities of the Dutch East India Company, who prescribed that their affiliates enter the Pacific by way of the Strait of Magellan, accused the two men of improper conduct for not following instructions.

The Development of the Ram

The Latin *rostrum,* the beaklike ram at the prow of a ship, was used for centuries as an offensive weapon to pierce enemy ships. However, on galleons and sailing ships it had a decorative function and also served for bracing the bowsprit.

The ram underwent various modifications during the centuries.

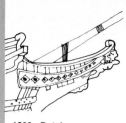

1600: Dutch

1640: English

1660: Dutch

1670: English

1670: French

1706: English

1708: English

1710: Spanish

1748: Danish

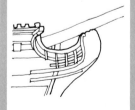

1759: English

The Galleon

When Philip II of Spain heard that his Invincible Armada had been destroyed, not so much by British naval firepower as by the fury of the elements, he is said to have exclaimed: "I sent my ships to fight the English not the wind and waves. May God be blessed." The backbone of Philip's armada were the galleons, those sailing ships that appeared toward the middle of the 16th century and remained the warship par excellence for a century and a half. The term first appeared in the 12th-century *Annali Genovesi* and was applied to a minor galley driven by 60-80 oars that was used for reconnaissance duty. The real galleon emerged in the course of the 16th century as a development of the galley. It was to combine the greater maneuverability of the galley with the requirements of long-distance sailing. The galleon was larger than the carrack, the outstanding 15th-century sailing vessel. The galleon was three times as long as it was wide, and the beam was two times its height. The bow of the galleon was still reminiscent of the galley, but the galley's long ram was modified. It was no longer an offensive weapon but provided support for the bowsprit. The sterncastle and forecastle were tall structures with two or more decks. The quarterdeck was elaborately decorated with wooden statues and allegorical figures, sometimes running the length of the quarterdeck as far as the mainmast. There were eight or ten gunports on the main deck for smaller pieces of artillery, and seven or eight cannons were installed on the upper stern decks. The main deck was not the most important, even though it was there that the complex maneuvers and rigging took place. The next deck down was more important. It was there that the heavy artillery was installed, obviously with the intent of giving the ship a better distribution of weight. A 16th-century galleon was about 130 feet long and more than 30 feet at the beam. Minor galleons had three masts and greater sail surface. The foremast carried three square sails. The lowest of these three sails was the largest and served to balance the mainsail. The mainmast also carried three square sails, while the mizzenmast carried a triangular lateen sail below and a square topsail. The larger galleons had four masts. The fourth mast, the one closest to the stern, the bonaventure, carried a lateen sail. At the stern there was a kind of outrigger for the lateen sheets. About half of the total sail surface was represented by the mainsail. Toward the end of the 16th century, there appeared a small square sail on a small mast set on the bowsprit.

The French, Spanish, and English fleets found the galleon to be their best warship. The notes of Matthew Baker, the English shipbuilder, provide valuable information about late 16th-century English galleons. The forecastle had a single deck only, and the ship was generally lower and sleeker than French and Spanish gal-

leons. The Dutch later developed a galleon in which the foremast was installed in front of the forecastle, while the sterncastle structures were lower and soberly ornamented.

The first battery of the galleons comprised some 20 improved culverins (133 mm., over ten feet long), and a second battery of demi-culverins, 9- or 10-pounders, was installed on the main deck. Portable cannons were installed on the quarterdeck and sterncastle. The crew, some 300-men strong, ate and slept in the batteries, while the captain and officers were lodged in the stern. The galleon saw military and merchant service alike. By the middle of the 17th century the galleon was well on its way toward becoming a powerful ship of the line.

The galleon came into being as a larger, more maneuverable, and faster successor to the carrack. The galleon carried fewer soldiers, for artillery was replacing hand-to-hand combat. On the earlier ships often there had been more soldiers than sailors aboard. Thus the structures of the forecastle and sterncastle were reduced, for there were fewer men aboard, and the ship became more streamlined and gained in speed.

In his youth, British admiral Lord William Monson had taken part in naval operations against the Spanish Armada. Speaking of the large carracks of an earlier day, Monson pointed out that the royal fleets of the time never made real voyages.

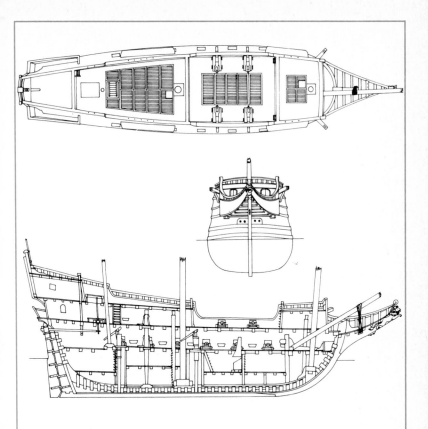

A typical 16th-century Dutch galleon. The bilges usually carried sand or stone ballast. The cargo, supplies, and equipment were stored in the holds above them. Above the holds was a battery deck with cannon ports. At the top level was the main deck, with the quarterdeck at the stern, where officers were quartered. The masts were firmly anchored on the lower decks, and bilge pumps were used to remove any water that leaked in.

They were never far from the coast. Indeed, with a fair wind they could get back to port within 24 hours. Such was the fleet of Henry VIII. But the galleons of Elizabeth's day did not expect to see the English coast for perhaps four, five, six months or more at a time. England was not at first a leader in galleon construction. The first leaders in the field, both technically and in navigation, were the Dutch and then the French.

Candia

The Venetian galleon was a magnificent combat ship. It was toughly built, and it was armored with metal plates to protect combatants on deck. However its massive structure made it very heavy and not easy to maneuver. The *Candia* was part of the impressive fleet that set out late in the summer of 1538, under the command of the Genoese admiral Andrea Doria (serving Emperor Charles V), to rid the seas of the galleys of Khair ed-din (Barbarossa), the pirate who had sworn allegiance to the Turkish monarch Suleiman and dominated the Mediterranean during the first half of the 16th century. Under Doria's command were assembled the fleets of Genoa, Venice, and the Papal States: 49 Genoese galleys; 81 Venetian ships, including galleys and galleons; and 36 papal galleys. Just before the battle began 30 Spanish galleys joined these forces. The Turkish ships were anchored in the Bay of Ambracia on the Greek coast. Doria tried in vain to get them out and finally withdrew to the island of Leucade in hopes that Barbarossa would come out. The Turks came out and attacked Doria's ships. While the rest of the fleet took up position for battle, the *Candia,* under the command of the Venetian Alessandro Condalmiero, fell behind because of light winds.

On September 28, 1538, the whole fleet of Turkish galleys attacked the stranded galleon in waves. At first the galleon did not reply to the enemy artillery fire. The first Turkish salvo split the Venetian ship's mainmast. Condalmiero ordered his crew not to fire on single Turkish galleys in the forefront but to skim their fire into the mass of galleys behind. This strategy proved to be highly effective.

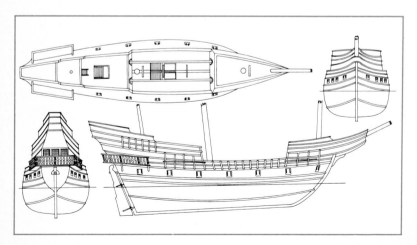

When the first wave of galleys was only a few hundred feet from the *Candia,* the Turks were overwhelmed by an avalanche of firepower. In earlier times, the decisive factors in naval combat had been maneuverability and successful boarding of enemy vessels. Now, instead, there were ships almost as immobile as castles and very heavily armed that could stand up to veritable sieges.

The Venetians lost the battle, but the *Candia* had demonstrated that a sailing vessel could outdo any galley in battle. And, indeed, the Battle of Preveza marked the end of the Mediterranean galley's career as a warship.

Type: **three-masted galleon**
Launching: **about 1530**
Length: **109 ft. (from the bowsprit)**
Beam: **28 ft.**
Depth: **13 ft.**
Displacement: **650 tons**
Armament: **first battery, sixteen 19-lb. culverins; second battery, sixteen 9-lb. demi-culverins**
Crew: **120 seamen; 160 soldiers**

Santissima Madre

The reconstruction and correct understanding of the sailing ships of the past is not always an easy task. Nevertheless it is conventional to classify the *Santissima Madre* as a galleon of the 16th century.

A tentative reconstruction of the 16th-century Venetian galleon can be made on the basis of the galleon model of 1540 in the Naval Museum in Madrid, the model in the Science Museum in South Kensington, London, and the notes compiled by the English master carpenter Matthew Baker, who built warships for the British navy.

Technical drawings of a galleon appear in a late 16th-century English manuscript which includes plans for the vessels that were built by Baker. A contemporary document describes one Venetian galleon as measuring approximately 135 feet in total length and more than 30 feet at its widest. Also helpful in reconstructing the galleon authentically are the studies that were carried out in 1884 by Eugéne Evrard.

It would seem that the Venetian galleon had a smooth-lined hull, altogether free of ornamentation. The captain's cabin, between the second and third deck toward the stern, provided a maximum of six feet headroom, while the soldiers aboard had some six inches less. The pilot and the boatswain had barely five feet headroom.

The masts were all built in a single piece. The foremast stood well forward toward the bow, while the mainmast and the mizzenmast were far to the stern. This arrangement of masts

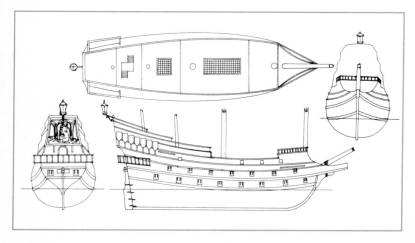

was typical until the middle of the 17th century.

This arrangement was the result of trial and error in an attempt to achieve the best balance of weight and sails.

The tops served for crewmen to maneuver the sails and also served as battle stations in combat. Protective plates were installed, and hand cannons could be installed. Pikemen and spear throwers were also sta-

Type: **four-masted galleon; five decks**
Launching: **about 1550**
Length: **137 ft.**
Beam: **29 ft.**
Depth: **12 ft.**
Armament: **12 culverins**
Sail surface: **11,836 sq. ft.**
Crew: **about 230 men**

tioned in the tops. The *Santissima Madre* is a typical example of what Italian naval construction could produce in the 16th century.

On March 22, 1588, the mainmast of the galleon *San Martin* carried the insignia of Don Alonzo Pérez de Guzman, Duke of Medina-Sidonia, the admiral in command of the Spanish Armada that Philip II sent against the English. The *San Martin* led the largest fleet of its day, with some 130 ships, 8,000 seamen, and 19,000 soldiers. It comprised galleons from Biscay, Castille, and Andalusia; the Guipuzcoa galleons under the command of Miguel de Oquendo; Eastern galleons; the *urcas* of Juan Gomez de Medina; the xebecs of Don Antonio de Mendoza; the Neapolitan galleasses; and the Portuguese gal-

Type: **three-masted galleon**
Launching: **about 1567**
Length: **123 ft. (from the bowsprit)**
Beam: **31 ft.**
Depth: **15 ft.**
Armament: **first battery, eighteen 18-lb. culverins; second battery, twenty-two 9-lb. demi-culverins; eight small hand cannons; four assault culverins**
Crew: **117 seamen; 300 soldiers**

leys of Don Diego Medrano. Among the 67 ships that escaped the English artillery and the fury of the elements was the *San Martin.* Thus the *San Martin* was a participant in the first modern naval battle, a battle that was to mark the beginning of the decline of the Spanish navy.

After the Battle of Gravelines (August 8, 1588), in the waters between Calais and Dunkirk, the Spanish Armada's fate was sealed. The Spanish admiral decided to head north along the English coast and around Ireland in order to avoid the English fleet waiting for him to the south. The *San Juan* was one of the surviving ships that set out on August 9 on the sail north, but just beyond the Orkneys a storm blew up and 19 galleons foundered on the rocks and sank. The captain of the *San Juan,* Vice Admiral Juan Martinez de Recalde, landed his crew on the Irish coast because they were without food or water. They

Type: **three-masted galleon**
Launching: **about 1576**
Length: **131 ft. (from the bowsprit)**
Beam: **32 ft.**
Depth: **16 ft.**
Displacement: **970 tons**
Armament: **first battery, eighteen 18-lb. culverins; second battery, ten 9-lb. demi-culverins; four hunting culverins; 16 smaller guns**
Crew: **119 seamen; 70 soldiers**

carried arms and hoped to find provisions. Nevertheless, many of the sailors died of hunger and thirst, and by the time the ship returned to Spain the crew had been reduced to 18 men.

There are conflicting accounts of this 16th-century English ship. There are those who maintain that the *Great Harry* was no more than a second name applied to Henry VIII's carrack the *Henry Grace à Dieu*. Others contend that it was an altogether different ship built some years after the *Henry*. It seems more likely, however, that the *Great Harry* was a reconstruction of the *Henry,* and so it followed that the carrack would have been rebuilt as a galleon. The superstructures of the *Henry* were eliminated, and the rigging was more functional. Cannons were installed in batteries along the sides of the ship, and ports

Type: **four-masted galleon (reconstruction, 1540, of the carrack *Henry Grace à Dieu*)**
Length: **198 ft.**
Beam: **27 ft.**
Depth: **15 ft.**
Displacement: **1,348 tons**
Armament: **48 bronze cannons; 56 smaller guns**
Crew: **568 seamen; 400 soldiers**

were installed for them. Although the *Harry* was faster and more maneuverable than the *Henry,* it still served only as a royal ship.

It was destroyed in 1552 when a fire broke out aboard the ship, so the *Great Harry* never saw any significant combat duty.

The *Judith*'s name is forever linked with the name of one of the most famous sailors in the history of England, Sir Francis Drake. Drake was born in Devonshire, veritable cradle of navigators and adventurers. Although the family was of humble origins and modest means, they were related to one of the richest families in Plymouth, the Hawkins. The Hawkins family were the owners of the *Judith,* and Drake was given command of the ship in 1567, when he was about 20 years old. He sailed with two other galleons on a slaving voyage between West Africa and South America. The English were at-

Type: **three-masted galleon**
Launching: **about 1559**
Length: **121 ft. (from the bowsprit)**
Beam: **29 ft.**
Depth: **14 ft.**
Displacement: **736 tons**
Armament: **sixteen 18-lb. culverins; ten 9-lb. demi-culverins**
Crew: **120**

tacked by the Spanish off the island of San Juan de Ulua. Drake's ship managed to escape without damage, and even though Hawkins later accused him of having retreated without fighting, the reasons for the quarrel could not have been very deep, since the two continued to maintain their friendship.

81

Golden Hind

The *Golden Hind* was a minor galleon that had originally been called the *Pelican.* It was renamed in honor of Lord Hatton, whose coat of arms featured a golden hind and who promoted Drake's voyage of circumnavigation. Despite its relatively small size, though no smaller than many other Renaissance exploration ships, it was a remarkably seaworthy vessel.

It was a relatively unadorned ship, the only decoration being at the stern. The forecastle was low, and the quarterdeck and forecastle were of the same height. The upper deck was barely three feet higher. The ship had five square sails, including the one on the stempost of the bowsprit, and one lateen sail carried by a long yard on the mizzenmast. The forecastle did not protrude outside the bow, and in this it followed the standard galleon pattern. The forecastle was totally integrated with the bow of the ship. Forward of the forecastle were the crew's sanitary facilities.

The helmsman had a small covered cabin at the foot of the quarterdeck and a fairly unobstructed view of the deck and riggings. The horizontal tiller had a vertical handle that made the rudder easier to operate.

On December 13, 1577, Sir Francis Drake set out with the *Golden Hind* and four other ships on the most famous voyage in English naval history. He carried sealed orders from Queen Elizabeth, and he may have hoped to discover the long-sought Northwest Passage when he reached the coast of California. The *Golden Hind* sailed to the Strait of Magellan and encountered furious storms that held up the passage for almost two

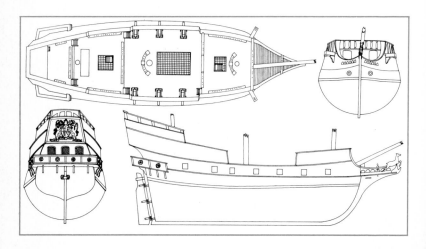

months and sank two of Drake's ships. Drake finally reached Valparaiso, where he attacked a large Spanish galleon. The *Golden Hind* proceeded along the coast of Chile, attacking Spanish ports and shipping, including the galleon *Cacafuego,* which surrendered without a shot being fired. Drake continued his voyage to California and then set out across the Pacific to the Moluccas. After almost three years at sea the expedition returned to Plymouth. Not

Type: **three-masted galleon**
Launching: **about 1560**
Length: **86 ft. (from the bowsprit)**
Beam: **14 ft.**
Depth: **9 ft.**
Displacement: **100 tons**
Armament: **first battery, fourteen 18-lb. culverins; second battery, twelve 9-lb. demi-culverins; various portable guns**
Crew: **146**

only was the *Golden Hind* the first English ship to circumnavigate the world, it was a financial success as well, showing a profit of 500,000 pounds sterling on the voyage.

Revenge

When Queen Elizabeth heard that Philip II's armada was about to attack England, she is reputed to have remarked that she had nothing to fear from a man who had taken 12 years to learn the alphabet. It is clear that the queen was confident of her seamen and ships. Another story is told of Sir Francis Drake in Plymouth on July 29, 1588. He was playing bowls with Lord Howard of Effingham, the admiral of the English fleet, when a breathless Captain Fleming of the *Golden Hind* arrived to tell him that the Spanish Armada had been sighted off the coast. Drake took the news calmly and remarked: "We have time enough to finish the game and beat the Spaniards, too."

The next day Drake was at the command of his galleon, the *Revenge,* on the trail of the armada. On the night of July 31, Lord Howard's *Ark Royal* was following the poop lantern of the *Revenge.* Somehow the lookout lost sight of it for a while and later thought he had found it again. The next morning it turned out that it was not the *Revenge* they had been following but the Spanish flagship. Meanwhile the *Revenge* had altered her course and captured the damaged Spanish ship *Nuestra Señora del Rosario,* earning Drake 45,000 ducats of prize money.

Subsequently the *Revenge* took part in the action off the Isle of Wight in pursuit of the *Santa Ana.* And on August 8 it took part in the decisive action at Gravelines. Medina-Sidonia's Spanish fleet, with its munitions almost exhausted and bad weather in the offing, headed north in retreat.

The Revenge joined the ranks of legendary ships three years after the armada's defeat. Now the flagship of

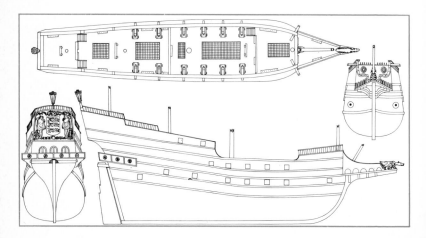

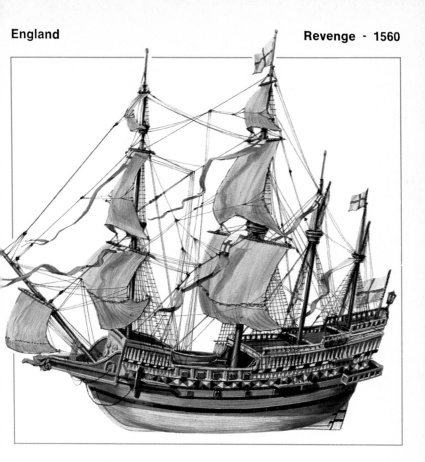

Sir Richard Grenville, she was part of a squadron whose mission was to capture Spanish treasure ships. Lying in wait off the Azores, the 16 English ships, commanded by Lord Howard, were surprised by a Spanish fleet of more than 50 warships. All but Grenville and the *Revenge* managed to escape. Though surrounded, Grenville decided to fight; he and 130 of his 150-man crew were killed.

Tennyson immortalized the ship and her crew in the ballad "The Re-

Type: **four-masted galleon**
Launching: **about 1560**
Length: **121 ft. (from the bowsprit)**
Beam: **29 ft.**
Depth: **15 ft.**
Displacement: **976 tons**
Armament: **first battery, sixteen 18-lb. culverins; second battery, fourteen 9-lb. demi-culverins; various portable guns**
Crew: **135**

venge." "We shall live to fight again and to strike another blow," he wrote, quoting one of the gunners, but the galleon sank in a storm right after the battle.

The first English ship to be called the *Victory* was a two-decked galleon. Under the command of John Hawkins, the *Victory* was part of the English fleet that defeated the Spanish Armada. When the fleet was assembled at Plymouth, Lord Howard, the English admiral, is reputed to have exclaimed that he would rather live among those noble ships than anywhere else in the world.

The *Victory* played a leading part in one of the actions off Gravelines on the French coast. Together with Howard's flagship, the *Ark Royal,* the

Type: **three-masted galleon**
Launching: **1571**
Length: **106 ft.**
Beam: **42 ft.**
Depth: **14 ft.**
Displacement: **870 tons**
Armament: **first battery, twenty-eight 18-lb. culverins; second battery, twenty 9-lb. demi-culverins; twelve portable guns**
Crew: **120 seamen; 240 soldiers**

Victory attacked the 650-ton Spanish urca *Gran Grifon,* which had become separated from the rest of the armada. There was a furious exchange of fire, and under this barrage the English were forced to withdraw.

The English fleet that waited in Plymouth Harbor for the Spanish Armada consisted of only 34 regular ships, under the command of Lord Howard of Effingham. But these ships were backed up by a host of merchantmen and lightships. A total of 197 ships were assembled to fight off the Spaniards. The *Triumph,* a royal war galleon, was a typical example of what English shipwrights could produce.

The Spaniards considered boarding and hand-to-hand combat decisive in naval actions and carried a great number of soldiers on their ships.

Type: **four-masted galleon**
Launching: **about 1576**
Length: **128 ft. (from the bowsprit)**
Beam: **31 ft.**
Depth: **16 ft.**
Displacement: **890 tons**
Armament: **first battery, eighteen 50-lb. culverins; twenty 18-lb. culverins; second battery, six 9-lb. demi-culverins**
Crew: **189**

The English, instead, counted on maneuverability and firepower, and the construction of the *Triumph* was most compatible with this strategy. Under the command of Martin Frobisher, it was the first ship to attack the Spaniards in the decisive Battle at Gravelines.

Ark Royal

The little we know about the construction of the *Ark Royal* we owe to the drawings and notes left by the master shipwright Matthew Baker, perhaps the finest shipbuilder of his day. The scale of the construction was 4:2:1. The ship was four times as long as it was broad in the beam, and its breadth was twice its height. Nevertheless the *Ark Royal* varied in the height of its superstructures. The forecastle had a single deck, and there was an area forward of the castle for handling the bow riggings and for sanitary facilities. The main deck between the castle and the mainmast was exposed to enemy fire, so the *Ark Royal* carried colored awnings that hung over the sides to cover the crew at the riggings.

The *Ark Royal* had four masts. The foremast stood on the forecastle. The mainmast stood roughly in the middle, the mizzenmast stood on the quarterdeck, and the bonaventure stood on the second deck. The mizzenmast and the bonaventure carried lateen sails.

Another innovation was the vertical handle of the rudder bar. Thus the helmsman could watch the sails. Earlier practice had required that he sail by compass alone with directions from an officer on the quarterdeck.

The *Ark Royal* fitted English tactical ideas perfectly. A naval encounter should rely on artillery fire and not on hand-to-hand combat. The *Ark Royal* was heavily armed with 133 mm. culverins that had taken the place of the squat 165 mm. cannons. The range of the *Ark Royal*'s culverins was about 300 feet. During the operations against the Spanish Armada, the *Ark Royal*,

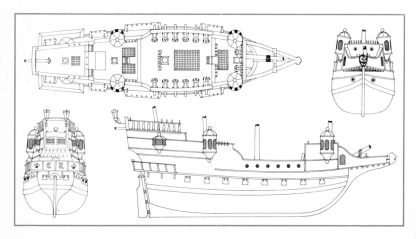

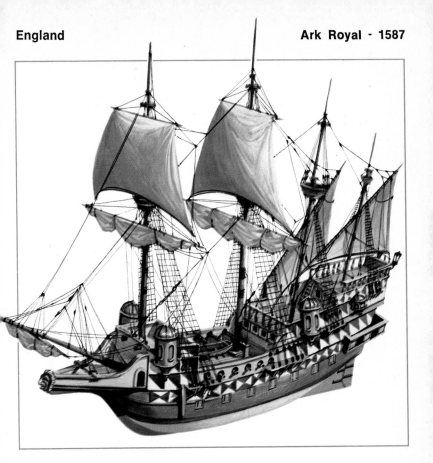

which had been launched the year before, flew the insignia of Lord Howard of Effingham, the commander in chief of the English fleet. Among the actions in which the *Ark Royal* was involved during the far-flung battle was a joint attack, with the *Victory,* on the Spanish urca *Gran Grifon* at Gravelines. The urca proved too formidable for the English galleons.

The British fleet consisted of 197 ships with some 16,000 men, while

Type: **four-masted galleon**
Launching: **1587**
Length: **122 ft. (from the bowsprit)**
Beam: **approx. 29 ft.**
Depth: **approx. 16 ft.**
Displacement: **approx. 880 tons**
Armament: **first battery, sixteen 18-lb. culverins; second battery, twelve 9-lb. demi-culverins; smaller portable guns**
Crew: **190 seamen (40 gunners); 70 soldiers**

the Spaniards, under the command of the Duke of Medina-Sidonia, had some 27,000 men. But the English fleet out-gunned the armada, and its ships were more maneuverable.

Mayflower

In the spring of 1957 Alan Villiers sailed an exact replica of the *Mayflower* across the Atlantic, following the route that had taken the Pilgrim Fathers to Plymouth Rock in 1620. Villiers' experience suggests much about the performance of 17th-century English galleons. The lower deck of the old *Mayflower* had served as cargo space, so there was little headroom for the hundred-odd passengers who made the crossing in 1620. However it was not unusual for seamen's quarters to have low ceilings. The *Mayflower* could develop reasonable speed, even with light winds, because of its small draft and sails suited to the prevailing winds of the Atlantic. The high sterncastle seemed to present problems, but Villiers proved it did not. He believed that such a small

ship should sail very well, and he made a point of the fact that world transport was carried out on such small ships from the time America was discovered until the 19th century.

The original *Mayflower* was put at the disposal of the Pilgrim Fathers by English merchants. Of the 102 pilgrims that sailed, only 35 had broken from the Church of England and were from the English Separatist Church in Leiden, Holland. Two ships had been chartered for the voyage, the *Mayflower* and the *Speedwell,* but the *Speedwell* was in such poor condition that it had to put back to land, and the 35 Separatists who were aboard were transferred to the *Mayflower.* They set sail in September 1620, and on November 20 the coast of North America was sighted. Their original

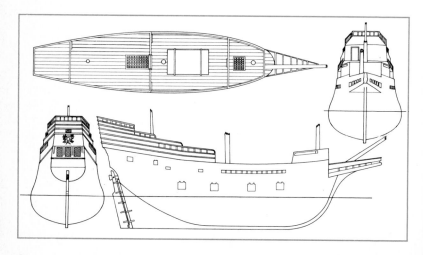

intention had been to land in Virginia, where the Virginia Company had agreed to rent land to them, but strong winds drove the ship farther north, and they landed at Cape Cod. Members of the group went ashore and declared the land inhospitable for settlement. The ship continued on and finally landed at Plymouth Harbor, and it was here that a permanent settlement was established.

The first months were hard, but by the time the *Mayflower* set sail for

Type: **three-masted galleon**
Launching: **1615**
Length: **65 ft.**
Beam: **26 ft.**
Depth: **11 ft.**
Displacement: **180 tons**

the return to England (in April 1621) the Plymouth Colony had taken root, although only half of the original pilgrims were still alive.

The replica, *Mayflower II,* can be visited in the harbor at Plymouth, Massachusetts.

The date was June 11, 1666. The second Dutch War was raging in the northern seas. The Dutch admiral De Ruyter was at sea off the coast of Dunkirk, and the Four Days' Battle was about to begin. Among the English ships was the *Henry*, commanded by Vice Admiral Sir John Harman. A Dutch fire ship had rammed it on the starboard side. Lieutenant Thomas Lamming managed to disengage the two ships. A second fire ship approached, and the crew of the *Henry* panicked. Sword in hand, Lamming quelled the crew, and the fire was put out. A third fire ship approached, but it was sunk by cannon fire. The Dutch vice admiral Evertzen called out from his ship to Harman, urging the Englishman to surrender. "It has not come to that yet," Harman exclaimed. The *Henry* fired a broadside that killed Evertzen. The *Henry* limped back to the port at Harwich for repairs and was in action again the next day.

Type: **three-masted galleon**
Launching: **about 1658**
Length: **128 ft. (from the bowsprit)**
Beam: **30 ft.**
Depth: **17 ft.**
Displacement: **1,100 tons**
Armament: **first battery, sixteen 18-lb. culverins; second battery, twelve 9-lb. demi-culverins; several smaller guns**
Crew: **190**

The *St. Michel* typifies the transition in construction techniques from the large 16th-century galleon to a more modern vessel. The *St. Michel* was well on the way to those later ships which were to offer firepower and great seaworthiness. Most important of all was its increased maneuverability. Built in Chatham of solid English oak and Baltic pine, the *St. Michel* could stand comparison with the finest ships produced by Dutch naval yards.

On June 7, 1672 (when the *St. Michel* was 23 years old), during the Battle of Solebay, between the Dutch and Franco-British fleets, the large

Type: four-masted galleon
Launching: **about 1668**
Length: **154 ft.**
Beam: **31 ft.**
Depth: **19 ft.**
Displacement: **865 tons**
Armament: **first battery, twenty-four 18-lb. culverins; second battery, twelve 9-lb. demi-culverins; eight stone launchers**
Crew: **150 seamen; 30 gunners; 170 soldiers**

English galleon took the Duke of York aboard. The duke had abandoned his flagship, the *Royal Prince,* when Dutch shells had smashed the mast. The *St. Michel* was so heavily battered during the battle that the duke had to transfer ships once again.

Built in Holland for Frederick William the Great Elector of Brandenburg, this small galleon is typical of late 16th-century naval construction. Frederick ordered many such ships from neighboring shipyards to build up the fleet of his emerging nation. The ship still has a gallery all the way around the stern, above the decorative elements that center on the coat of arms of Lubeck. The *Roter Löwe* had very advanced riggings for its time, and they were remarkably simple in concept. On the first battery deck, where the 12 main cannons were installed, there were two bilge pumps with single handles, and a double winch

Type: **three-masted galleon**
Launching: **1597**
Length: **132 ft. (from the bowsprit)**
Beam: **26 ft.**
Depth: **13 ft.**
Displacement: **unknown**
Armament: **first battery, twelve 24-lb. guns; second battery, four 18-lb. guns; eight 9-lb. culverins**
Crew: **unknown**

for yards and anchor.

The bowsprit was inclined slightly to starboard. The captain's cabin was near the helm, certainly not the place for a good night's sleep. Although the overall dimensions of the *Roter Löwe* are known, its displacement and size of the crew are not.

The main feature of the *Eendracht* was that the lines of its superstructures were considerably lower and smoother than those of contemporary English and French vessels. Indeed, the Dutch were the first to realize that high superstructures were a serious impediment to maneuverability and speed. This problem was even greater when maneuvering in shallow waters, when quick changes in direction were of the utmost importance.

The *Eendracht* was blown up with all its crew on June 13, 1665, when battling the Duke of York's flagship, the *Royal Charles,* during an engagement in the second Dutch War.

Type: four-masted galleon
Launching: **about 1647**
Length: **148 ft. (from the bowsprit)**
Beam: **33 ft.**
Depth: **16 ft.**
Displacement: **1,126 tons**
Armament: **first battery, twenty 42-lb. cannons; second battery, sixteen 24-lb. cannons; twelve 19-lb. cannons; eight 9-lb. culverins**
Crew: **226 seamen; 360 soldiers**

It is worth pointing out again that until the 18th century, shipbuilding was a craft industry. There were no fixed standards for shipbuilding, and ships of the same category could be strikingly different from each other. The *Eendracht* represents the result of trial and error coupled with past experience.

This fine galleon was the flagship of Maarten Tromp, the first in a long line of Dutch seamen. During the first Dutch War, 1652-54, the *Brederoe* played a leading role at the Battle of Dungeness. Tromp commanded a fleet of 81 vessels with 2,200 cannons and 8,000 men. He faced a force of 42 ships, with 1,400 cannons and 5,800 men, under the command of Robert Blake. The *Brederoe* fought off Blake's *Triumph* and the *Bonaventure* at the same time and managed to capture the latter.

Legend has it that Tromp hung a broom from the top of the mast to

Type: **three-masted galleon**
Launching: **about 1650**
Length: **129 ft. (from the bowsprit)**
Beam: **30 ft.**
Depth: **15 ft.**
Displacement: **1,112 tons**
Armament: **first battery, twelve 19-lb. culverins; second battery, twelve 9-lb. demi-culverins**
Crew: **146 seamen; 220 soldiers**

mark the fact that he had swept the English from the sea. Tromp lost his life aboard the *Brederoe*. He was struck down by an English bullet on August 10, 1653, during the Battle of Scheveningen, the last battle of the first Dutch War.

What strikes one first about the *Lerwich,* a 17th-century Dutch galleon, is the disappearance of all the heavy superstructures that characterized earlier ships of this type. The quarterdeck is lower and the forecastle has been all but replaced by a continuation of the main deck. Thus the forward rigging and sails were much easier to handle.

The basic armament of this ship consisted of front-loading bronze cannons. These medium-caliber weapons were installed three or four feet higher than were such weapons on English ships. This arrangement did not help

Type: **three-masted galleon**
Launching: **about 1662**
Length: **134 ft. (from the bowsprit)**
Beam: **31 ft.**
Depth: **15 ft.**
Displacement: **1,109 tons**
Armament: **first battery, sixteen 24-lb. cannons; second battery, eight 9-lb. cannons**
Crew: **180**

balance the ship, but this was compensated for by greater draft. Since the cannons sat higher it was not necessary to close the ports of the lower battery when the sea was rough. Thus the ship could maintain full firepower even during inclement weather.

97

Zeven Provincien

The United Provinces of Holland won full independence and recognition as an independent state with the Peace of Westphalia in 1648. The Dutch fleet of more than 1,700 ships absorbed nine-tenths of the traffic of English ports. Conflict with England was inevitable, and scarcely four years after the Peace of Westphalia, Holland and England were at war. There were three Dutch wars with England over the next decades.

In 1672 the Dutch fleet was commanded by one of the greatest naval officers in history, Michiel Adriaanszoon De Ruyter. The Dutch fleet consisted of 78 ships, with 4,188 guns, 24 escort ships, 36 fire ships, and 19,930 men. The English, allied with the French, had 84 men-of-war, 17 frigates, 23 fire ships, 4,954 guns, and a total of 30,500 men. The Battle of Solebay took place on June 7, 1672. The *Zeven Provincien* attacked the *Royal Prince* and smashed her mast. At the end of the encounter, the English had lost the *Royal James* and eight other ships, and the French *Superbe* was badly damaged. One Dutch ship had been sunk, and the *Stavoren* had been captured by the enemy. De Ruyter's flagship was badly damaged, but it managed to reach the port of Walcheren.

Admiral Michiel De Ruyter, "the man who was worth an army," died on April 29, 1676, during the Battle of Augusta, which took place between Cape Santa Croce and Syracuse, Sicily. He was faced with the French fleet commanded by Admiral Duquesne, and was on the quarterdeck urging his men on when a cannonball took off almost all of his right leg.

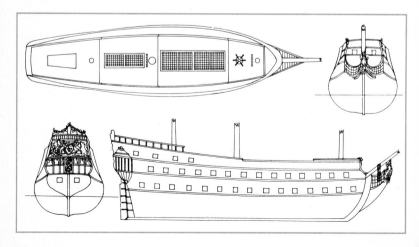

Type: **first-rate three-decked ship**
Launching: **1665**
Length: **205 ft.**
Beam: **43 ft.**
Depth: **20 ft.**
Displacement: **1,427 tons**
Armament: **first battery, thirty 42-lb. cannons; second battery, thirty 24-lb. cannons; third battery, twenty 12-lb. cannons; twenty smaller guns, 3-, 6-, and 9-pounders**
Crew: **743**

Derfflinger

What we know about 17th-century vessels is usually fragmentary. But we know that sometime about 1685 an older galleon, perhaps the *Wolkensauli,* was rechristened in honor of Marshal Derfflinger, the victor at the Battle of Fahrbellin.

It is also definitely known, however, that the name *Derfflinger* appears in building plans dating from the year 1675, so it is difficult to assign a date to the ship bearing this name. It is from the plans, of course, that we have learned what we know about the *Derfflinger*'s technical characteristics, armament, and dimensions.

It was a four-decked ship with some original features. For example, most of its weapons were on the main deck, while the first deck carried only two cannons. The deck below the sterncastle held six cannons and gives us an idea of what life on board a fighting ship must have been like at that time. There were several ports for the cannons, a gangway over the winch, and several other openings as well. The wind must have whistled through this "closed" deck at all hours of the day.

The bilge of the *Derfflinger* had stone ballast. The sails were maneuvered by a winch under the quarterdeck. The helmsman stood in a well but had a clear view of the forward part of the ship. The *Derfflinger* was overhauled in 1683, and its armament was modified. Six 23-pound cannons and two 12-pounders were added, and the crew was increased by 20 men.

The only decoration carried by this ship was a carved figure of Marshal Derfflinger on the stern.

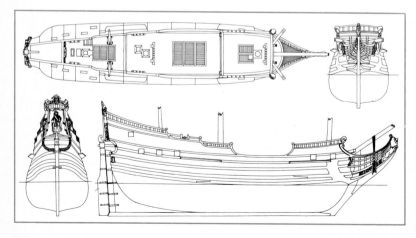

Type: **transition from galleon to flute**
Launching: **about 1675**
Length: **129 ft. (from the bowsprit)**
Beam: **26 ft.**
Depth: **19 ft.**
Displacement: **760 tons**
Armament: **twelve 23-lb. cannons**
Crew: **86**

The *Elefanten* is another example of the longevity of the caravel, which was first a coastal vessel and then became the ocean-going ship of famous navigators.

While naval construction was developing more advanced ships like the galleon, North Sea countries were still using the caravel, the proportions of which were not radically different from those of the larger galleon. The Swedish caravel *Elefanten,* built in the second half of the 16th century, was built with *franc-bord,* or carvel, planking rather than clinker planking. That is to say, the planks of the hull

Type: **northern caravel**
Launching: **about 1560**
Length: **108 ft. (from the bowsprit)**
Beam: **25 ft.**
Depth: **12 ft.**
Displacement: **450 tons**
Crew: **86 seamen; 100 soldiers**

were laid flush, and not overlapping. The stern of the *Elefanten* was square, and the rudder was installed in the center.

Construction of a high sterncastle and forecastle was a characteristic feature of the caravels, the ships that, small as they were, had first opened the ocean routes to navigation.

The *Piet en Paul,* a large galleon built in Copenhagen at the beginning of the 17th century, was in some ways an extremely advanced ship for northern Europe. The height of the holds, for example, was much greater than in other contemporary ships. More cargo could be carried, and the gundeck was sturdier. The ship was built to Dutch design, and the *Piet en Paul's* hull was varnished with a mixture of white lead, bitumen, and sulphur. This mixture was considered poisonous for shipworm, a marine clam of the family Teredinidae that secretes an enzyme which is deadly

Type: **three-masted galleon**
Launching: **about 1603**
Length: **138 ft. (from the bowsprit)**
Beam: **32 ft.**
Depth: **20 ft.**
Displacement: **910 tons**
Armament: **first battery, eighteen 18-lb. culverins; second battery, twelve 9-lb. demi-culverins**
Crew: **164 seamen; 90 soldiers**

to wood. A complex crane and pulley system was used to install the masts, which weighed several tons. In 1626 the galleon got stuck in the sand, and the Swedes applied a kind of camel technique to free the ship. Caissons were attached to the ship and sunk. Then the water was pumped out of the caissons, and the ship was freed.

Vasa

It was the spring of 1628, and the Thirty Years' War was raging (1618–1648) when a new three-masted galleon entered the fleet of Gustavus II Adolphus, King of Sweden. This was the *Nya Vasa*.

Dutch and Swedish craftsmen and artisans, under the direction of Henrik Hybertsson, built a magnificent ship. The sterncastle was over 60 feet high, almost 50 feet above the waterline. The mainmast was about 180 feet high. The ship had balconies, cupolas, arabesques, relief carvings, and more than 700 sculptures in gilded wood. On August 10, 1628, the ship set out on its maiden voyage to Alvsnabben, near Stockholm. It was hauled as far as Södermalm, where it began hoisting its sails. A few hundred feet from the islet of Beckholmen, a sudden wind struck from starboard and water entered through the gunports. A few minutes later the ship had sunk, in barely 100 feet of water. About 50 persons lost their lives, and some 100,000 riksdaler were lost, the equivalent of some $50 million. It was a national calamity. Salvage operations were begun at once. The Englishman Ian Bulmer managed to turn the ship upright and remove part of the masts. In 1664 Hans Albrecht von Treileben of Sweden and Andreas Peckell of Germany used a pneumatic bell and recovered 53 of the 60 cannons. In 1954 Anders Franzen and Arne Zetterstroem, with the Swedish underwater naval school, began salvage operations again, and on April 24, 1961, the *Vasa* was brought to the surface. It was in remarkably good condition and is now kept in dry dock in Stockholm, a valuable example of 17th-century ship construction.

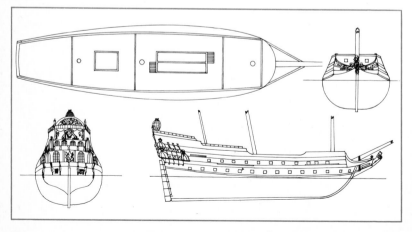

Type: **three-masted galleon**
Launching: **1627**
Length: **230 ft. (from the bowsprit)**
Beam: **35 ft.**
Depth: **14 ft.**
Displacement: **1,400 tons**
Sail surface: **12,375 sq. ft.**
Armament: **first battery, twenty-eight 24-lb. cannons; second battery, twenty-two 24-lb. cannons; third battery, two 1-lb. cannons, eight 2-lb. cannons, six 6-lb. mortars**
Crew: **133 seamen; 300 soldiers**

Couronne

The *Couronne* was the first all-French ship in design and construction and one of the finest ships in the history of sail. The launching of the *Couronne* was the result of the efforts of Cardinal Armand Jean du Plessis, Duke of Richelieu, who had concentrated naval authority in his own hands in 1627. Richelieu became Grand Master of Navigation and kept this function until his death in 1642. He may justly be considered the founder of the French navy.

He established schools for seamen, shipwrights, naval technicians, and engineers and founded shipyards and foundries. He organized French military ports (Le Havre in the north and Toulon in the south) and summoned Dutch and Italian builders to take part in the reconstruction of the French fleet. Richelieu also imported a number of Dutch galleons to be used as models both by the designers and the carpenters.

Built by master shipwright Charles Morieur of Dieppe, the *Couronne* became the model for other ships. It took the wood of an entire forest to build it.

The galleon was more than 150 feet in length overall, one of the largest ships of its day. It was also one of the sturdiest built. The two gundecks were about 6 feet in height and accommodated a total of 72 cannons.

Two stern decks stood high above the ship's waterline, and these were trapezoidal in shape, with the short end to the stern. The upper deck was smaller than the lower deck, and this feature was picked up by later ships. The forward bulkhead had two gun emplacements, and the small deck in

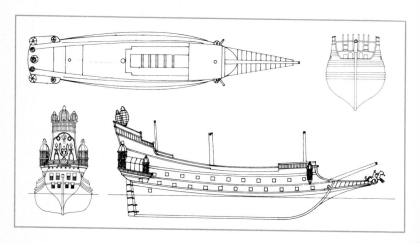

front of the forecastle was low and clear for firing. The bowsprit was installed with its base in the forecastle itself.

The *Couronne* was an elaborately ornamented vessel. At the stern were gilded wooden statues and allegorical figures, and at the front of the ship was a figurehead of Hercules killing the Hydra.

The ship had a displacement of more than 1,000 tons and made an enormous impression when it joined

Type: **three-masted galleon**
Launching: **1636**
Designer: **Charles Morieur**
Builder: **La Roche Bernard**
Length: **150 ft. (from the bowsprit)**
Beam: **50 ft.**
Depth: **23 ft.**
Displacement: **1,087 tons**
Armament: **first battery, thirty-two 18-lb. culverins; second battery, twenty-four 9-lb. culverins; third battery, sixteen 6-lb. culverins**
Crew: **638**

the Biscay squadron in 1638, for at that time the *Couronne* was the largest fighting ship that had ever appeared in European waters.

When Cardinal Richelieu began taking an interest in the French navy, he found a shipbuilding industry inferior to that in the advanced shipyards of Holland and England. Richelieu turned to the Dutch for guidance and secured five galleons to serve as models in the new shipyards he was building. Among these five ships was the *Saint Louis*. This ship had some original features for the time. Hand-to-hand fighting was no longer decisive in naval engagements; it was cannon fire that determined the outcome of the battle. Thus the main deck had a wooden grating to protect the crew if part of the mast were to

Type: **three-masted galleon**
Launching: **1626**
Length: **144 ft. (from the bowsprit)**
Beam: **29 ft.**
Depth: **15 ft.**
Displacement: **865 tons**
Armament: **first battery, twenty 32-lb. cannons; second battery, twenty-four 24-lb. cannons; eight 9-lb. demi-culverins; four guns forward and astern**
Crew: **310**

collapse under artillery fire, and gratings were applied to deck and forecastle so that the smoke of the cannons could escape.

The *Saint Louis* was a three-master with five square sails. The mizzen-mast carried a lateen sail and a topsail, while the bowsprit carried spritsails.

Type: **three-masted galleon**
Launching: **about 1643**
Length: **162 ft. (from the bowsprit)**
Beam: **32 ft.**
Depth: **17 ft.**
Displacement: **1,076 tons**
Armament: **first battery, eighteen 32-lb.
   cannons; second battery, ten 12-lb. can-
   nons; twelve 24-lb. cannons; several
   smaller pieces, 3 to 6 lbs.**
Crew: **402, including soldiers**

Some scholars hold that the galleon is a typically Spanish invention. As the galleon spread from the Mediterranean north, the type underwent several modifications and variations. Thus a great many ships were constructed that could be classed in one category or another. The *Norske Löwe* was a kind of northern galleon. The Dutch were the first to build this type of ship in the north, and it soon became popular in the Scandinavian countries. The *Norske Löwe,* the first Swedish two-decker, had the characteristic low sterncastle of Dutch ships.

There was little decoration, and the smooth lines were not unlike those that were to characterize the man-of-war or ship of the line that was to appear a few decades later. The *Norske Löwe* was the first ship to carry iron cannons, instead of bronze, with black powder charges. This was the only explosive then in use.

109

The Danish galleon *Sophia Amalia* was built for the Baltic fleet and took part in the first Northern War against the Swedes (1654–1660), which came to an end with the Peace of Copenhagen.

The *Sophia Amalia* was built almost entirely of oak, the basic material used in shipbuilding until the end of the 18th century, when teak came to be preferred. The keel was almost 30 inches thick in the middle, the timbers were half as thick, and the hull planks were up to 20 inches thick. The deck planks were 4 or 5

Type: **three-masted galleon**
Launching: **1650**
Length: **155 ft. (from the bowsprit)**
Beam: **31 ft.**
Depth: **16 ft.**
Displacement: **1,118 tons**
Armament: **first battery, twenty-four 42-lb. cannons; second battery, twenty-two guns from 12 to 24 lbs.**
Crew: **585**

inches thick, and the deck beams were almost twice as thick. The *Sophia Amalia* was a good example of the "wooden fortresses" which dominated the seas for two centuries. They were gradually replaced by the sleeker, faster frigates and schooners.

Spanish galleon, 1588

Flemish galleon, 1593 (model in the Naval Museum, Madrid)

The need for ships that could make trans-Atlantic crossings, ride well with the wind, and carry large cargoes was responsible for the birth and development of the galleon throughout Europe. It was smaller than the largest galleys but faster and easier to handle than the carrack. The galleon was an extremely tough vessel and stood up well in combat. But it did not stand up well to bad weather, because of the imbalance between the upper and lower part of the ship, the lower part with its heavy artillery and combined weight of the large crew (up to 800, including seamen and soldiers).

The Venetian Republic had started building galleons in the first half of the 16th century. A contemporary document mentions a galleon about 135 feet long overall and almost 100 feet long at the waterline. It was over 30 feet wide at the beam. The construction proportions were 4:3:1.

The first technical drawings of a galleon appear in an English manuscript of about 1586, the *Fragments of Ancient English Shipwrightry.* The manuscript contains plans and sections of English warships built by Matthew Baker in the years before the Spanish Armada sailed up the English Channel.

Venetian galleon, 1548

English galleon, late 16th century (after Matthew Baker's plans)

Flags on the Sea

Flags have been flown at sea since ancient times, when navigators carried symbols to identify their vessels. Originally the same flags were flown at sea and on land, but in the middle of the 17th century different flags began to be used at sea. Later different flags were carried by warships and merchant ships.

Spain
royal flag of Castille and Leon

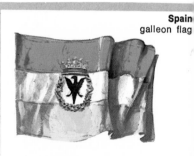

Spain
galleon flag

England
royal flag of William of Orange

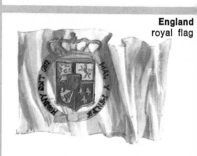

England
royal flag

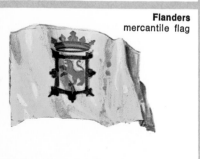

Flanders
mercantile flag

Holland
flag of the city of Hoorn

France
royal flag

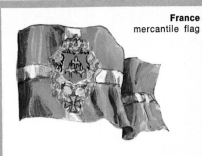

France
mercantile flag

Denmark
royal flag

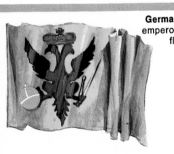

Sweden
royal flag

Germany
emperor's
flag

Russia
czar's flag

Brandenburg
Great
Elector's
flag

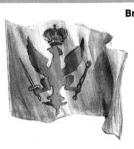

Brabant
state banner

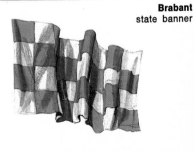

113

Ships' Decorations

For about three centuries large sailing vessels carried a wealth of ornament, especially at the stern. About the time of the Stuarts and Cromwell in England, and at about the same time in France and elsewhere, painted decoration was replaced by gilded carvings. Even warships took on a flamboyant air, thanks to the garlands, statues, columns, low reliefs, and elaborate lanterns created by famous artists and sculptors.

Men-of-War

Several advances were made in the 17th century that were to result in the development of the man-of-war. The first was the British innovation of the battle line. In 1653 the Fighting Instructions of the British Admiralty established the line of battle as the most efficient combat tactic. Such a formation could obtain optimum results if every ship in line maintained the same speed, could maneuver in the same way, and was sufficiently armed that it would not find itself face-to-face with a ship of superior firepower. Thus military ships came to be classified by firepower and velocity. The first, second, and third rate ships of the line were combat ships. The fourth rate included convoy escort ships and exploration

ships. The fifth rate also included exploration ships as well as signal vessels, while the sixth rate was assigned to ships used for coast guard duty.

The second innovation of the 17th century, perhaps the most important, was establishment of technical criteria for shipbuilding. In meeting these standards sails were improved, as was the armament of ships.

About the middle of the 17th century the ship of the line had taken on its traditional form, and in the course of the next two centuries it was to become a perfect military instrument. One of the pioneers of the new naval architecture was the Englishman Anthony Deane, who carried out some of the first fundamental

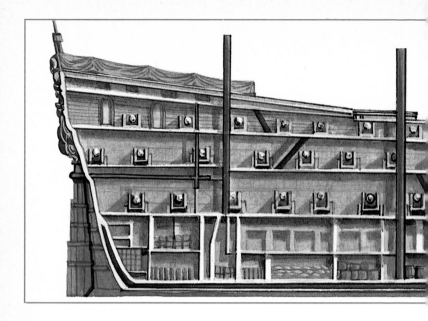

studies of the relationship between weight loads and hull shape. Toward the end of the 17th century, the warships of the French fleet, fast and well-balanced, were considered the best in Europe.

The capital ship of the European fleets was extremely sturdy. In part this was due to the adoption of double timbers, the framework that branched out from the keel and was the main structural element of the ship. Thus the ship's reinforcement was literally doubled. Oak was the primary mate-

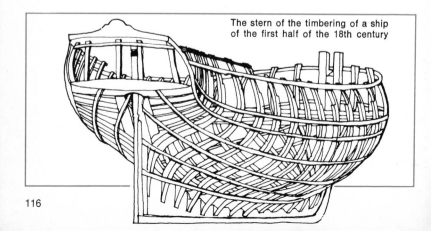

The stern of the timbering of a ship of the first half of the 18th century

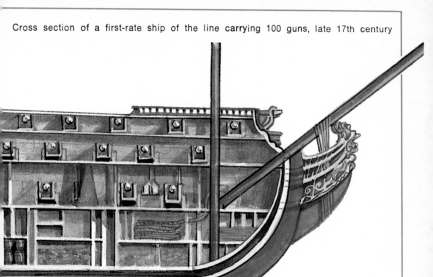

Cross section of a first-rate ship of the line carrying 100 guns, late 17th century

rial in ship construction until teak was introduced at the end of the 18th century. Yards, masts, and spars were almost always made of fir. The oak planking of the ship was attached to the timbers by large cone-shaped wood dowels, instead of metal nails which deteriorated quickly. The thickness of the double-layered hull was sometimes as much as two feet and could stand up to the heaviest artillery fire of the period. It took some 2,000 oak trees to build a ship, and curved elements were carved directly from the trunk for greater strength. The hull below the waterline was protected from corrosion by a coating of tar and inch-thick elm planks. Thus shipworm did not reach the actual hull of the ship.

In England copper plates were first applied to the hull in 1761. Until the end of the 18th century the hull was grayish in color because of the mixture of sulphur, tallow, and lead paint (mixed with fish oil and tar) that was applied. Later mineral tar was used, and then the hull below the waterline acquired the black color that was to remain characteristic of sailing ships until about the middle of the 18th century.

Until the end of the 19th century warships were painted with yellow and black stripes. The gunports, painted red, opened in the yellow zones. Later yellow was replaced by white. The inside of the warship was painted ochre. In the 17th century ship decoration reached its apex, under the influence of baroque style. From stem to stern ships were decorated with gilded carvings, and even gunports were adorned with sculptured garlands. Elaborate pavilions were erected both at the bow and stern, and gorgeous lanterns were installed.

Over a period of time these elaborate decorations gradually disappeared, both for reasons of cost and for efficiency. Though the decorative elements may have been stylish, they were of course no aid to navigation.

By 1750 decoration had almost entirely disappeared, although the application of figureheads at the bow continued, usually to symbolize the name of the ship.

In 1705 the wheel tiller was introduced in place of the bar tiller. The square stern survived until 1804, when the English naval architect Robert Seppings built a round stern for the second-rate warship *Namur*. The new stern was sturdier and more practical. There were usually three lower decks, built to make the most functional use of the space available. The masts (main, mizzen, and fore) were constructed in three sections, and each section carried a square sail. In early versions the mizzenmast carried a lateen sail, but this was later replaced by a trapezoidal sail, and the yard was replaced by two smaller spars. The lower one was the boom and the upper one was a gaff.

This sail came to be known as a spanker and was soon joined by an upper sail, the gaff topsail. In 1750 all navies did away with the stempost on the bowsprit, a feature that had

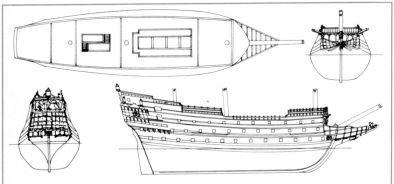

The *Sovereign of the Seas,* nicknamed the "Golden Devil" for its elaborate decorations, the work of Gerard Christmas based on drawings by Van Dyck. This ship was larger than any built before.

appeared during the development of the galleon. It was replaced by the jib boom, which carried jib sails and flying jibs. Staysails were also added between the masts to increase maneuverability. The riggings were also improved.

A host of pumps and bilge pumps made their appearance at this time. The galley was in the forecastle, while officers continued to be quartered in the sterncastle.

Cannons ranged from 3-pounders to 42-pounders. And vessels were divided in all navies, albeit with some variation, by number of cannons. The first rate included ships with more than 100 guns; the second rate, 80–98 guns; the third rate, 64–74 guns; the fourth rate, 44–56 guns; the fifth rate, 32–36 guns; the sixth rate, 24–28 guns. Tonnage varied from a maximum of 5,000 tons to a minimum of 1,500 tons.

Another advantage to the line of battle was that it protected the one weak point of the warship, the stern. There were not enough bulkheads at the stern to prevent a cannonball from shattering the stern and causing significant damage the full length of the deck.

The ship of the line reached its highest peak of development during the Napoleonic Wars. But the development of artillery with increased calibers was to mark the end of the ship of the line. It survived in most navies until 1870 and a decade more in the British navy.

For two centuries the ship of the line dominated the seas, but the new era of technology was to bring to an end the age of sail.

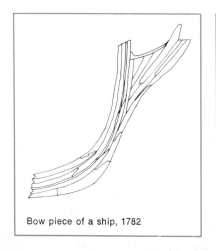
Bow piece of a ship, 1782

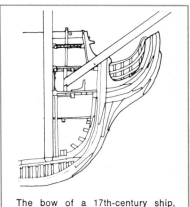
The bow of a 17th-century ship, showing the position of the bowsprit

Royal Sovereign

It is quite probable that in the second half of the 17th century there was no other ship sailing European seas as famous as the *Royal Sovereign.* It was designed initially in 1637 by the famous British shipwright Phineas Pett for Charles I of England. Baptized the *Sovereign of the Seas,* it saw several years' service as a three-decker. Later Peter Pett, Phineas' son, overhauled the ship and turned it into a two-decker, making it better balanced and more maneuverable. Its size was reduced, but not its armament, which consisted of more than 100 guns. The heavier cannons were installed on the lower gundeck. The ship was more stable with this arrangement, but water came in through the gunports.

At the Battle of Beachy Head in 1690, during the War of the Grand Alliance, the English fleet faced a French fleet under the command of the Count of Tourville. The *Royal Sovereign* was commanded by Admiral Arthur Herbert, Earl of Torrington. The battle was going in favor of the French, who supported the cause

1637 - Sovereign of the Seas

of the deposed James II. The *Royal Sovereign* engaged several ships during the battle, including the *Content,* the *Entreprenant,* and the 60-gun *Apollon.* Although the English ship was more heavily armed, it had to withdraw before the French ships. The British admiral was held responsible for the failure of the battle, and although he was exonerated, he was never given another ship. The *Royal Sovereign* was destroyed in a fire in 1696.

Type: **first-rate ship with two decks**
Designer: **Peter Pett**
Launching: **1654**
Reconstruction: **1654–1660**
Length: **234 ft.**
Beam: **49 ft.**
Depth: **24 ft.**
Displacement: **1,541 tons as *Sovereign of the Seas;* 1,637 tons as *Royal Sovereign***
Armament: **first battery, twenty-four 42-lb. cannons; second battery, twenty 24-lb. cannons; third battery (main deck), twenty-two 18-lb. cannons; smaller guns, from 9 to 12 lbs.**
Crew: **780 men**

Resolution

"Nothing equals the beautiful order of the English at sea. They bring all their fire to bear on those who come near them." These are the words of the Comte de Guiche, who was present at the Four Days' Battle (June 11–14, 1666), during the second of the three Dutch wars.

De Guiche went on to remark that the British ships advanced like a line of cavalry while the Dutch vessels darted out of the ranks. The line of battle was considered the optimum strategy by the English, provided all the ships could maintain the same speed, were equally armed, and could avoid facing more heavily armed vessels.

The *Resolution,* a magnificent three-decked ship with 100 cannons, was in this line of battle. The ship had been built to plans by Anthony Deane,

and the relationship between loaded weight and hull had been carefully studied. The lower gundeck was about four feet above the waterline so that water did not pour in through the gunports.

In 1652 the *Resolution* was part of the naval squadron commanded by Sir George Ayscue that attacked and destroyed a Dutch convoy on July 13 between Cape Blanche and Cape Gris Nez on the Normandy coast. On October 8, 1652, the *Resolution* took part in the action commanded by Admiral Robert Blake against the Dutch ships of Admiral de With, during the first Dutch War. The ship took part in the Four Days' Battle in 1666, and it was present on May 13, 1672, when Charles II reviewed the Anglo-French fleet assembled at Plymouth to face the Dutch.

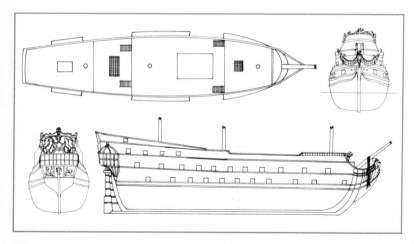

Type: **second-rate ship, three decks**
Launching: **1650**
Length: **195 ft.**
Beam: **42 ft.**
Depth: **20 ft.**
Displacement: **1,541 tons**
Armament: **first battery, thirty 42-lb. cannons; second battery, thirty 24-lb. cannons; third battery, ten 18-lb. cannons; 30 smaller pieces**
Crew: **630**

Royal Charles

Built at Woolwich by order of Oliver Cromwell, this superb three-decked ship was originally called the *Naseby.* (The ship carried a gilded figurehead representing Cromwell.) It was the flagship of Lord Edward Montagu, and in 1660 it carried Charles II to England. In honor of this deed, the ship was rechristened the *Royal Charles.*

The *Charles* was captured by the Dutch in one of the boldest actions of the second Dutch War. The plan was developed by Admiral De Ruyter. He hoped to capture or destroy British ships that were in dry dock on the Medway. On June 6, 1667, a Dutch fleet of 51 ships of the line, 3 frigates, and 14 fire ships left Helder under the command of Van Ghent. After passing through a furious storm, the ships entered the estuary of the Thames on the night of the 17th.

When news reached London that the Dutch were on the river, English business came to a halt, banks stopped payment, and a host of citizens gathered up their belongings and fled, according to the report of the times. On the 22nd the Dutch broke the chain that blocked the Medway, where they found 18 of the larger British ships anchored. They set half-a-dozen on fire and captured the *Royal Charles,* which they towed away.

This bold enterprise was the concluding episode of the second Dutch War, and hostilities were suspended for another five years by the Treaty of Breda (July 31, 1667).

The *Royal Charles* represented a rich prize, because the ship was armed with some of the first cannons expressly cast for the British navy. Casting cannons was a difficult craft, and the Dutch, Italians, Germans, and

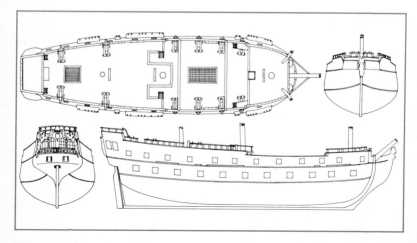

Scandinavians were masters of it. It was, however, still an imperfect craft, and calibers were only approximate. The shot was not always perfectly matched, and there were frequent accidents on board resulting in injury and death to the cannoneers. The cannons of the *Royal Charles* were elaborately decorated with the arms of the king and his admirals.

The captured ship also carried lighter arms, including mortars that could fire at a 45° angle. There were

Type: **second-rate ship, three decks**
Launching: **1655 (as the *Naseby*)**
Length: **184 ft. (from the bowsprit)**
Beam: **41 ft.**
Depth: **20 ft.**
Displacement: **1,400 tons**
Armament: **first battery, twenty-two 32-lb. cannons; second battery, twenty-two 28-lb. cannons; third battery, twenty-two 18-lb. cannons; eight attack guns; twelve 9-lb. guns; six portable cannons**
Crew: **670**

also small terra cotta receptacles full of grapeshot and powder (a sort of early hand grenade) and small revolving cannons.

125

Type: **first-rate ship, three decks**
Launching: **1670**
Length: **151 ft. (keel)**
Beam: **54 ft.**
Depth: **25 ft.**
Displacement: **1,395 tons**
Armament: **first battery, twenty-eight 32-lb. cannons; second battery, twenty 24-lb. cannons; third battery, twenty-six 24-lb. cannons; quarter-deck, ten 18-lb. cannons; eight attack cannons; two 9-lb. cannons**
Crew: **750**

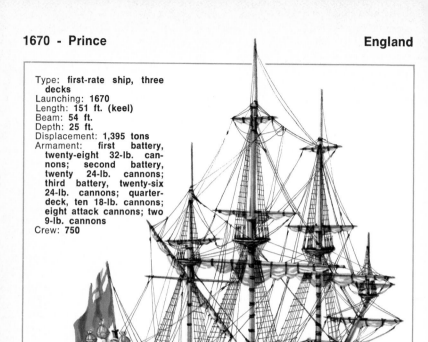

The construction plan of the 100-cannon first-rate ship *Prince* is in Sir Anthony Deane's *Doctrine of Naval Architecture,* at Magdalene College, Cambridge. The Science Museum in South Kensington, London, has one of the best models of this ship. As was typical of ships built at this time, the decks and platforms were very solidly built, and the whole structure of the ship was massive and heavy. The draft was consequently greater. The stern of the *Prince* was elaborately decorated, but not all of the decorative elements were gilded. Most of the British ships built around 1660 limited gilding to the royal coat of arms.

Type: **second-rate ship, three decks**
Launching: **1690 (the date the model was built)**
Length: **193 ft.**
Beam: **39 ft.**
Depth: **18 ft.**
Displacement: **1,296 tons**
Armament: **first battery, twenty-eight 32-lb. cannons; second battery, fourteen 24-lb. cannons; third battery, ten 18-lb. cannons; ten 9-lb. cannons; eight attack cannons; twenty-six smaller portable pieces**
Crew: **657**

The *St. George* was a three-decked ship with 96 cannons. It was built at a time when it had become common to create small scale models before beginning construction of the ship itself. In fact, as early as 1649, when Oliver Cromwell overthrew the reign of King Charles II, the British Admiralty asked shipwrights to present models along with the technical plans of the ships they planned to build.

Models of the ships of the Admiralty built around the middle of the 19th century provide us with the most accurate source of information about the techniques of shipbuilding of that time. The model of the *St. George* is in the collection of Henry Huddleston Roges and still has its original sails.

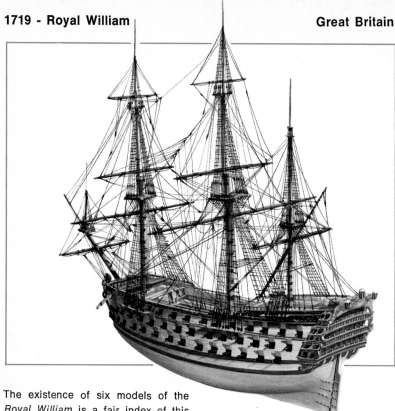

The existence of six models of the *Royal William* is a fair index of this vessel's importance in the history of shipbuilding. Built in 1719, it was the third to be called *Royal William* and was a reconstruction. At the time it was not uncommon to demolish a ship and reuse its salvageable parts. And, indeed, the first *Royal William*, which was launched in 1692, was a reconstruction of the 1670 *Prince*.

During its lifetime the *Royal William* took part in the naval operations that raised the seige of Gibraltar in 1782. It was also involved in the attempt to salvage the 100-gun *Royal George*,

Type: **first-rate ship, three decks**
Launching: **1719**
Length: **226 ft.**
Beam: **42 ft.**
Depth: **20 ft.**
Displacement: **1,600 tons**
Armament: **first battery, thirty-four 32-lb. cannons; second battery, twenty-eight 24-lb. cannons; third battery, twenty 18-lb. culverins; eighteen 9-lb. demi-culverins**
Crew: **736**

which had foundered at Spithead. The *Royal William* was finally assigned to port duty at Portsmouth and was demolished in 1813.

At Spithead on August 28, 1782, the most important ship of the line in Lord Howe's fleet, the *Royal George,* foundered and sank. Some 900 people lost their lives, including 300 who were aboard as visitors. A court-martial concluded that some of the bulkheads gave way when water poured in during loading, attributing this to simple deterioration. But the Royal George was only 26 years old when the tragedy occurred. Generally the wooden ships of the time did not deteriorate so rapidly.

From 1839 to 1843 attempts were made to demolish the wreck, which

Type: first-rate ship, three decks
Launching: **1756**
Length: **220 ft.**
Beam: **41 ft.**
Depth: **20 ft.**
Armament: **first battery, twenty-eight 42-lb. cannons; second battery, twenty-four 32-lb. cannons; third battery, twenty-two 24-lb. cannons; ten 12-lb. cannons; ten 9-lb. and six 6-lb. cannons**
Crew: **826**

was an obstacle to shipping. Finally a ton of explosives was used, and what remained of the proud ship was blasted out of the water.

Victory

The English historian Philip Watts called the *Victory* the Royal Navy's Westminster Abbey. The ship has been preserved in dry dock at Portsmouth. Designed in 1759 at the Old Single Shipyard at Chatham, the *Victory* was the fifth British ship to be so named. The first was a merchantman of 1560, demolished in 1608; the second was one of the last galleons (1620–90). In 1715 the name was given to the former *Royal James,* and in 1737 a first-rate ship of the line with 110 cannons was launched with the same name. This ship was wrecked seven years later. The fifth *Victory* was six years in the building and was finished in 1765. Elm beams some 18 inches thick were used for the keel, while the timbers were of English oak. There were three layers of planking. Each layer, in Baltic oak

to the waterline, was 5 inches thick.

The great ship lay in dry dock for 13 years for continuous repair because of shipworm damage. Finally on May 8, 1778, the *Victory* set sail for its first military action against the French off Ushant. Two years later the *Victory*'s hull was lined to the waterline with 3,923 sheets of copper weighing about 17 tons.

The ship had an intense career until 1805, when, under the command of Horatio Nelson, it took part in the Battle of Trafalgar. Lord Nelson fell to the deck of his ship, mortally wounded by French rifle fire from the captured *Redoubtable.*

Every year on the anniversary of the battle, the *Victory*'s signal flags are raised with Nelson's message to the fleet, "England expects that every man will do his duty."

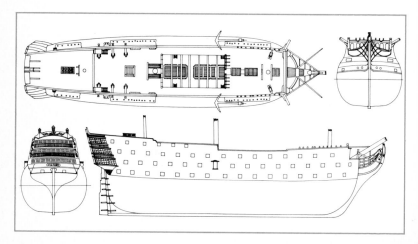

Type: **first-rate ship, three decks**
Launching: **1765**
Builders: **John Lock and Edward Allin**
Length: **228 ft.**
Beam: **52 ft.**
Depth: **25 ft.**
Displacement: **3,225 tons**
Armament: **first battery, thirty-two 42-lb. cannons; second battery, twenty-eight 24-lb. cannons; third battery, thirty 12-lb. cannons; main deck, twelve 12-lb. cannons**
Crew: **850**

San Felipe

When the *San Felipe* was launched in February 1693 at the La Coruña naval yards, the Spanish navy was a far cry from the formidable force it had been in earlier times.

No expense had been spared in building the *San Felipe*. It had a powerful double hull, constructed with internal and external planking, and was extremely sturdy. The garboards (the first two planks that were fitted into the massive bar keel) were of oak, as were the planks along the waterline and those around the main deck. These planks or plates were some 25 feet long and 10 inches thick. The rest of the shell of the hull was built of elm, oak, and pine. The strips of the various planks tended to swell or shrink with the strains of the ship, so the seams between them were caulked with tar or pitch. For additional sealing, the entire hull was treated with a mixture of vegetable tar and resin. On top of that mixture a layer of wadding was applied, consisting of animal skins and tarred ropes, and another layer of inch-thick oak planking was laid over the wadding. This final layer was nailed down with broadheaded nails set so close together they almost entirely covered the keel, thus providing further protection from corrosive marine elements.

The *San Felipe* carried bronze cannons, which had greater resistance to wear and were more manageable than iron cannons. To have a better understanding of the size of the ship, it is worth mentioning that the *San Felipe*'s two anchors weighed almost 18,000 pounds. The anchor cables were almost two feet in diameter.

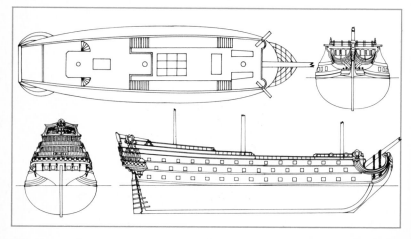

Two smaller anchors, weighing half as much, had cables one foot in diameter. The two-foot diameter ropes were called "master ropes," and the smaller ones were known as "second ropes" or "mooring ropes."

The *San Felipe* had capstans in two sizes to operate the anchors. The larger one was made up of two bell-shaped gearings, with one chamber on the first deck and the other on the second deck. Thus this bigger capstan could be operated simul-

Type: **first-rate ship, three decks**
Launching: **1693**
Length: **207 ft.**
Beam: **54 ft.**
Depth: **22 ft.**
Displacement: **1,890 tons**
Armament: **first battery, fifty 32-lb. cannons; second battery, thirty 24-lb. cannons; third battery, twenty-two 18-lb. cannons; eight 9-lb. culverins**
Crew: **846**

taneously at two levels, increasing the power that could be applied.

The *San Felipe* was never involved in any combat and was demolished in 1736.

Phénix

The original plans of the *Phénix* appear in two albums known as the *Atlas de Colbert,* which are now preserved by the Hydrographic Service of the French navy. The atlas is named for Louis XIV's minister, Jean Baptiste Colbert, who played a decisive role in the reorganization of French merchant shipping. The two volumes were probably prepared by Colbert especially for the king.

The construction plans were the work of the shipwright Coulomb, who worked in Toulon. The building criteria were simple, not to say rough. The number of cannons was decided first and the ship was built around the armament. After the caliber of the first and lower battery was determined the dimensions of the gunports could be decided on, as well as the distance between one weapon

and the next. Thus, the number of cannons established the length of the ship simply by adding the widths of the gunports to the widths of the intervening spaces. From that point on the keel length could be established, as well as the width of the beam, and the number of decks and their respective heights.

Needless to say, this manner of construction led to striking differences between ships of the same type. It was not until 1670 that a council was set up in the various ports to establish uniform criteria for ship construction, and even then the rules were not always followed.

What was particularly striking about the *Phénix* was its waterline, which did not follow the line of the keel. This proves that the shipwrights of the time did not have a clear idea

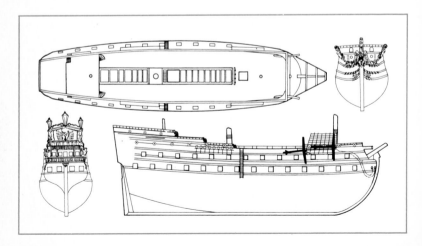

of the significance of the waterline, and it was only through trial-and-error experience that seamen learned to distribute cargo in a sensible manner aboard ship.

One captain noted that his ship made faster progress at night, when most of the crew was asleep in the bow. Finding himself in pursuit of a British frigate by day, he sent all of the unoccupied crew members to their quarters in the bow, increased his speed, and overtook the enemy.

Type: **second-rate ship, three decks**
Design: **1664**
Length: **190 ft.**
Beam: **40 ft.**
Depth: **19 ft.**
Displacement: **1,500 tons**
Armament: **first battery, thirty-four 42-lb. cannons; second battery, twenty-eight 24-lb. cannons; third battery, twenty-two 18-lb. cannons**
Crew: **684**

The *Phénix* was one of the last ships to have a bar rudder. The bar rudder was replaced by the wheel rudder, which had a cable that acted on the rudder bar.

Soleil Royal

The *Soleil Royal,* one of the most powerful of the French three-decked sailing ships, was built to regulations that laid down detailed instructions for the construction of naval vessels. This code was a first attempt to regularize shipbuilding and create a certain homogeneity among ships of the same class. The keel was, in accordance with the Naval Ministry's orders, to be built with boards approximately 18 inches wide. And, perhaps for the first time in the history of French shipbuilding, when selection was made of the wood to be used, consideration was given to the kind of seas the ship would sail. Also, the ship's lines were designed with actual maneuvers in mind.

The *Soleil Royal* was one of the most elaborately decorated ships of her time, and the stern was literally covered with gilded carvings. On June 22, 1690, she set off for the first of several naval operations against the English with all of her decorations overpainted in gray.

The *Soleil Royal* was the flagship of Admiral Hilarion de Cotentin Tourville, who led a fleet of three divisions, each of which included a first-rate ship of the line with a division commander aboard. The first division was Tourville's and carried white insignia. The rear guard division carried blue insignia. The third division carried navy blue and white insignia on the foremast.

The *Soleil Royal* had considerable firepower, carrying 106 cannons on three decks. The rigging was very advanced for the period, consisting of ten square sails, two jibs, and a lateen spanker on the mizzenmast.

The *Soleil Royal* played a leading part in naval actions against the

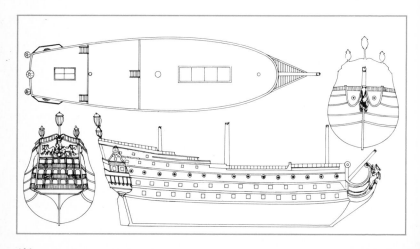

Type: **first-rate ship, three decks**
Launching: **1669**
Length: **200 ft.**
Beam: **43 ft.**
Depth: **21 ft.**
Displacement: **1,613 tons**
Armament: **first battery, thirty-six 42-lb. cannons; second battery, twenty-eight 24-lb. cannons; third battery, twenty-six 18-lb. cannons; ten smaller pieces, from 6 to 9 lbs.; six attack cannons**
Crew: **836**

English in the War of the Grand Alliance. Tourville had faced the British in the Battle of Beachy Head and had been victorious there against Admiral Arthur Herbert, Earl of Torrington. The *Soleil Royal* was involved in the Battle of Beveziers on July 10, 1690, and in the Battle of Barfleur on May 29, 1692, where, according to one observer, she looked like a tall fortress pouring out death on all sides from those 106 cannons.

Although the Battle of Barfleur was a victory for the French, it was fatal to the *Soleil Royal*. Badly damaged, the ship went aground on the Cherbourg coast on May 31, 1692. The English rammed it with a fire ship, and the *Soleil Royal* was destroyed.

Tourville was soundly defeated later at the Battle of La Hogue, and France's naval fortunes declined after that encounter.

The *Mirage* was built in the golden age of French sailing vessels and represents the transition from the large galleon to the more functional and improved ship of the line. The main deck as far as the forecastle was built of pine and teak, carefully caulked for waterproofing. The deck planks were attached to the beams, which supported the deck and reinforced the timbers. Iron nails covered with wood were used. The deck planking was five inches thick on the lower gundeck and four inches thick on the upper gundeck. The planking of the third deck was three inches

Type: **second-rate ship, three decks**
Launching: **unknown**
Length: **182 ft.**
Beam: **40 ft.**
Depth: **19 ft.**
Displacement: **1,245 tons**
Armament: **first battery, twenty-eight 32-lb. cannons; second battery, twenty-four 24-lb. cannons; third battery, eighteen 9-lb. cannons; eight 18-lb. cannons**
Crew: **543**

thick. The planking thickness was especially designed to be in proportion to the weight of the cannons. This harmony of weight relationships shows that the craft of shipbuilding could achieve remarkable results.

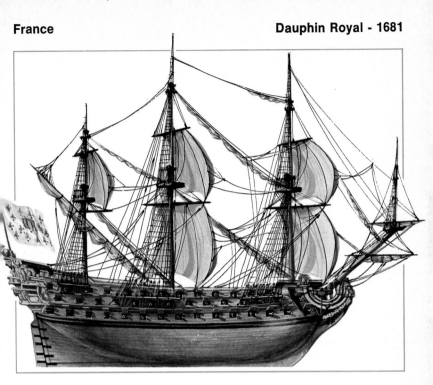

The *Dauphin Royal* was one of those large and majestic *vaisseaux du Roi,* the pride and glory of the French navy. The ship was outstanding in its technical features, sails, and armament. It was richly decorated, and contemporaries were struck by the lavishness of the decorations of the stern, bow, and superstructures. But the *Dauphin Royal* was noteworthy not only for its beauty. The ship also represented a marked advance in seaworthiness. Indeed, French ships of this period were considered the finest in the world.

The *Dauphin Royal* flew the insignia

Type: **first-rate ship, three decks**
Launching: **about 1681**
Length: **204 ft.**
Beam: **51 ft.**
Depth: **21 ft.**
Armament: **first battery, thirty-four 42-lb. cannons; second battery, thirty 24-lb. cannons; third battery, thirty-six 12-lb. cannons**
Crew: **854**

of Château-Renault during the Battle of Beachy Head in 1690. The French supported the claims of the deposed James II to the throne of England, while the united forces of Holland and England fought for William and Mary.

Royal Louis

The *Royal Louis,* a 112-cannon war-ship, was one of the largest and most heavily armed vessels of her time, and she had a remarkably long career.

The original version of the *Royal Louis* was launched at Brest in 1692. She had a very high sterncastle, and at the height where the third battery of cannons was located and at the main deck there were galleries that ran completely around the stern of the ship.

Almost a century later the ship was overhauled, and this was done in the same shipyard from which it had been launched. The sterncastle was removed, and the quarterdeck low-ered, which made the main deck look more horizontal. The general deck line was also lowered. The waterline was altered and the draft increased.

As for the sails, the spritsail, the small square sail on the bowsprit, was replaced by three jibs; these were fore-and-aft sails at the bow. The new *Royal Louis* had a sail surface of 31,656 square feet (compared to 26,911 square feet in the earlier ver-sion). The two galleries at the stern were also removed, and the ship took on a more streamlined appear-ance. The port sides, where the can-nons were located, also underwent a change in design when the ship was rebuilt.

The armament was kept intact, with very little modification. The heavier cannons were concentrated in the lower part of the ship—the first bat-tery deck. This provided greater sta-bility for the hull. There was another advantage to this arrangement: The heavier cannonballs shot from this

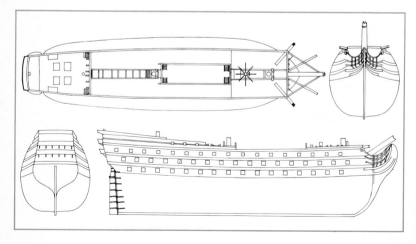

position would strike enemy ships close to the waterline and do more damage than if they had been fired from higher up. The first battery consisted of thirty 48-pound cannons. One round, then, totaled 1,440 pounds. The second battery consisted of thirty-two 18-pounders, or 576 pounds in a single round. The volume of this firepower is particularly impressive when one considers that these 17th- and 18th-century cannons had a very

Type: **first-rate ship, three decks**
Launching: **1692**
Reconstruction: **1780**
Length: **210 ft.**
Beam: **57 ft.**
Depth: **25 ft.**
Displacement: **2,130 tons**
Armament: **first battery, thirty 48-lb. cannons; second battery, thirty-two 18-lb. cannons; third battery, thirty 12-lb. cannons; sixteen 8-lb. cannons; four 4-lb. cannons**
Crew: **856**

short range, and in all naval battles of that time artillery fire was exchanged at close quarters.

141

Protecteur

The *Protecteur* was part of the 12-ship squadron that left Toulon on April 18, 1778, to carry the French diplomatic representative to America and to aid the colonists in their conflict with England. The squadron was under the command of Vice Admiral Charles Hector d'Estaing. D'Estaing had been an army officer before becoming a lieutenant general in the French navy in 1763. As a naval officer he had seen several campaigns in the waters of the Antilles.

Reaching America, the French fleet engaged in unsuccessful maneuvers off of Newport, Rhode Island, then headed for the West Indies. On July 6, 1778, d'Estaing's ships clashed with a British squadron commanded by Admiral John Byron off the island of Grenada. The British had held that island and also nearby St. Vincent, and d'Estaing had successfully taken them for France. Byron's flagship was the 98-gun *Princess Royal*. The reasons for Byron's attack have never been made clear, and the encounter itself was inconclusive, though three English ships were dismasted.

In this engagement the *Protecteur* was commanded by the French officer de Grasse-Limermont, and it seems likely that his ship was responsible for smashing the mast of the English ship *Cornwall*.

There is also a possibility that it was another ship named *Protecteur,* a 74-gun vessel, that was involved in this action. What is certain, however, according to French naval archives, is that a ship named the *Protecteur* went into construction in 1757, was launched in 1760, and retired in 1784.

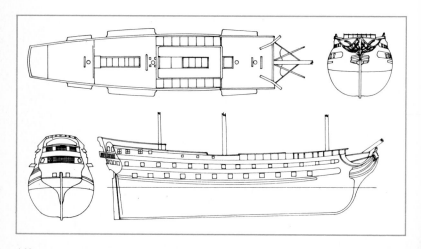

Type: **second-rate ship, two decks**
Launching: **1760**
Length: **185 ft.**
Beam: **37 ft.**
Depth: **20 ft.**
Displacement: **1,600 tons**
Armament: **first battery, twenty-six 24-lb. cannons; second battery, twenty-eight 12-lb. cannons; ten 8-lb. cannons**
Crew: **676**

Spartiate

The *Spartiate* is a classic example of 18th-century French naval architecture. This 74-gun ship was designed by the famous French naval engineer Jacques Noel Sané. He won a national competition for establishing standard models of construction for the first three classes of French ships of the line, 118-, 80-, and 74-gun ships. Sané's plans for each of the three classes provided the basis for French military shipbuilding during the next three decades.

The *Spartiate* was part of the naval squadron commanded by François-Paul Brueys d'Aigalliers that carried Napoleon's army from Toulon to Alexandria, Egypt, in May 1798. The *Spartiate,* together with the *Guerrier, Conquérant, Peuple Souverain, Aquilon, Franklin, Mercure, Orient, Tonnant, Heureux, Guillaume Tell, Genér-* *eux, Timoleon,* plus the frigates *Diane, Justice, Arthemise,* and *Sérieux* took part in the Battle of the Nile. The fleet flew the tricolor, the new revolutionary flag, with vertical stripes of red, white, and blue, which had been adopted on May 20, 1794. The French squadron was at anchor off Abu Qir, nine miles east of Alexandria, drawn up in a line about three miles from the coast. The English ships maneuvered between the French ships and the coast, blocking the French effort to prevent attack from the land side.

Nelson had been searching for the fleet for months, and at last he had found it. On August 1, at five o'clock in the afternoon, in Abu Qir Bay, the first two French ships felt the force of the advance English ships. The *Zealous,* the *Goliath,* the *Audacious,* and the *Orion* took up positions be-

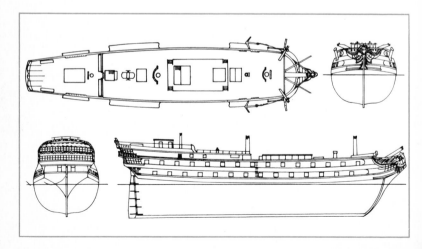

tween the French ships and the coast. Nelson in the *Vanguard,* with the *Bellerophon* and the *Majestic,* attacked from the other side and drew up to the *Orient,* the 120-gun French flagship. Despite a splendid defense (the two English ships of the line lost their masts), the French ship was defeated and burned. It exploded at ten o'clock that night. The *Spartiate,* under the command of Aristides Emériau, fought the *Vanguard.* The broadsides of the French vessel wreaked havoc on the English ship, and Nelson was wounded in the head. But Emériau soon had to surrender. The *Spartiate* had 49 holes

Type: third-rate ship, two decks
Launching: **1785**
Length: **178 ft.**
Beam: **36 ft.**
Depth: **19 ft.**
Displacement: **1,603 tons**
Armament: **first battery, forty-eight 32-lb. carronades; second battery, twenty-six 18-lb. carronades**
Crew: **660**

below the waterline on the port side and 27 on the starboard side. Water poured into the stricken ship. The cannons had been knocked out of action, one after another, and the powder stores were waterlogged. Nelson refused to accept the sword of his vanquished enemy. He had fought too well.

Type: **second-rate ship, three decks**
Designer: **J. N. Sané**
Launching: **1793**
Length: **216 ft.**
Beam: **50 ft.**
Depth: **22 ft.**
Displacement: **1,780 tons**
Armament: **first battery, twen-eight 18-lb. cannons; four-teen 24-lb. cannons; sec-ond battery, twenty-six 18-lb. cannons; third battery, twenty-eight 9-lb. can-nons; four smaller guns**
Crew: **774**

The *Sans Pareil* is a classic of French naval engineering of the late 18th century and was also the work of the noted engineer Sané. Her cannons could fire a variety of ammunition, including grapeshot and buckshot projectiles, making her a formidable fighting ship.

Following a tradition that had not totally disappeared by the end of the 18th century, the *Sans Pareil* carried

boarding troops. When the ship was engaged in combat, riflemen on the upper decks would provide covering fire for these troops. In that historic period artillery fire alone could not be counted on to sink enemy ships. In the next 50 years the practice of hand-to-hand fighting would prove in-effective, and superior cannon power would determine the outcome of a battle.

Type: **second-rate ship, three decks**
Launching: **1766**
Length: **233 ft.**
Beam: **49 ft.**
Depth: **23 ft.**
Displacement: **1,673 tons**
Armament: **first battery, thirty-six 42-lb. cannons; second battery, twenty-eight 24-lb. cannons; third battery, twenty 18-lb. cannons; sixteen other pieces**
Crew: **712**

Although the Spanish fleet of the 18th century did not have the power it had several centuries earlier, it was still able to provide the Napoleonic fleet with this powerful 100-gun ship, which played an important role in naval action against the English. The *Algeçiras* was present at Trafalgar on October 21, 1805, under the command of Rear Admiral Magòn, who lost his life in the engagement. The Spanish ship, ravaged by the broadsides of the *Aigle,* finally had to surrender on the morning of the 22nd. The English crew had to release the 270 Spanish crewmen in order to handle the damaged ship. In return for its freedom, the crew made hasty repairs to the vessel and then sailed the *Algeçiras* to Cadiz, risking shipwreck more than once on the perilous voyage.

Santissima Trinidad

The *Santissima Trinidad* was the most heavily armed ship of its day, carrying 130 cannons. It took four years to build the vessel at La Coruña shipyard. During the late 18th century great pains were taken in building exact scale models of ships before beginning the actual construction. These arsenal models, as they are called, were built by expert carpenters who gave a great deal of attention to creating miniatures with exact proportions and accurate details. Thus these artisans have provided us with valuable information about the ships of that time, since it is almost impossible to find original plans and specifications for them.

The hull of the *Santissima Trinidad* was built of timber cut down in the winter of 1776 and allowed to season for two years. The timbers for the "ribs" or "frames" of the hull were carved whole out of tree trunks that were carefully selected. They were then fired and in the process became so hard that it was impossible to scratch them, even with the sharpest knives or chisels.

Although the decorations on the stern were lavish, they could not compare with the decorations of earlier ships. By now sailing ships were considered war machines, and functionalism was the prime requisite.

The sterncastle of the *Santissima Trinidad* was only slightly higher than the main deck. The main deck had become an almost continuous structure with the forecastle. With such a large, open area the upper gundeck could carry cannons almost all the way to the bow.

As part of the Spanish fleet, the *Santissima Trinidad* took part in the Battle of Trafalgar. The Spanish,

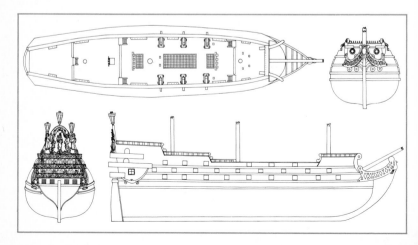

Type: **first-rate ship, four decks**
Launching: **about 1778**
Length: **206 ft.**
Beam: **54 ft.**
Depth: **25 ft.**
Displacement: **2,274 tons**
Armament: **first battery, forty-two 42-lb. cannons; second battery, thirty-six 24-lb. cannons; third battery, twenty-two 18-lb. cannons; fourth battery, twenty-two 9-lb. demi-culverins; eight attack cannons**
Crew: **836**

under the command of Admiral Gravina, were allied with the French. The *Santissima Trinidad* carried the flag of squadron commander Don Balthazar Cisneros Vicente. On the morning of October 21, 1805, the English fleet, under Lord Nelson, and the Franco-Spanish fleet, commanded by Admiral Villeneuve, caught sight of each other. Because of her great size the *Santissima Trinidad* was mistaken for the fleet's flagship, and Nelson, on his flagship *Victory,*

headed for her. She was soon dismasted and had to surrender. Villeneuve's flagship, the *Bucentaure,* was also forced to surrender to Nelson.

San Juan Nepomuceno

The *San Juan Nepomuceno* was a third-rate ship of the line and there were only minor differences between its structure and configuration and that of the frigates, the swift fighting ships that developed at the end of the 18th century. There were two features, in particular, that the third-rate ships and the frigates had in common. The main deck was relatively smooth compared with other ships of the class, and the stern was almost totally free of ornamentation.

However, the *San Juan Nepomuceno* was not especially fast or easy to handle, whereas the frigates were extremely maneuverable. It was not suited for reconnaissance or pursuit missions, nor was it a match for the slow and heavily armed 100-gun ships.

Like all Spanish ships of the period

it had a copper-bottomed hull. As early as the 16th century lead plating had been applied to hulls to protect them from shipworm. (This technique had been known as far back as the time of the ancient Romans.) In 1670 the English replaced lead with copper for the first time. True, the metal was subject to corrosion, but it protected the wood and stayed cleaner. By collecting less marine growth on its hull a ship could move much faster in the water.

The *San Juan Nepomuceno* took part in the Battle of Trafalgar, in which Lord Nelson's fleet ended the threat to Britain's supremacy on the high seas by defeating Napoleon and his Spanish allies. The ship was commanded by Brigadier General Cosmo Damian Churruca, who lost his life in the battle. She fought valiantly but

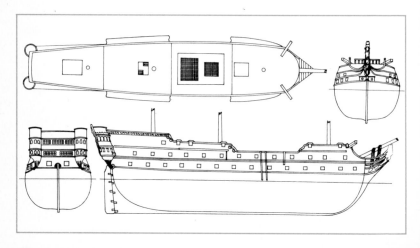

finally surrendered to Lord Collingwood, along with 11 other Spanish ships. A storm blew up the next day and there was no way to keep the captured ships under control. Collingwood burned several of them, and he brought the *San Juan Nepomuceno,* the *Bahama,* and the *San Ildefonso* to Gibraltar.

The hull of the *San Juan Nepomuceno* was kept in the port of Gibraltar as a floating memorial of the

Type: **third-rate ship, two decks**
Launching: **1779**
Length: **217 ft.**
Beam: **36 ft.**
Depth: **20 ft.**
Displacement: **1,500 tons**
Tonnage: **2,700 tons**
Sail surface: **10,760 sq. ft.**
Armament: **first battery, twenty-eight 36-lb. cannons; second battery (main deck), thirty 24-lb. cannons**
Crew: **637**

English victory. There is no information available as to what happened to it later.

1665 - Stora Kronan · Amaranth · Sweden

This was the first two-decked ship of the new Swedish fleet. During a voyage to the East Indies in 1668 an attempt was made to grow cress and lettuce on the ship to be added to the crew's diet in an effort to combat scurvy. This was perhaps the first such attempt to find a cure for the disease, which is caused by a deficiency of vitamin C. On long voyages scurvy was a greater threat to the crew than storms. For almost 200 years, from 1622 to 1815, the weekly rations of Swedish seamen included 5 gallons of beer, 4 pounds of salted beef, 6 ounces of butter, and 12 ounces of cheese. None of these

Type: **third-rate ship, two decks**
Launching: **1665**
Length: **164 ft.**
Beam: **38 ft.**
Depth: **16 ft.**
Displacement: **1,212 tons**
Armament: **first battery, twenty-eight 32-lb. cannons; second battery, twenty-six 24-lb. cannons; smaller pieces, from 9 to 12 lbs.**
Crew: **598**

foods contained the necessary ascorbic acid. There is no record that the experiment on the *Stora Kronan Amaranth* succeeded. In the mid-18th century a British naval officer determined that limes were effective in combating scurvy, and eventually the disease was overcome.

Although Brandenburg, in northeastern Germany, did not have many ports, it played an important part in the maritime life of the period, thanks to the initiative of its leaders. Frederick William, the Great Elector, who ruled from 1640 to 1688, was particularly aware of the need to create a strong naval force and levied a special tax to provide funds for acquiring ships. Aware of the inability of his own small country to engage in shipbuilding, he purchased vessels from other European shipyards.

The *Wappen Von Hambourg* was built in Holland. It was one of the first ships in history to carry a wheel

Type: **three-decked ship**
Launching: **about 1669**
Length: **145 ft.**
Beam: **29 ft.**
Depth: **17 ft.**
Displacement: **897 tons**
Armament: **first battery, thirty 32-lb. cannons; second battery, eighteen 24-lb. cannons; third battery, four 9-lb. cannons**
Crew: **176**

rudder, which may have been installed only experimentally. It consisted of a simple wheel with a cable acting on a rudder bar. The wheel was much easier to handle than the bar, and some years later the wheel became standard equipment.

153

The Golden Age

Revolutionnaire, French first-rate ship with three decks and 114 cannons

Association, French second-rate ship with three decks and 98 cannons

The large warship reached its peak of perfection in the late 18th century, due to the genius of the French naval engineer Jacques Noel Sané. After his time the construction of sailing vessels was not substantially modified.

Because of improved technology, naval yards in the 18th century were able to build warships that weighed as much as 2,000 tons and merchant ships up to 600 tons.

In every country construction techniques were closely guarded secrets,

Languedoc, French second-rate ship with two decks and 80 cannons

Peuple Souverain, French third-rate ship with two decks and 64 cannons

Etats de Bourgogne, French first-rate ship with three decks and 120 cannons

Franklin, French second-rate ship with two decks and 80 cannons

and it was extremely difficult to get into shipbuilding yards. Designs were often based on shipwrights' traditions passed on from generation to generation. The general design of merchant ships was not much different from that of warships.

Saint-Esprit, French armed merchantman

Valmy, French first-rate ship with three decks and 120 cannons

Steering Systems

The movement of the rudder determines the direction a ship will take. In ancient times the rudder consisted of two long oars, one on each side of the stern. The rudder over the stern was probably introduced in the late Middle Ages. Wheel attachments developed in the 17th century.

Station of the helmsman in a 15th-century carrack

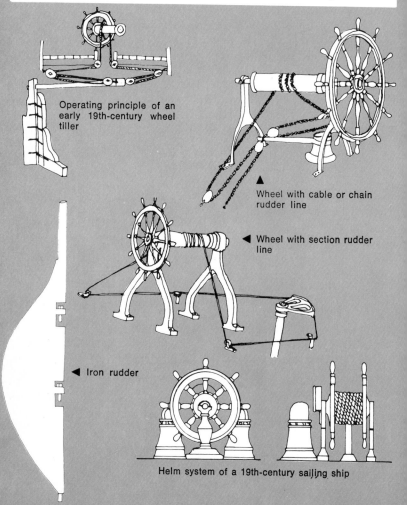

Operating principle of an early 19th-century wheel tiller

Wheel with cable or chain rudder line

◀ Wheel with section rudder line

◀ Iron rudder

Helm system of a 19th-century sailing ship

The Frigate

Almost all of the large sailing vessels of the past centuries were derived from earlier types of ships, generally smaller oar-driven ships. The frigate was no exception to this rule. In the 18th century this large military and merchant vessel began to replace the sixth-rate ship, and when it increased in size it became the outstanding ship of its time.

The etymology of the name is not clear, but it is certain that the ship developed in the Mediterranean. The Spaniards applied the term to a small merchant vessel that plied the seas between Spain and its South American colonies in the late 16th century. In the 17th century a small ship, scarcely more than 30 feet long, was called a frigate. It had two masts with lateen sails and 12 oars. About the same time the name was used in northern waters to describe the fast pirate ships that were based at Dunkirk or Ostend and raided along the English Channel and the Atlantic coast.

But it was the English who first built a ship officially known as a frigate. This was a fast vessel of approximately 400 tons that appeared about 1646. It had most of the features that later were to characterize the outstanding ship of the golden age of sail. A single deck ran from stem to stern, and the forecastle was small and low. The quarterdeck ran almost half its length, and there was a large hatch for storage amidships. Between the gunports were housings for oars, which were still employed when the ship was in port or if it was becalmed.

Sometime after the middle of the 17th century the term frigate was also applied to merchant vessels that were particularly fast. Indeed, what was to typify the 18th-century frigate was its large quantity of sail and its great speed.

As mentioned before, the British Admiralty's Fighting Instructions of 1653 made provision for the line of battle and divided warships into six rates. The sixth rate comprised single-decked ships, about 100 feet long, with some twenty 9-pound guns, and a displacement of about 500 tons. It was from this class of ship that the frigate emerged in the course of the 18th century. The size of the ship increased, the superstructures were reduced to a minimum, and the armament was increased. This development was particularly rapid in the French navy, and when English ships managed to capture French vessels they did not hesitate to copy desirable new features.

The dimensions of a typical 18th-century frigate were as follows: length overall, about 180 feet; length at waterline, about 150 feet; beam, about 40 feet. For the sake of comparison, a third-rate ship of the line, with 74 guns, was about 190 feet long overall, about 160 feet at the waterline, and about 50 feet at the beam.

Although the French made many improvements in the frigate's design, the English were responsible for an important innovation in artillery. This was the carronade, a large-caliber gun that was particularly light in weight. It became very popular because it could fire both ball and shot and required only three men to operate it. The carronade, or smasher, was invented in 1779. Although its range was shorter than other guns it could fire heavier shot. Therefore it was ideally suited to short-range combat and wreaked havoc with masts and crew.

The frigates often carried three or four mortars that could fire grenades at a 45° angle. Small moveable guns, descendants of the 16th-century culverin, were installed along the gunwales for use in close-range fighting. Because boarding missions and hand-to-hand combat were still common practice, the frigates also carried contingents of marines.

Mention has been made of the frigate's speed. This speed was due not only to its streamlined shape but also to its increased number of sails. Staysails had made their appearance about 1670 and were widely used on smaller vessels. This new type of sail, derived from the lateen sail, was rigged on stays between the masts. Staysails were also installed on the bowsprit and replaced the older square sails. With these new sails ships could tack faster and close haul better than before. The

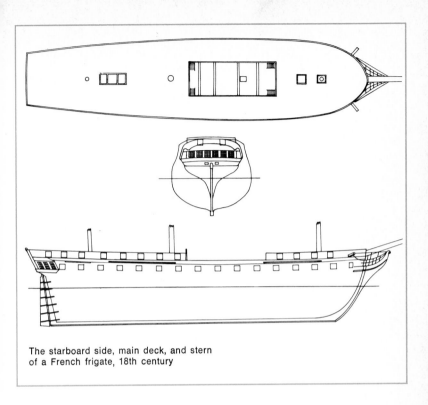

The starboard side, main deck, and stern
of a French frigate, 18th century

forward staysails were called fore
topmast staysails. The outer ones
were called jobs. About the middle
of the 18th century the frigate was
equipped with a spanker gaff, a diag-
onal spar attached to the mizzenmast
to replace the yard that carried the
lateen sail. Thus staysails could also
be installed between the mainmast
and the mizzenmast. As a result of
these changes manipulating the sheets
was simplified. All in all, the frigate
was faster and easier to handle than
earlier sailing vessels.

Another innovation appeared during
the Napoleonic Wars. This was the
introduction of the boom, the horizontal spar at the bottom of the mizzenmast's lateen sail. The bowsprit
was also reinforced, since it had to
carry more sail. The three sails of the
principal masts were augmented by a
fourth sail. This was the main royal
sail. Gallants and royals appeared on
the mizzenmast above the spanker.
The frigate carried a total of 18 sails.

Depending on sailing conditions
and for combat maneuvers, other

small sails were also used. Small square sails were used if there were light winds.

The frigate was well-suited to running battles, and it was an excellent ship for convoy escort and patrol duties. During the Anglo-French conflicts of the 18th and 19th centuries the larger English frigates were given heavier armament, enabling them to take part in a broader range of actions. Frigates also saw duty on reconnaissance missions and were used on exploratory voyages and for carrying messages. In battles they often served a valuable purpose by towing larger vessels out of the line of fire. Indeed, it became a convention for larger ships never to fire on frigates during sea battles.

The life of the captain of a frigate was more varied than that of the captain of a larger vessel. The latter often undertook long voyages and endured monotonous port blockades. Also, as a result of raiding forays, many frigate captains accumulated considerable fortunes.

The final development of the frigate took place in America. In 1794 Barbary Coast pirates had seized a number of American merchant vessels and in response to this piracy the Congress of the United States authorized the construction of six frigates to protect American shipping. But the bill carried the proviso that if peace was established with the Algerian corsairs none of the ships was to be finished. Keels were laid for the *United States,* the *Constitution,* and the *Constellation,* but when President Washington did sign a treaty with the Algerians little more was done. Then, in 1797, in response to a French decree that threatened the welfare of American ships and the lives of American seamen, Congress gave President Madison the power to finish the construction of the three frigates. By the close of that year they were all launched and went on to make memorable names for themselves in American naval history.

All of the ships were designed in 1794 by Joshua Humphreys, who was recognized as the finest designer in America. A Quaker from Philadelphia, his talents were known to President Washington and the two met together to discuss the construction of the new ships. In his designs Humphreys drew upon his knowledge of the English and French methods of construction but added his own considerable expertise. For much of his innovative approach he drew upon his observations of the long, sleek Baltimore clippers that skillfully maneuvered in Delaware Bay. He incorporated the best of the clipper features with those of the existing frigates, and the result was a longer, faster ship that could carry heavier armament.

Experienced seamen were skeptical, and the first launchings were far from successful, but after adjustments were made the new models proved

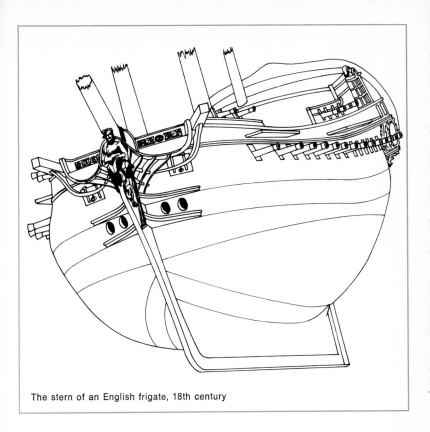

The stern of an English frigate, 18th century

Humphreys right, and soon the American frigates far surpassed those of Britain and Europe.

By the end of the Napoleonic Wars the frigate had become the most popular ship in the main navies of the world. The British fleet, for example, had 126 ships of the line, most of them third-rate ships, and 145 frigates. The frigate had the same sail surface as a ship of the line, but it was lighter and faster and one of the most effective ships of its time.

About 1860 the age of the frigate drew to a close. Steam-driven ships gradually replaced sailing ships in the navies of the world, and even the fast clippers eventually gave way to steamships in merchant fleets.

But the name has survived in present-day navies. The modern frigate is an entirely different vessel, but it performs many of the same functions as its illustrious predecessor.

Berlin

The facts that can be verified about the frigate *Berlin* are chiefly connected with a naval encounter in which this ship distinguished itself. In 1676 the *Berlin* captured the Swedish postal schooner *Maria* without firing a single shot. The *Maria* was carrying documents containing important information about the movements of the Swedish fleet, information of great interest to Frederick William, the Great Elector of Brandenburg. This is one of the earliest examples of naval espionage.

The *Berlin* was built in Holland and was acquired for the Great Elector's fleet by the superintendent of the navy, Benjamin Raule. A few years later it was Raule who urged his sovereign to strengthen his fleet with the *Friederick Wilhelm,* one of the best-armed frigates of the period.

The *Berlin* represents a sort of link between the old sixth-rate ship and the new fast frigate. The *Berlin*'s hull had the full smooth lines and excellent sails that were to make frigates fast and highly maneuverable vessels. This is why a ship like the *Berlin,* much smaller and less heavily armed than a first- or second-rate ship, could attack and defeat larger and better-armed vessels. The only decoration on the *Berlin* was at the stern, which carried the Brandenburg black bear. The second gundeck housed two classic elements: the hand-operated bilge pump to keep the hold dry and the winch for yards and sails. The bow of the ship had taken on the elegant and graceful lines that were to characterize later sailing vessels.

The *Berlin* had a long and active

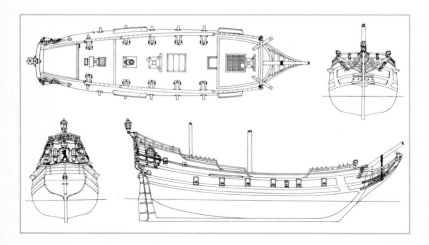

life. Under the command of Captain Melle, it took part in the Battle of Weser. In November 1675, under Cornelius Rees, it engaged the French *Royal de Dunkerque* and forced it to withdraw. On August 2, 1677, still under Rees, the *Berlin* sank the Swedish ship *Enhorm* and, single-handed, captured two others, the *Leopard* and *Diederik*. The following year the *Berlin* took part in landing operations at Rugen. In 1680, under the command of Captain Claes, it

Type: **two-decked frigate**
Launching: **1675**
Builder: **Zeeland shipyard, Holland**
Length: **75 ft.**
Beam: **20 ft.**
Depth: **19 ft.**
Displacement: **approx. 350 tons**
Armament: **first battery, twelve 7-lb. cannons; second battery, six 5-lb. cannons**
Crew: **100**

took part in naval operations against the Spanish on the coast of Flanders and in the West Indies. In 1688 the *Berlin* was captured by ships of the Dutch West India Company.

Friederick Wilhelm

The *Friederick Wilhelm zu Pferde,* one of the largest frigates built in Lubeck, was commissioned by the Great Elector of Brandenburg. At first it looked as if the expenses of building this ship and the high cost of maintenance would outweigh her benefits. Four years went by after the *Friederick Wilhelm*'s launching before the ship even entered the Brandenburg fleet.

The ship was heavily armed, and the stern was richly ornamented. Her general lines and armament were similar in concept to those of the smaller ships of the line, but also included more modern features in its smoother form.

The ship was originally assigned to the defense of the port of Emden, which at that time was threatened by French ships. But the *Friederick Wilhelm* had an excellent opportunity to show her worth in offensive action when Jean Le Sage took command in 1691. Le Sage was an experienced seaman who knew how to get the most out of a ship. On July 27, 1692, Le Sage attacked three French ships off the Cape Verde Islands. One of the French ships was a third-rate ship of the line. The battle raged throughout the afternoon, and by evening the French ships were smoking wrecks. On October 30, 1693, the *Friederick Wilhelm* outfought a 70-gun French ship: After an hour of broadsides the French ship sank with more than a thousand men aboard. This battle was also fatal to the *Friederick Wilhelm.* A fire broke out aboard, and the ship went down. The bold Jean Le Sage was not among the survivors.

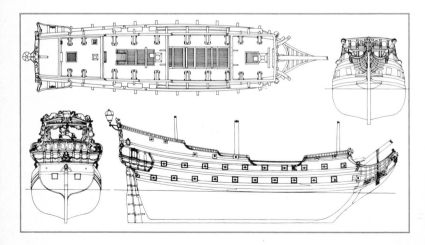

Brandenburg

Friederick Wilhelm - 1681

Type: **three-decked frigate**
Launching: **1681**
Builder: **G. C. Peckelhering, Lubeck**
Length: **195 ft.**
Beam: **33 ft.**
Depth: **22 ft.**
Displacement: **900 tons**
Armament: **first battery, twenty-two 32-lb. cannons; second battery, twenty 24-lb. cannons; third battery, fourteen 9-lb. cannons**
Crew: **250**

Sirène

The *Sirène* offers an excellent example of those features that put the French frigate ahead of similar contemporary ships. She was designed by Frederik Henrik Chapman, a member of the Swedish Royal Academy of Science, for the king of France. Chapman's *Architectura Navalis Mercatoria* (*Architecture of Trading Ships*), published in Stockholm in 1769, contains an extremely detailed account of the calculations that went into the design of the ship, together with a full technical study of the hydrodynamics involved. It was not long before Chapman's time that shipbuilding was still a question of trial and error and a good shipwright's "eye." With Chapman, shipbuilding was put on a scientific basis. Chapman's notes to his plans for the *Sirène* contain the remark that this frigate was an excellent sailing ship and could stand up to high winds. These words were written barely a century after the time when all that was needed to flood and sink a ship was to leave the gunports open. The construction of sailing vessels had indeed come a long way, and shipbuilding was now far more than the rough craft it had been in earlier times.

The *Sirène*'s smooth clean lines were the result of Chapman's extensive study of water resistance. The extremely low quarterdeck added to the sleekness of the ship, giving her a clean, graceful profile. The front of the bow carried the figurehead of a lovely mermaid, the body ending in the curve of a serpent.

The *Sirène* was an extremely fast ship, and it did not take many sailors to handle her rigging. The ship's duties, typical of her class, included

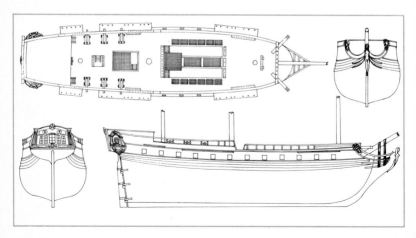

the pursuit of enemy convoys, several voyages of exploration, and the capture of smaller armed ships. The *Sirène* had only one covered gundeck. The second battery was divided between the open deck and the area below the quarterdeck.

The ship also carried a large contingent of marines for offensive and defensive actions. These soldiers were used for landing missions. In these engagements they were supported by the ship's guns. They, in

Type: **two-decked frigate**
Launching: **1700**
Length: **151 ft.**
Beam: **40 ft.**
Depth: **21 ft.**
Displacement: **667 tons**
Armament: **first battery, twenty-six 8-lb. cannons; second battery, eight 4-lb. cannons**
Crew: **286**

turn, backed up the artillery with rifle fire when battles involved close combat. Sometimes they were used to board enemy ships, fighting hand-to-hand with the opposing crews.

Pomone

The main difference between the *Pomone* and a standard ship of the line was the second battery of cannons it carried. The position of the cannons on the *Pomone* was as follows: The 36-pound guns were on the first (lower) gundeck and the 24-pound guns and several smaller guns were on the main deck, the quarterdeck, and the forecastle. The gunpowder and explosive charges were stored in a hold at the stern. Above the powder magazine was another area for bread and biscuit storage. A shaft from the main deck down the middle of the powder magazine accommodated the bilge pump tubes.

About six feet below the main deck was another deck with planking that could be removed when there was bulky cargo to be stored. This moveable deck ran almost the length of the ship, from the bow to several feet short of the stern. The first hold, which was adjacent to the powder magazine, was called the wine hold. A larger hold, the water hold, extended toward the bow. It was in the bow that the cannonballs were kept. The food stores, the large hold, and other storage sections had hatches that opened onto the moveable deck, providing easy access to these areas. On the sides of the false deck were depositories for weapons, perishable foods, officers' supplies, and various replacement parts. There were also a small infirmary and surgeon's quarters on this deck. A passageway between the hull and the various holds ran along the sides of the ship. This tunnel made it possible to inspect the hull and carry out any necessary repairs.

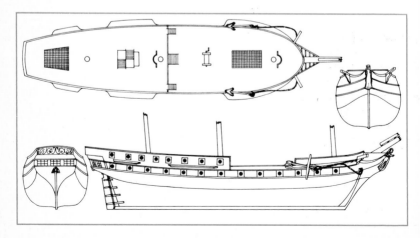

The captain's cabin was below the low quarterdeck, as were the officers' quarters. These areas were separated from one another by moveable bulkheads. The tolling of the ship's main bell, which was located on the forward part of the quarterdeck, regulated all of the crew's duties.

Beneath the forecastle were located the kitchens and supply quarters. At the end of the main deck,

Type: **two-decked frigate**
Launching: **1794**
Length: **181 ft.**
Beam: **40 ft.**
Depth: **20 ft.**
Armament: **first battery, thirty-two 36-lb. cannons; second battery, twenty-six 24-lb. cannons; eight 9-lb. demi-culverins**
Crew: **342**

toward the bow, a bulkhead with two doors gave access to the platform of the ram.

Winchester

The *Winchester,* one of the first frigates built by the British navy, was a sixth-rate ship and had only one gundeck for the 74 cannons it carried. It was fully rigged. The foremast and the mainmast carried square sails, while the mizzenmast carried a lateen sail that was supported by a long boom. The canvas for the sails of the *Winchester* came from France, from the village of Olonne nell'Aunis, where the best sail canvas was made. During this period most of the canvas for sails came from France. The sails were woven of cotton and hemp, and for additional strength they were reinforced by strips of heavier sailcloth, sewn an inch or so apart.

The *Winchester* had a square stern with a large, ornately decorated opening. Through this, light and air passed to a large area where partitions had been erected to create the captain's and officers' quarters. Below this area was a tunnel (a feature that was eliminated from later vessels) the floor of which was formed by the quarterdeck projecting from the stern. The tunnel was protected throughout its length by a richly decorated railing.

At the bow of the ship was an elaborate figurehead supported by heavily ornamented struts. The ship's ram, the beak at the prow for piercing enemy ships, was made up of several pieces, and a bulkhead separated the ram from the other sections of the ship. The ram was connected to the prow with long pieces of wood, which were also ornately decorated. Between these pieces of wood was the platform of the figurehead, and

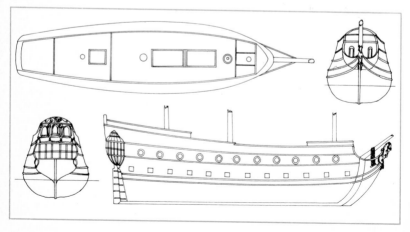

the sanitary facilities for the crew were located here.

There were two hawseholes on either side of the ram. The hawseholes were leaded to protect the wood from water dripping from the anchor cables. In addition, a semicircular wooden projection kept the cables from rubbing against the hull and possibly damaging the ship.

The *Winchester* was a very ad-

Type: **three-decked frigate**
Launching: **1695**
Length: **183 ft.**
Beam: **39 ft.**
Depth: **19 ft.**
Displacement: **1,570 tons**
Armament: **first battery, thirty-two 32-lb. cannons; second battery, twenty-four 24-lb. cannons; third battery, eighteen 9-lb. cannons**
Crew: **456**

vanced ship for its time. It was demolished in 1746, having served in the British navy just over 50 years.

Quebec

Frederik Henrik Chapman, naval architect and member of the Swedish Royal Academy of Science, designed the *Quebec* for the British navy. The Swedish designer included the plans of the *Quebec* in his *Architectura Navalis Mercatoria,* published in Stockholm in 1769 to illustrate his studies of hydrodynamics and ship-building.

The *Quebec* entered the British fleet the year it was launched. She was a fourth-rate ship. This was the rating given to the frigates, the newer ships that were being built in various navies. The frigates had originally emerged from the sixth-rate ships but soon became established as a class in themselves.

On February 6, 1778, Benjamin Franklin signed a treaty of alliance with France on behalf of the new nation across the Atlantic, and hos-

tilities with England soon broke out. On October 4, 1779, the *Quebec* was involved in one of the most dramatic episodes of the Anglo-French conflict at sea. Under the command of Captain George Farmer, the *Quebec* was sent on a reconnaissance mission to Brest. In the middle of the English Channel the *Quebec* came upon the French warship *Surveillante,* under the command of the Chevalier Du Couëdic de Kergoualer, which was also reconnoitering the English fleet at anchor at Plymouth. The furious battle began about 11 o'clock in the morning. After exchanging fire for over an hour, both ships had smashed masts and heavy casualties, including both captains. Farmer lost an arm, and Du Couëdic had two head wounds and a bullet in his stomach. As the two ships drew together for boarding a fire broke out on the

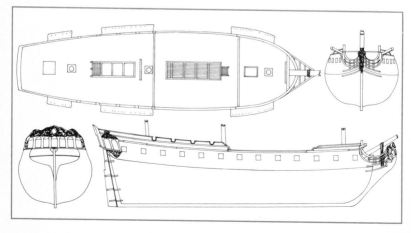

Quebec. Instead of attacking, the French undertook a rescue operation. Sixty-eight English crewmen were saved, but Captain Farmer preferred to go down with his ship. The *Quebec* had a short but glorious career, as did her captain. (Horatio Nelson had served as a midshipman under Farmer.)

After completing the rescue the damaged *Surveillante* managed to reach the port of Quessant in Normandy. There were 70 warships at

Type: **two-decked frigate**
Launching: **1770**
Length: **157 ft.**
Beam: **34 ft.**
Depth: **17 ft.**
Displacement: **1,320 tons**
Armament: **first battery, twenty-six 32-lb. carronades; second battery, twenty 4-lb. carronades**
Crew: **480**

anchor at Quessant when the *Surveillante* hobbled into port, and they gave the ship a hero's welcome. Du Couëdic died from his wounds three months later, on January 7, 1780, at the age of 40.

Serapis

The three-decked *Serapis* was a typical 18th-century English frigate. It was a three-masted ship. The foremast carried foresail, fore-topsail, and fore-topgallant sail. The mainmast carried mainsail, main topsail, and main-topgallant sail. The *Serapis* represented a development of the English sixth-rate ship, but it was larger and had heavier armament. The quarterdeck reached almost to the mainmast. Two gangways along the sides of the ship connected the quarterdeck to the forecastle. They constituted another area above the main deck. In between was room for supplies, masts, yards, and lifeboats. The quarterdeck and forecastle had large gunports. Offensive cannon were oriented toward bow and stern. Along the gangways between quarterdeck and forecastle nets could be stretched

over iron bars offering the crew protection from enemy rifle fire.

The *Serapis* was involved in a celebrated episode of the American Revolution. In 1779 John Paul Jones was in France representing the American naval forces. The French gave him a ship, the *Duc-de-Duras,* which was rechristened the *Bonhomme Richard.* Jones set sail on August 14, 1779, aboard the *Bonhomme Richard* at the head of a squadron. Jones cruised the waters of Ireland and Scotland and took a number of prizes. Returning to France by way of the North Sea his small group of ships ran into a convoy of 41 English ships coming from the Baltic, escorted by the *Serapis* under the command of Captain Richard Pearson.

Battle was engaged off Flamborough Head, between Newcastle

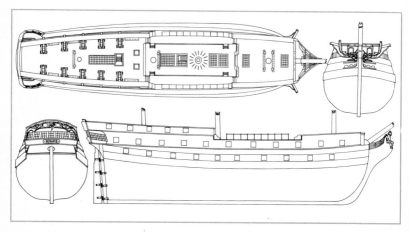

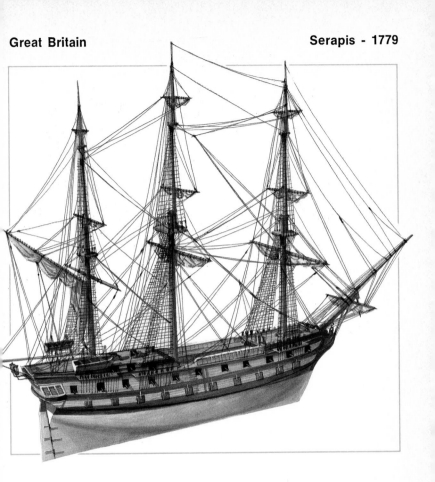

and Hull. John Paul Jones opened fire by moonlight. The two ships exchanged fire for more than three hours. Two 18-pounders exploded on the *Bonhomme Richard* and knocked out the lower battery. And the *Serapis* pounded away. When asked to surrender, Jones replied, "I have not yet begun to fight." In a daring action Jones and his men boarded and captured the *Serapis* while the *Bon-*

Type: **three-decked frigate**
Launching: **1779**
Length: **209 ft.**
Beam: **44 ft.**
Depth: **22 ft.**
Displacement: **1,280 tons**
Armament: **first battery, twenty-four 24-lb. cannons; second battery, twenty 18-lb. cannons; other smaller pieces**
Crew: **350**

homme Richard sank to the bottom of the sea. Jones sailed the damaged *Serapis* triumphantly into French waters.

Bounty

The *Bounty* was a rebuilt merchant ship under the command of Captain William Bligh when the famous mutiny took place. Bligh had served as navigator of the *Resolution* on Captain Cook's second voyage and ended his career as a vice admiral, but he is most remembered for his association with the *Bounty.* The ship set out from Spithead in December 1787 on a mission to transplant breadfruit trees from Tahiti to the West Indies. The ship reached Tahiti without incident and remained there for five months.

It was only after the *Bounty* left Tahiti that mutiny broke out. The cause is usually attributed to Bligh's iron discipline. Certainly life on board an 18th-century ship was in marked contrast to what life must have been ashore in Tahiti.

For reasons not fully known Bligh was excessively rude and insulting to his second officer Fletcher Christian, finally accusing him of theft, and Christian led the uprising in April 1789. Bligh was set adrift in an open boat with 18 members of the crew who refused to join the mutiny. Bligh managed to reach Timor, some 4,000 miles away, and then returned to England.

Meanwhile the *Bounty* headed back to Tahiti, where 16 mutineers went ashore. Christian and the others headed for Pitcairn Island, where they settled. In 1808 some American whalers went ashore on Pitcairn and found the descendants of the mutineers, as well as one survivor, Alexander Smith. Descendants of the mutineers still live on Pitcairn. Those of the mutineers who landed at Tahiti

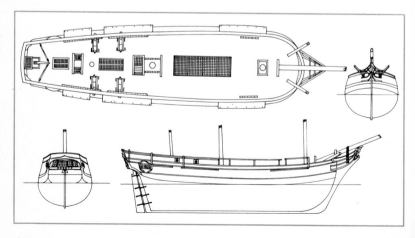

were captured by Captain Edwards of the frigate *Pandora* and taken back to England for court-martial. Three of them were executed.

Bligh saw duty in the South Seas again, and he was governor of New South Wales from 1805 to 1808, when a mutiny broke out, this time led by the deputy governor. He died in London in 1817 with the rank of vice admiral.

A replica of the *Bounty* was built for the 1962 movie production, and

Type: **armed merchant frigate**
Launching: **1787**
Length: **180 ft.**
Beam: **45 ft.**
Depth: **21 ft.**
Displacement: **980 tons**
Armament: **twenty-four 18-lb. cannons**
Crew: **46**

this replica has been authentically outfitted as a marine museum and can be visited in Vinoy Basin, St. Petersburg, Florida. On shore is a replica of the longboat in which Captain Bligh and the 18 seamen made their voyage to Timor.

Torborg

The frigate was an extremely popular ship in smaller 18th-century navies, but the finest examples (until the appearance of the large American frigates) belonged to the English and French fleets. Other nations in northern Europe lost no time in acquiring the new shipbuilding techniques and turned out some very fine frigates. The *Torborg,* built in Sweden, was one such ship. It was the work of one of the finest naval architects of the time, Frederik Henrik Chapman. Chapman had also designed ships for the navies of other nations and was recognized as an outstanding authority on ship construction.

The *Torborg*'s quarterdeck reached as far as the mainmast, and the forecastle was about 50 feet long. Sturdy bulwarks ran along the quarterdeck

and forecastle. There were seven gunports on each side of the quarterdeck and four on each side of the forecastle. The *Torborg*'s foremast, like that of all contemporary ships, was fitted inside the hull. Below and back of the base of this mast was the main powder magazine, where the black powder charges were prepared. There was a second munitions magazine at the stern, below the officers' quarters. The storeroom, which was large enough to accommodate provisions for six months, was also at the stern. Water and liquor were kept in the hold in barrels. Amidships, between two gangways, was a large hatched area for storing sails and extra spars and mast. The lifeboats that the ship carried were stored in this area.

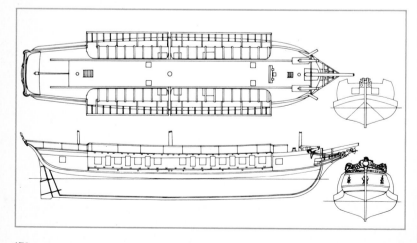

Type: **three-decked frigate**
Launching: **1770**
Length: **180 ft.**
Beam: **41 ft.**
Depth: **25 ft.**
Displacement: **1,790 tons**
Armament: **first battery, thirty 18-lb. cannons; second battery, twenty-two 32-lb. carronades; four 9-lb. attack cannons**
Crew: **315**

Havfruen

This Danish ship is an excellent example of the 18th-century frigate, the outstanding small warship of its time. The 40-gun *Havfruen* had the characteristic sails of the frigate that made it a fast fighter. It illustrates particularly the evolution in the rigging of the sails that distinguished the frigate from the earlier sixth-rate ships. The *Havfruen* carried ten square sails: four on the foremast, four on the mainmast, and two on the mizzenmast. There were also five staysails between the masts, three jibs at the bow, and a spanker at the foot of the mizzenmast. The two-decked *Havfruen,* however, is an impressive example of the frigate not only because of the number of sails it carried, but also because of the unusual height of its masts. The mainmast, for example, was over 200 feet high and went down some 25 feet inside the hull. These figures

give some idea of what must have been demanded of the crew for them to have to handle such an enormous sail surface. The small warship was manned by a crew of only 326.

There were 12 other supplementary sails available to increase speed when in pursuit of enemy vessels or to take advantage of light winds. These were attached to the foremast and the mainmast. Even the spanker, the trapezoidal sail on the mizzenmast, had a supplementary sail. Finally, the *Havfruen* had four additional studding sails that could be installed on the sides of the ship, almost at the waterline.

The quarterdeck was very low and seemed lower still because of its bulwarks. It was almost parallel to the forecastle. The 18th-century sailing vessel was becoming ever more streamlined.

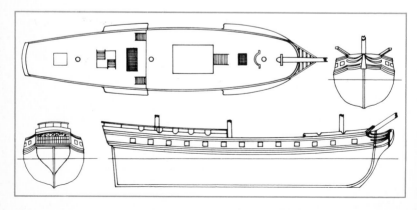

For the most part the cannons were installed on a single covered gun-deck. The additional guns that were installed on the open deck had to have special emplacements at certain points along the bulwarks so that they would not topple over the edge.

The *Havfruen* found a happy compromise between fast lines and firepower, and there was a kind of friendly rivalry between the men behind the cannons and the men who handled the riggings.

Type: **two-decked frigate**
Launching: **1789**
Length: **214 ft.**
Beam: **46 ft.**
Depth: **23 ft.**
Displacement: **1,300 tons**
Armament: **first battery, twenty-six 18-lb. cannons; second battery, fourteen 8-lb. cannons**
Crew: **326**

Constitution

By the close of the Revolutionary War the American navy had virtually ceased to exist as a fighting force. In 1794, in response to raids on American shipping in the Mediterranean by Barbary Coast pirates, Congress authorized the construction of six large frigates and the keels were laid for three—the *United States,* the *Constitution,* and the *Constellation.* Work on the ships slowed when a peace treaty was signed with the Bey of Algiers, but in 1797, when French privateers threatened American merchant ships, construction resumed at a fast pace, and all were launched in 1797. Plans also went ahead to build the other three—the *President,* the *Chesapeake,* and the *Congress.* All of the ships were built to the design of Joshua Humphreys of Philadelphia.

The *Constitution* represented an advance over contemporary British and French frigates. She had two decks, three masts, and full rigging. She was almost as big and solid as a ship of the line. Although classified as a 44-gun frigate, the *Constitution* carried over 50 guns.

The *Constitution's* most glorious victory was against the British frigate *Guerrière* on August 19, 1812, off the coast of Halifax. It was in this battle she acquired the nickname "Old Ironsides," when the enemy's cannonballs couldn't penetrate her tough oak hull. Captain Isaac Hull was in command. The two ships engaged in a furious exchange of cannon fire. The *Constitution* shot away the *Guerrière's* main yard and mizzenmast, and the British ship's other masts were so badly damaged it could only wallow helplessly in the rough seas. The *Guerrière's* captain,

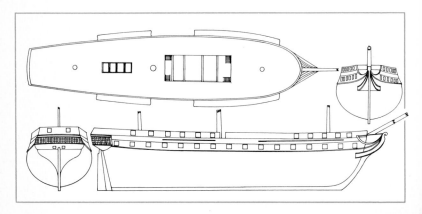

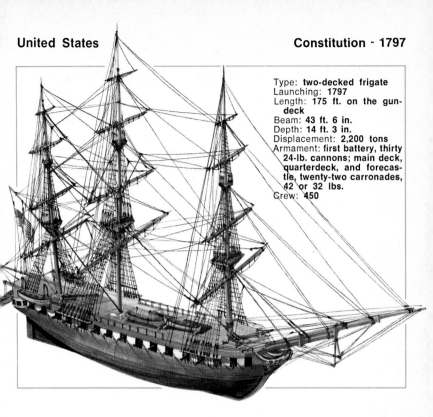

Type: **two-decked frigate**
Launching: **1797**
Length: **175 ft. on the gun-deck**
Beam: **43 ft. 6 in.**
Depth: **14 ft. 3 in.**
Displacement: **2,200 tons**
Armament: **first battery, thirty 24-lb. cannons; main deck, quarterdeck, and forecastle, twenty-two carronades, 42 or 32 lbs.**
Crew: **450**

James Dacre, surrendered his ship.

Later the same year the *Constitution* won another frigate duel; this time William Bainbridge was her captain. The enemy ship was the *Java,* commanded by Henry Lambert. This battle took place off the Brazilian coast. Early in the fighting Bainbridge was shot in the right leg but remained at his post. The *Java* was sinking under the force of the American broadsides, and the victors rushed to save the British crew, including the mortally wounded Captain Lambert.

In 1830 the *Constitution* was condemned to be broken up. A young Bostonian, Oliver Wendell Holmes, wrote a stirring poem, "Old Ironsides," in her defense, and when it was published public response was so overwhelming the ship was rebuilt. The *Constitution* continued in service for nearly 50 more years, seeing duty as a training ship and during the Civil War. She was retired in 1897. Now restored as a floating maritime museum, the *Constitution* can be visited at her berth in the U.S. Naval Shipyard in Boston Harbor.

Constellation

The third large American frigate, the *Constellation,* was also designed by Joshua Humphreys. In some ways it anticipated the principal features of 19th-century American sailing ships. The frigate was almost as large as a ship of the line and had a large sail surface. It was maneuverable and fast and well-armed. It carried twelve large square sails on its three masts, a spanker on the mizzenmast, three jib sails, and six staysails.

The masts were built in three sections and could be dismounted easily. These three sections were the lower mast, the topmast, and the topgallant mast. The joints of the three sections were banded in iron. The tops were roughly square-shaped though rounded on the forward side. They were the foretop, the maintop, and the mizzentop.

The yards were made of pine, prism-shaped toward the center and truncated at the ends. The shape of the yards was an innovation of Humphreys's. The yards that carried the sails had additional spars for supplementary sails, and these were attached by iron rings. These additional spars were sometimes called outriggers.

Gunports were arranged along the sides of the ship, and they were opened and closed by a system of cables. The second battery, with its carronades, had black-and-white painted mounts.

The *Constellation,* under the command of Thomas Truxtun, proved her merits in two engagements with French frigates in the Caribbean. On February 5, 1799, she sighted and closed in on the *Insurgente* and after half an hour of withering gunfire, forced her to surrender. One year

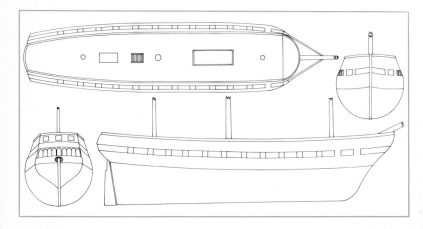

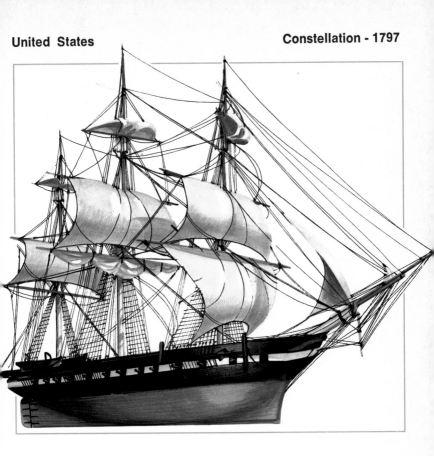

Type: **two-decked frigate**
Launching: **1797**
Length: **177 ft.**
Beam: **45 ft.**
Depth: **20 ft.**
Displacement: **1,140 tons**
Armament: **first battery, thirty 24-lb. carronades; second battery, twenty-two 42-lb. carronades**
Crew: **368**

later, in February 1800, the *Constellation* overhauled the *Vengeance,* a 54-gun vessel, off the coast of Trinidad. When the French ship opened fire Truxtun had his crew load and fire as fast as possible. From early in the morning until past midnight the battle raged. The *Constellation* lost its mainmast and could not follow the *Vengeance.* The French ship escaped, but four days later, battered and with a shattered hull, she ran aground at Curaçao. The *Constellation* limped into the harbor in Jamaica, still the victor in the battle.

The *Constellation* later saw active duty in the Mediterranean against Algerian pirates.

Independence

The *Independence* was one of a group of heavier ships of the line built during the War of 1812. The British blockade of the United States during the war had made it obvious that there was a need for heavier vessels that would be capable of dispersing the large enemy ships that had blocked the ports. Until this time the United States had put its faith in the frigates and sloops to protect its interests at sea, and while these fast ships had been effective in battles where quick maneuverability was required, they did not have the firepower necessary to combat bigger ships.

The *Independence,* along with the *Washington* and the *Franklin,* was designed by William Doughty. Doughty had been an assistant to Joshua Humphreys, and many of Humphreys's theories were incorporated in the construction. From lessons learned by the performance of the frigates and from knowledge gained by studying the heavier British and European vessels, Doughty made some modifications in the design of the *Independence* and her sister ships.

The armament on the *Independence* was heavier than originally planned. She had been designed to carry 32-pound guns but 42-pounders were later installed. The long guns were carried below and carronades above. The carronade was developed about 1778 by the Carron Company of Scotland. It was lighter than the iron guns in use at that time, but it had a larger caliber and greater power, even though the barrel was shorter. More important, it required fewer men for handling. Made of cast iron, the carronade was installed on a sliding mount to absorb its recoil. It

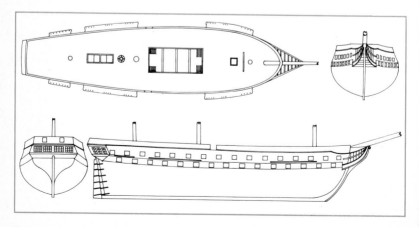

was a squat weapon, yet effective at short range.

The *Independence* carried a variety of shot other than the usual cannonballs. There was special shot for damaging masts, chain balls, and grapeshot, to mention a few.

The *Independence* was one of the first American ships to be copperplated. The nails were also copper, and this provided total protection against shipworm, which had been such a menace to earlier wooden ships.

By the time the 74-gun ship was finished and fully armed the War of 1812 had ended, so she never

Type: **line-of-battle ship**
Launching: **1815**
Length: **190 ft. 10 in.**
Beam: **54 ft. 7 in.**
Depth: **24 ft. 4 in.**
Displacement: **2,243 tons**
Armament: **74 guns; 42-pound cannons below; carronades above**
Crew: **790**

saw action. In 1815 William Bainbridge, now a commodore in the United States Navy, took the *Independence* to Algiers. Commodore Stephen Decatur was there securing indemnity for American ships that had been seized by privateers in the war, and the *Independence* and eight other vessels were sent as a show of force to reinforce Decatur's demands.

A New Way of Fighting

Keulse Galy, Dutch frigate, 1747

Petten, Swedish frigate, 1756

The first frigates carried 24 or 28 guns and a crew of about 160 men. Toward the middle of the 18th century armament was increased to 32–36 guns, and by the end of the century to more than 40 guns, usually mounted on a single gundeck.

There is no way of determining when the frigate made its first appearance on the world's seas. During the Battle of Lepanto (1571), the term frigate was applied to some of the oar-powered galleys that were on reconnaissance and pursuit duty.

At the peak of its development, the frigate had one covered gundeck and a second battery on the main deck, which were given some protection by the quarterdeck and forecastle.

In 1748 the British Admiralty codified the structural features and armament of the frigate and outlined its specific tactical functions. Smaller than ships of the line, it was assigned to running combat. Masts and sails were consequently increased.

Glasgow, English 50-gun frigate

Liverpool, English 50-gun frigate

Forth, English 50-gun frigate

United States, American 52-gun frigate

The ultimate success of the frigate was due to its lower cost of construction. Also, it could be handled efficiently by a relatively small crew, between 250 and 300 men, far fewer than were required for the battleships with their heavy firepower.

The Americans had a particular aptitude for getting the greatest speed from their sails. Perhaps the large frigates of the end of the 18th century represented the acme of frigate construction. These fast ships could outmaneuver ships much larger than themselves.

The fighting techniques of American frigates, counting on speed and maneuverability, had a decisive influence on conventional sea warfare as it had been practiced for centuries.

The French frigates, among the finest ships built in Europe, had slightly inclined bows and sterns. This created a slight concavity by the keel. These ships took the sea well and were highly maneuverable.

Erie, American 44-gun frigate

Lutine, French 52-gun frigate

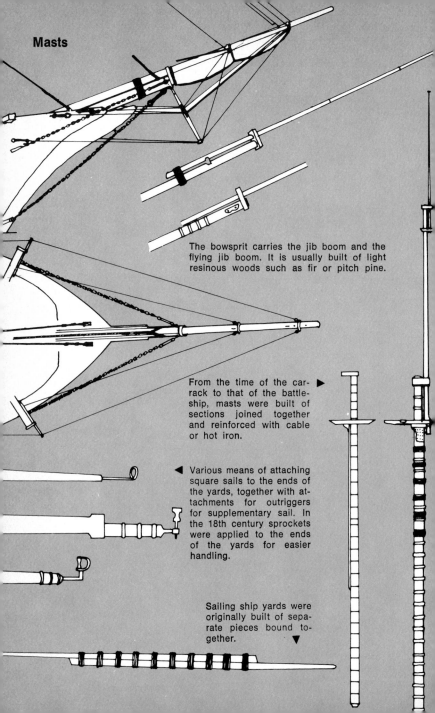

Masts

The bowsprit carries the jib boom and the flying jib boom. It is usually built of light resinous woods such as fir or pitch pine.

From the time of the carrack to that of the battleship, masts were built of sections joined together and reinforced with cable or hot iron. ▶

◀ Various means of attaching square sails to the ends of the yards, together with attachments for outriggers for supplementary sail. In the 18th century sprockets were applied to the ends of the yards for easier handling.

Sailing ship yards were originally built of separate pieces bound together. ▼

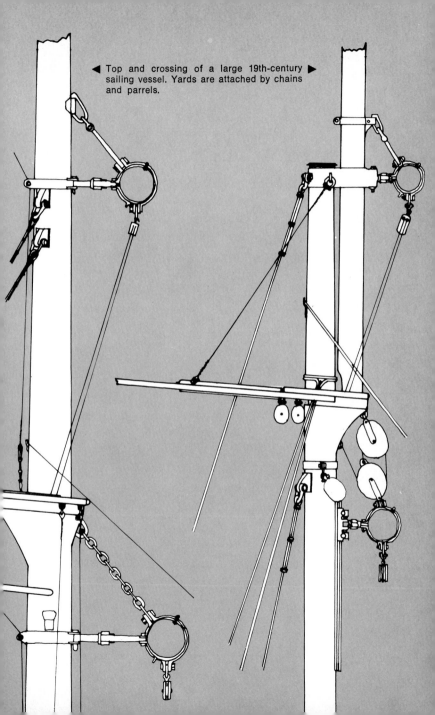

◀ Top and crossing of a large 19th-century ▶ sailing vessel. Yards are attached by chains and parrels.

Lanterns

Poop lantern,
16th century

English (*Great
Harry*), 16th century

English (*Golden
Hind*), 16th century

Spanish, early
17th century

Dutch, 17th
century

English, mid-17th
century

French, 1750

Swedish, 17th
century

Danish, 18th
century
▼

Spanish, late
18th century
▼

Portable lantern, late 18th
century
▼

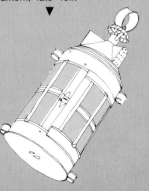

The Brigantine

The sailing ship known as the brigantine was of northern origin, and the name was first applied to a proper sailing vessel about the middle of the 18th century. Until the end of the 17th century the ship that carried the name of brigantine was a smaller version of the galley, the queen of oar-driven ships. That brigantine was about 50 feet shorter than the galley and carried 20 oars, 10 per side. Each oar was operated by two rowers. The early brigantine had no castles, and the oars were backed up by one or two masts carrying lateen sail. The bow of the ship carried a ram for smashing enemy vessels.

The name brigantine was also applied to a square sail that narrowed at the top and was carried on the mizzenmast of smaller square-rigged sailing vessels. This sail was the predecessor of the spanker.

An early brigantine weighed about 150 tons. It had a bowsprit with a small square sail at the bow, square sails on the foremast and mainmast, as well as a spanker with gaff and boom. The small square sail on the bowsprit balanced the ship when the wind was from behind. This sail was perforated so that spray and water would run off at once. This sail was gradually replaced by jib sails. The brigantine also carried supplementary sails and staysails.

Early in the 19th century, especially in the Mediterranean, the brigantine was equipped with a large course on the mainsail, which increased the ship's speed. This version was generally known as a brig. Another development was the addition of a third mast for greater speed. This ship was known as a bark. The third mast was the mizzen, which carried a spanker and a gaff topsail. The bark saw various types of merchant service on Atlantic routes, and it could reach very large sizes. The Italian *Lazzaro* of 1892, for example, weighed 1,246 tons and was some 200 feet long. The Italian *Precursore,* which was launched at Lavagna in 1899, weighed 1,486 tons.

Another variation was the schooner bark. These ships also carried a large mainsail with a triangular sail above. Fore-and-aft sails required smaller crews, so the ships were more economical to operate, but if these sails were too large they became extremely difficult to handle. Therefore, the ships were always relatively small.

In the Mediterranean countries a variation was developed that was somewhere between the brig and the schooner. This ship was designed to have high speed and larger cargo capacity. It carried small square sails on the upper part of the masts. The tonnage of this type of ship was about 900 tons. The rigging was imitated in a host of two-masters in most of the world's merchant navies. Thus the French had a kind of cross between a brig and a schooner, the Italians had a small military vessel known as a *bombarda,* and the English had a kind of xebec. All of these ships combined ease of handling with economy of operation and were popular everywhere.

Because of all the variations on the basic brig theme, it is hard to establish rigid classifications for these ships. Nevertheless it is no exaggeration to say that the brig was one of the most popular ships in the world for about a century and a half.

It should be pointed out again that the brigantine (or brig) sailing ship had no structural relationship to the earlier oar-driven ship that carried the same name. It is not infrequent that the same name is used to indicate different kinds of vessels. The sailing brigantine was a northern development and bore no resemblance to its medieval Mediterranean namesake.

Simple and functional as the brigantine's sails were, they nevertheless underwent several modifications as new types of sailing vessels came on the scene. The changes can be seen in one of these newer ships, the schooner. In size, speed, and ease of handling, the schooner was not unlike the brig. The Spanish merchant ship *Juanita* was somewhere between a brig and a schooner. This ship made its appearance in the last quarter of the 18th century. It was a coastal sailing ship and also served Mediterranean routes. Its rigging dif-

Type: **hermaphrodite brig**
Launching: **1775**
Length: **122 ft.**
Beam: **27 ft.**
Depth: **16 ft.**
Displacement: **683 tons**
Crew: **32**

fered from that of the brigantine and resembled that of the schooner.

The bowsprit carried two jibs. The foremast carried three square sails. The mainmast carried two topsails but no mainsail. It had a spanker sail instead. What made it different from a brigantine were the two topsails on the mainmast.

Type: **brigantine**
Launching: **1786**
Length: **80 ft.**
Beam: **22 ft.**
Depth: **11 ft.**
Displacement: **432
   tons**
Crew: **16**

The structure of the English brig *Symondiets* perfectly suited the tactical requirements of the period. Like other smaller ships, the *Symondiets* was destined for escort duty, scouting and reconnaissance, and convoy escort for merchant ships. Such brigs often found themselves in action against larger and more powerfully armed vessels.

The *Symondiets* was a single-deck brig with mixed armament and large sail surface. The square sails were reefed so that the amount of sail surface exposed to the wind could be reduced in bad weather without taking down the entire sail.

The principle of reefing had been applied for some time, but only with the development of advanced sail-making did it become a practical reality. On the *Symondiets* the lower sails carried two reefs, while the upper sails carried four. The spanker had three rows of reefs.

Originally the *Tonnant* was a brigantine. It carried eighteen 24-pound guns and four carronades, all of them installed on the main deck. It was a typical merchant ship adapted for military purposes. Piracy was in a certain sense officially recognized by several nations, and many privateers carried letters of authorization for arming their ships. Although the Congress of Paris of 1856 banned privateering, there were still pirate raids carried out by Spain, Mexico, and the United States, which had refused to sign the international agreement.

The *Tonnant* roamed the seas for

Type: **armed, three-masted brigantine**
Launching: **1793**
Length: **105 ft.**
Beam: **21 ft.**
Depth: **16 ft.**
Displacement: **620 tons**
Armament: **eighteen 24-lb. cannons; four hand carronades**
Crew: **127**

many years, the Atlantic being her favorite hunting ground. She preyed on English merchant ships in particular, those on their way back from the West Indies with valuable cargo. The *Tonnant* carried a great deal of sail for a ship of her size, seven square sails, two jibs, and a larger spanker on her mizzenmast.

From the Mediterranean to the Atlantic

Brasile, Italian brigantine, 1816

Maddalena, Genoese brigantine, 1818

The brigantine, a characteristic 19th-century sailing vessel, was the most popular sailing ship in the Sardinian and Neapolitan navies. These fast modern ships (almost as fast as the clippers) sailed to Chilean and Peruvian ports after 1815. They doubled Cape Horn and often went as far as the Dutch East Indies.

The routes sailed by Italian brigantines between 1830 and 1840 were infested with pirates. Many Sardinian brigantines carried light cannons and rifles to fight off pirate raids in the Greek archipelago.

The tonnage of Italian brigantines ranged from 150 to 300 tons, and sometimes was as much as 500 tons. Brigantines from Liguria ventured on the routes to Cape Horn and South America, while Neapolitan brigs followed the merchant routes to the Indian Ocean.

The two-masted brig-schooner, with square and trapezoid sails, was the classic Italian sailing ship until the middle of the 19th century. A few remained in service until 1870. The last Mediterranean brig-schooner, the *San Pubblio,* an Italian-built Maltese ves-

Fortunato, Ligurian brigantine, 1838

Selz, Italian brigantine-schooner, 1845

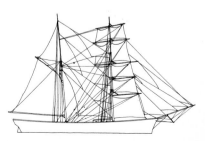

Segesta, Italian brick, 1863

Cincinnato, Italian bark, 1873

sel, was still in service in 1912.

Although the brigantine was generally a merchant ship it continued to use painted ports along its sides, both at gundeck level and at the level of the main deck, a reminiscence of earlier times.

Between 1860 and 1890 the bark was the pride of Italian seafarers. Derived from the French *brick,* its displacement ranged from 400 to 1,000 tons. It had three masts. The foremast and mainmast had square sails, while the mizzenmast carried trapezoidal sails. Its average length

was about 150 feet. Thousands of these ships were built between 1850 and 1903.

The last barks displaced 2,000 tons, and until 1870 they successfully plied the routes to Argentina, Uruguay, Chile, and Peru carrying immigrants. Some barks were still in service during World War I.

Italian brigantines were built in Liguria, at Gaeta, on the island of Procida, in the Sorrentine peninsula, at Ancona and Chioggia, in Trieste, Lussimpiccolo, Fiume, Sabbioncello, and along the Dalmatian coast.

Sicilia, Italian bark, 1875

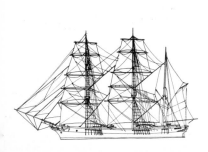

Fortunata, Italian brick, 1878

Cannon batteries were installed on various gundecks with their barrels pointing out of gunports. They were strung out the length of the ship. Smaller guns were installed on the quarterdeck and forecastle. Gunports at the bow made it possible to fire on fleeing ships, while those at the stern made running defense possible.

Gundecks

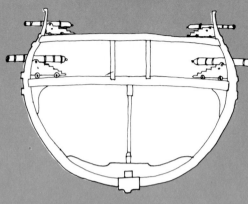

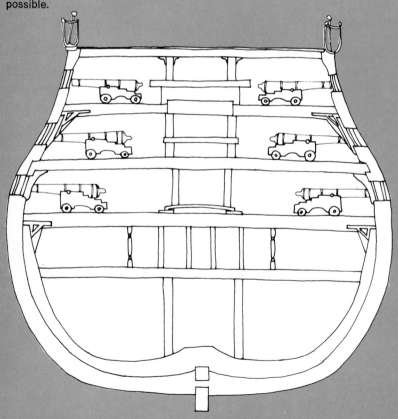

The Corvette

It was in the second half of the 17th century that the term corvette was first applied to a long, single-masted, oar-driven vessel. The name itself was not new, however. As early as Roman times the name *corbita* was applied to a small merchant vessel that was used chiefly for grain transport. (*Corbita* comes from *corbis*, "basket," and may allude to the round-bellied form of the hull.) It is not impossible that the round-bellied medieval ship ultimately derived from the Roman vessel. Another theory, however, is that *corbita* referred not to the vessel described above but to the reed-woven top at the head of the mast. The top was basket-shaped.

In the 18th century corvette was the name applied to an oarless vessel with two square-sailed masts (the mainmast and the foremast) and a square-sailed bowsprit. By the middle of the 18th century the corvette was larger and was classified as a sixth-rate ship. It had three masts. At first the mizzenmast carried a lateen sail; later it carried a spanker. The corvette had up to 24 guns installed on the main deck. It was a fast and highly maneuverable ship and was assigned scouting and communication duty. During the course of the Napoleonic Wars, the French navy made extensive use of the corvette against British sloops. The finest corvettes were produced in the 18th and 19th centuries, especially in the United States. It survived into the age of steam, and the name is still applied to a small, fast warship used for convoy and antisubmarine duty.

The *Rattlesnake* was the first ship that was all-American in design and construction. It was built by W. Peck with private capital. The American authorities assigned it to running battle duty. The ship was heavily armed for its tonnage. Its riggings made it very fast and maneuverable. Particularly noteworthy were the jib sails. This American corvette had its baptism of fire at the Battle of Chesapeake Bay on September 5, 1781. A French fleet under the command of Admiral Paul de Grasse fought alongside the Americans against the English ships of Admiral Thomas Graves.

The *Rattlesnake* went to the Mediterranean in 1803 under the command of Commodore Preble on a mission against Tripoli. After serving in the Atlantic the ship was disarmed in October 1817.

Type: **corvette, three masts, square sails**
Designer: **W. Peck (1779)**
Launching: **1780**
Length: **175 ft.**
Beam: **26 ft.**
Depth: **7 ft.**
Displacement: **420 tons**
Armament: **10 carronades on the single deck**
Crew: **95**

Type: **coastal cutter**
Launching: **1790**
Length: **42 ft.**
Beam: **16 ft.**
Depth: **6 ft.**
Displacement: **16 tons**
Armament: **eighteen 18-lb. cannons; four carronades**
Sail surface: **753 sq. ft.**
Crew: **10**

One of the smallest sailing vessels of the 18th and 19th centuries was the cutter. The cutter originated in England as a coastal sailing vessel. The *Aldebaran,* a distinguished member of this class, had a light and streamlined hull that cut through the water. Some sources suggest the cutter's name came from this characteristic.

The *Aldebaran* saw duty as a coast guard vessel and against smugglers.

The *Aldebaran* had a tall single mast, and the bowsprit, which carried three jibs, could be withdrawn for anchoring. The sail was outsized for the dimensions of the ship, and the vessel sailed at a steep angle when the wind came across the sides.

The Spanish navy classified the *Sebastian Gumà* as a corvette although it carried no armament. It was a merchant ship, but it had the hull of the fast fighting ship.

The *Sebastian Gumà* was built in the shipyards of Palma on Majorca, and saw service in the Ferreira merchant fleet of Lisbon, the same company that was to buy the famous clipper ship *Cutty Sark* a few years later.

Despite its low tonnage and small size, the *Sebastian Gumà* made 25 Atlantic voyages in its career. It sailed between the ports of Portugal and

Type: **three-masted corvette**
Builder: **naval shipyard, Palma, Majorca**
Designer: **naval shipyard, Palma, Majorca (1873)**
Launching: **1875**
Length: **150 ft.**
Beam: **35 ft.**
Depth: **7 ft.**
Displacement: **467 tons**
Crew: **45**

northern Europe and made voyages to the United States and Canada.

During a violent storm in September 1905, the ship foundered on reefs off the coast of Morocco. During its career with several shipping companies, the *Sebastian Gumà* sailed over 200,000 miles.

More and More Sails

Orlgosktovet, Danish corvette, 1743

Aurore, French corvette, 1766

The corvette comes between the bark and the frigate in size and sail. Like the bark, the corvette was three-masted and very fast. In addition it was sturdily built and was the preferred ship for scientific expeditions in the 19th century.

But the corvette was preeminently a military ship and carried up to 24 guns. The corvette could be up to 170 feet long and 35 feet at the beam. The masts were tall, and the mainmast could be up to 190 feet high.

Smaller corvettes were also built. These two-masted vessels, like the sloop, were assigned to coast guard duty. These ships carried 18 guns, and they often carried oars to be used for maneuvering in shallow coastal waters.

The corvette carried an enormous amount of sail. It carried from 8 to 14 square sails, and up to 11 staysails. Corvettes were chosen for the first military experiments with steam-engine propulsion.

Diligente, French corvette, 1783

General Pike, American corvette, 1813

Naval Artillery

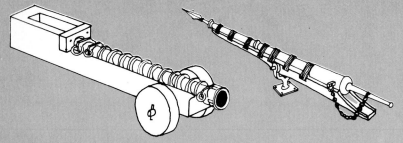

Iron-staved bombard mounted on a two-wheeled wooden mount. It may have been part of the armament of the English carrack *Mary Rose*, 14th century.

An iron springal with a harpoon-like projectile, 13th century.

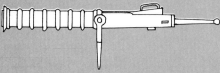

15th-century portable bombardelle.

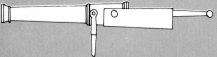

15th-century portable musket.

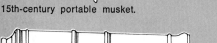

17th-century bronze demi-culverin.

18th-century bronze naval cannon.

16th-century bronze culverin.

Firearms were used aboard ship as early as the middle of the 13th century, but it was only in the 15th century that artillery was systematically employed. From the 16th century on, cannons were installed on wheeled mounts and arranged on more than one deck.

The first arrangement of gun batteries may have been originated by the French. The development of artillery was slow, and it was only after 1860 that rifle-bored cannons replaced smoothbore guns.

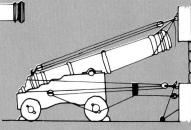

French 18th-century iron cannon with a system of cables and pulleys for recoil.

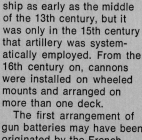

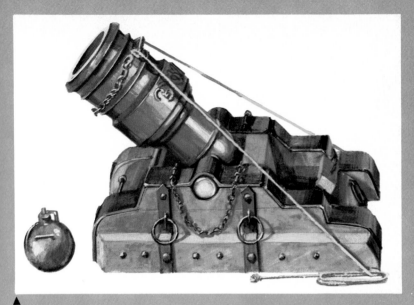

A 17th-century naval mortar. The projectile has a wooden fuse.

The proportions of naval cannons were improved in the 18th century. They were smaller and sometimes tougher than land cannons.

Scientific Voyages

Vast areas of the world were still virtually unknown at the beginning of the 17th century. Navigators, lacking sufficient scientific information, often contented themselves merely with finding new commercial outlets and bringing home precious cargoes, but in the course of another century improved conditions, new interest in discovery, the establishment of such scientific organizations as the English Royal Society and the *Académie des Sciences* in France, and the publication of such theoretical works as Padre Fournier's *Hydrographie* (1642) made it possible for navigators to set out on their voyages with a great deal of knowledge.

The century between 1740 and 1840 may be considered the golden age of naval exploration. Ships were specially fitted for such voyages and became veritable floating laboratories. The world map of the seas was soon to take its final form. Prior to this time unexplored coasts were indicated by vague outlines, and mythical islands dotted the seas. This came to an end, and by the middle of the 19th century the world's seas had been fairly well mapped. The Pacific Ocean attracted 18th-century navigators who hoped to find the *Terra australis incognita,* the large continent intuited by Ptolemy. The eventual discovery of Australia was to make an important contribution to the expansion of the British Empire.

After 1760 naval exploration gained an added impetus. Between 1764 and 1790, ten round-the-world scientific voyages were undertaken with important results. These voyages included John Byron's (1764–1766), the voyage of Samuel Wallis and Philip Carteret (1766–1768), and the three voyages of Captain Cook between 1768 and 1779. Then there were the explorations of Bougainville, the scientific expedition of La Perouse, Marchand, and the Spaniard Malaspina. The scientific information brought back from these voyages was of inestimable value, and some of the publications that resulted were read as avidly as novels.

Although much had been accomplished, much remained to be done, including the detailed mapping of the newly discovered areas and more detailed scientific studies.

Again it was Englishmen and Frenchmen, joined by Americans, who led in this new phase of exploration. Thus by 1815 most of the world, except for the polar regions, had been explored at least roughly. The period 1815–1840 saw another intense wave of exploration by sea. There were the voyages of Dumont D'Urville (1826–1829 and 1837–1840), the voyage of the *Beagle,* with Charles Darwin aboard, and the six-ship expedition under the command of American scientist Charles Wilkes, which went around the world.

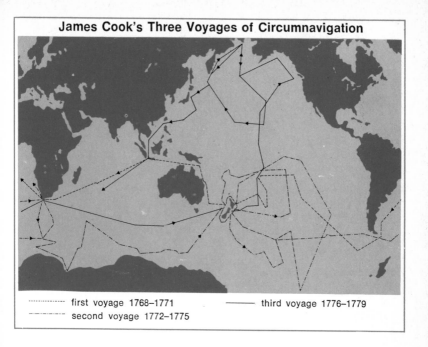

James Cook's Three Voyages of Circumnavigation

·············· first voyage 1768–1771
―·―·―·― second voyage 1772–1775
——— third voyage 1776–1779

The year 1840 marked the end of the great sailing voyages of exploration. The coastlines of the world were well-mapped, and future studies would be concerned with mapping the ocean and sea bottoms. Oceanography was to become a key area of research after the second half of the 19th century.

Even though warfare made it an instrument of death, the large sailing ship was also one of the most important instruments for the progress of civilization.

The sailing ship was to claim its place on the more important commercial routes of the world until the beginning of the 20th century, but this was its swan song. However, when the sailing ship withdrew from the center of the stage it left a heritage of important scientific discoveries behind. Two centuries of exploration also saw technical improvements in naval vessels, and new navigation equipment and instruments were tested. The conditions of life aboard ship were also much improved, and cures were found for a number of the diseases that had long plagued seamen.

Thus the large sailing ship made a contribution to discovery, to commerce, and to science.

Boudèuse

Louis Antoine de Bougainville, gentleman, scientist, and soldier became a navigator to explore the seas. The scientific world of the day was intrigued by the enigma of the famous *Terra australis.* Many people believed that there was an immense and fertile continent in the southern hemisphere. An expedition was organized in France in 1766, with the backing of the naval minister, Choiseul, to explore the South Pacific in search of the mythical Australian continent. A large frigate was outfitted with great care for this enterprise. The three masts were of Riga wood, and the riggings were made in Nantes, while the sails were made in Angers. The *Boudèuse* proudly carried a splendid figurehead in gilded wood. It was the figure of a woman with a sulky expression on her face, and this gave the ship its name, "The Pouter."

The proportions of the *Boudèuse* were 4:1. It was four times as long as it was broad at the beam. The ship carried a crew of 237 men. The *Boudèuse* was accompanied by a second ship, the *Etoile,* a flat-bottomed round-sterned flute.

On December 8, 1766, the expedition set out on the great voyage. Louis XV's instructions were clear. Every place that Bougainville landed, he was to plant the French flag and draw up all the necessary documents to assure the possession of those places by the French crown. The journey included Rio de Janeiro, Buenos Aires, Montevideo, and the Strait of Magellan in 42 days. After a long voyage the *Boudèuse* carried the flag over the waters of the Pacific. The expedition reached Ta-

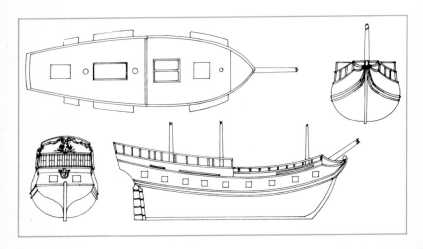

hiti and spent a month there.

The *Boudèuse* spent another month sailing in the vicinity of the Great Barrier Reef and visited Samoa and the New Hebrides. It was at this time that it was discovered that one of the crew was a woman, Jeanne Barre, who became the first woman to sail around the world. Finally the *Boudèuse* reached Java, the possession of the powerful Dutch East India Company. The ship was repaired and the crew rested up before beginning the voy-

Type: **two-decked frigate**
Launching: **1760**
Length: **134 ft.**
Beam: **35 ft.**
Depth: **16 ft.**
Displacement: **1,260 tons**
Armament: **first battery, twenty-four 24-lb. cannons; second battery, twelve 9-lb. cannons**
Crew: **237**

age home. The *Boudèuse* proceeded to the Cape of Good Hope and anchored at St. Malo on March 16, 1769.

211

Endeavour

In front of the British Admiralty stands the statue of a man whose name will always be associated with the great scientific voyages of the 18th century, James Cook.

The great Pacific explorer was born in 1728, the son of a farm laborer. After serving aboard coal ships, James Cook joined the British navy in 1755. By 1757 he had his master's papers. He studied and increased his theoretical and practical knowledge. In 1768 the Royal Society gave him command of a scientific expedition to the South Pacific.

The ship was the *Endeavour,* a sturdy bark well-suited for navigation in unknown water. The foresail and the mainsail were square-rigged, and its mizzenmast was rigged fore and aft. The *Endeavour* was a Whitby-built collier, and the navy had taken it especially for a mission to Tahiti. It was built of English oak with a re-inforced hull. The ship was special-ly fitted out for astronomical and scientific observations. Its official mission was to observe the passage of Venus in front of the sun, which was to take place in June 1769. This could be observed in ideal conditions in Tahiti. Cook had further instruc-tions to look for new lands, the mythical *Terra australis* in particular.

On August 25, 1768, the *Endeavour* set sail from Plymouth making for Cape Horn. In addition to the crew, there was an astronomer, Charles Green; the botanist Joseph Banks, later president of the Royal Society; and the Swedish botanist Daniel Solander. A great deal of scientific

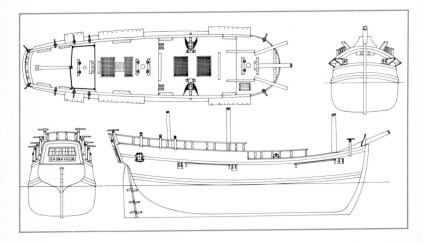

equipment was carried on board, including equipment for distilling sea-water.

The *Endeavour* reached Tahiti in April 1769 and made its observations of the eclipse. It then proceeded to New Zealand, where it remained until March 1770. In this period Cook charted about 2,400 miles of coastline. With some difficulty the ship overcame the Great Barrier Reef and reached the Torres Strait and went on to Java. Thanks to strict diet and

Type: **bark**
Launching: **1762**
Length: **98 ft.**
Beam: **32 ft.**
Depth: **19 ft.**
Displacement: **378 tons**
Crew: **53**

scrupulous cleanliness the crew had remained healthy early in the voyage, but many fell ill and died on the homeward journey. When Cook reached England in July 1771, he had lost 43 men.

Astrolabe

The *Astrolabe* was built as a transport for cavalry troops (carrying up to 46 horses) and christened *Coquille.* The ship earned its place in history because Jules Sébastien Dumont D'Urville came aboard as a lieutenant. An expert seaman, Dumont D'Urville was also gifted with scientific talents. Under the command of Gautier, Dumont D'Urville took part in a hydrographical research campaign in the Mediterranean and in the Black Sea. On August 11, 1822, D'Urville set off on his first round-the-world scientific voyage. This time the *Coquille* was commanded by Duprey, and Dumont D'Urville was the second officer.

The expedition covered 25,000 miles in the Pacific without losing a single man. The information the ship brought back was published in 1825 and filled seven volumes and four atlases.

The *Coquille* was rechristened *Astrolabe,* in honor of the ship of another great French navigator, Jean-François de La Perouse, who had disappeared at sea in 1788. The new *Astrolabe* set out on April 25, 1826, on another round-the-world voyage, this time under the command of Dumont D'Urville.

This was a particularly fruitful voyage. D'Urville charted some 2,500 miles of Pacific coast, corrected the position of some 150 islands, and found evidence of La Perouse's shipwreck on the Vanikoro atoll in the reef barrier of the Santa Cruz Islands. On March 25, 1829, the *Astrolabe* dropped anchor at Toulon.

On September 7, 1837, the command of the refurbished *Astrolabe* was again entrusted to Dumont D'Urville. This time the ship's destination was Tierra del Fuego and the Antarctic. The first attempt to reach the

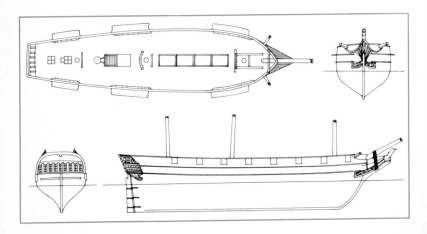

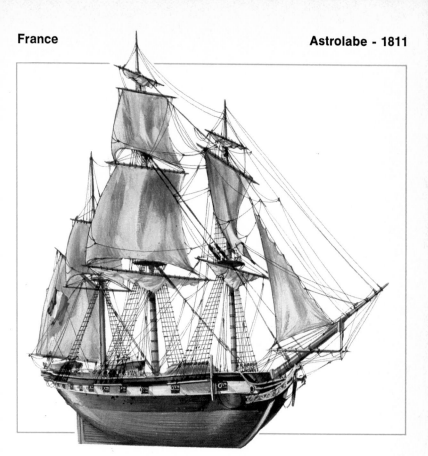

Antarctic was blocked by ice at 65° south latitude.

After a stop at Valparaiso and a cruise in the Pacific, Dumont D'Urville tried again. On January 18, 1840, the *Astrolabe* again headed south. This time Dumont D'Urville was more successful. He discovered the Adelie coast, so named for his wife. After a stopover at Hobart, the ship returned home, reaching Toulon on November 7, 1840. In 38 months at sea, 24 men had died and 17 had been put ashore ill.

Type: **three-masted corvette**
Launching: **1811**
Length: **102 ft.**
Beam: **28 ft.**
Depth: **12 ft.**
Displacement: **380 tons**
Armament: **fourteen 6-lb. cannons**

The *Astrolabe* made another voyage along the coasts of South America between 1847 and 1850, but without its valorous captain, who had been killed in a railway accident near Verdun on May 8, 1842. This French ship ended its legendary career in 1851.

215

Beagle

Many ships are remembered in the annals of naval history because of famous battles or because of the bravery and courage of their crews. A special place in these ranks was earned by the *Beagle,* a 10-gun brigantine that was transformed into a bark by the addition of a mizzen-mast. The ship was modified to make it more maneuverable when it was assigned to service in the great coral barriers of the South Seas. On December 27, 1831, the *Beagle* set sail from Plymouth on its greatest adventure. The ship was under the command of Captain Robert Fitzroy. The object of the voyage was scientific exploration of the Southern Atlantic and Pacific oceans.

There was a 22-year-old naturalist aboard, Charles Darwin.

Darwin had studied medicine and then decided on the ministry, but the sea and nature held a greater fascination than the church for the young man. The *Beagle* crossed the Atlantic without incident and reached the coast of Brazil. Then it proceeded to Patagonia, where Darwin saw fossils of prehistoric animals. A storm lasting 24 days blew up around Cape Horn, but the cruise along the Chilean coast was uneventful and the ship reached the Galápagos, which had been discovered in 1535 by Tomàs de Berlanga, bishop of Panama.

The voyage continued to Tahiti, New Zealand, Cape of Good Hope, and finally England again, where the *Beagle* dropped anchor on October 2, 1836.

It was a good voyage, and the ship

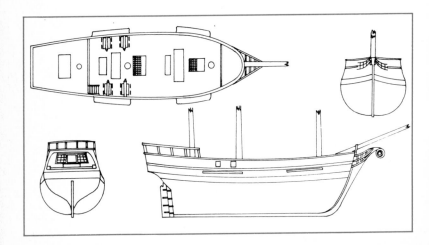

proved its worth. It had been at sea for five years in a row without serious accident, and the crew was intact. Not that the voyage had been without incident. On January 13, 1833, a violent swell all but swamped the bark and carried off two of the lifeboats, but the captain of the *Beagle* was an experienced navigator, and the incident was soon forgotten. In

Type: **bark**
Launching: **1817**
Length: **94 ft.**
Beam: **24 ft.**
Depth: **12 ft.**
Displacement: **350 tons**
Armament: **ten 6-lb. cannons**
Crew: **26**

1859, Darwin published his *Origin of Species,* much of which was based on the extensive observations he made while aboard the *Beagle.*

19th-Century Voyagers

François Peron: 1800–1804

Peron led the first French scientific expedition to measure deep-sea temperatures.

Nicolas Baudin: 1800–1803

Baudin's expedition set out to complete the exploration of the west and south coasts of Australia. About 20 zoologists, botanists, astronomers, and mineralogists took part. Baudin lost his life on the homeward voyage.

Ivan F. Krusenstern: 1803–1806

Krusenstern led the first Russian round-the-world scientific expedition and published several works based on the voyage.

William Scoresby Jr.: 1807–1822

Scoresby led one of the longest and most fruitful English oceanographic campaigns around Greenland and Spitzbergen.

Otto Von Kotzebue: 1815–1826

Two round-the-world voyages led by Admiral Kotzebue of the Russian navy obtained important information about surface currents in high and low latitudes.

Louis de Freycinet: 1817

De Freycinet sailed the *Uranie* to the farthest southern regions after charting Timor, Guam, and New Guinea.

Fabian G. Von Bellingshausen: 1819–1821

The expedition led by this Russian naval officer circumnavigated the continent of Antarctica.

Fury, the English frigate used by William E. Parry on his Arctic expedition

William E. Parry: 1819–1820

This British Arctic explorer led several expeditions in search of the Northwest Passage. His flotilla's western penetration of the polar ice pack in the 1819–1820 expedition was a record unbroken for 149 years. Earlier Parry had been second in command to John Ross. Both Ross and his nephew James Clark Ross were noted polar explorers, the latter more famous for discoveries in Antarctica.

F. Duperrey: 1822–1825

This expedition completed the work begun by De Freycinet, covering 50,-000 miles in the Pacific and collecting a large amount of scientific data.

Jules Sébastien Dumont D'Urville: 1822–1840

Dumont D'Urville sailed around the world three times, charted some 2,500 miles of Pacific coast, and corrected the location of some 150 islands. He led the second and third expeditions.

Hecla, another of the ships used by Parry in his Arctic expedition

Charles Darwin: 1831–1836

The famous English naturalist sailed aboard the *Beagle* under the command of Fitzroy, collecting scientific information.

Charles Wilkes: 1838–1842

Wilkes led a six-ship expedition to study tides and currents along the North American coast and in the Antarctic, carrying out geological and mineralogical studies as well.

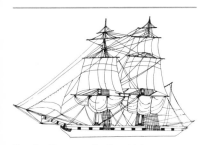

Uranie, the corvette in which Louis de Freycinet sailed to the South Pacific in 1817

James Clark Ross: 1839–1843

Ross led an expedition to the southern seas and to the Antarctic, carrying out studies on terrestrial magnetism, deep-sea temperatures, and botanical and biological subjects.

Wyville Thomson: 1872–1876

Thomson led a long campaign on the English expedition of the *Challenger* in the Pacific, the Indian Ocean, and the Atlantic.

George E. Belken: 1874–1875

Belken did oceanographic research in the Sea of Japan and in the North Pacific.

Alexander Agassiz: 1877–1880

Agassiz led an American expedition in the Caribbean and along the coasts of Mexico and Florida.

Alberto di Monaco: 1885–1922

Di Monaco made a host of oceanographic studies from the Cape Verde Islands to Spitzbergen and from the Mediterranean to Newfoundland.

S. O. Makarov: 1886–1889

Makarov led a Russian round-the-world expedition to study sea temperatures, currents, and tides.

Victor Hensen: 1889

Hensen led the German expedition in the North Atlantic.

Fridtjof Nansen: 1893–1896

Norwegian explorer Nansen sailed the *Fram* among the icebergs of the north.

Light Arms

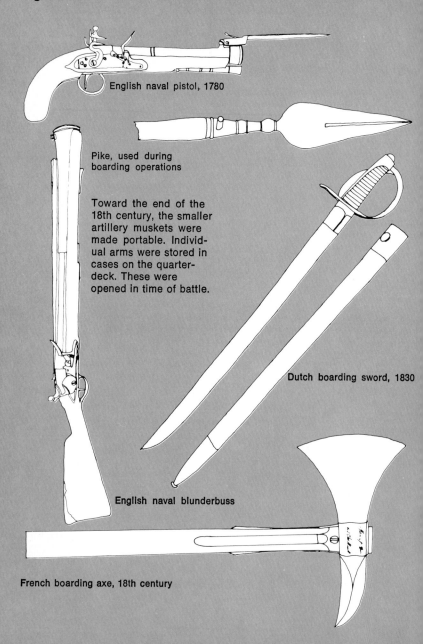

English naval pistol, 1780

Pike, used during boarding operations

Toward the end of the 18th century, the smaller artillery muskets were made portable. Individual arms were stored in cases on the quarterdeck. These were opened in time of battle.

Dutch boarding sword, 1830

English naval blunderbuss

French boarding axe, 18th century

The Great Century of Sailing

In the 19th century, the sailing vessel reached its greatest popularity and the peak of its technical evolution. Under the impulse of the Industrial Revolution, sailing vessels grew larger and larger. But the arrival of steam power dealt sailing vessels a lethal blow. The great sailing days were coming to an end. The ship of the line that had dominated the seas for almost two centuries inevitably gave way to the new armor-plated ships with their steel hulls. The age of steam, the internal combustion engine, the turbine, and finally the jet engine were to change the shape of ships.

But before the age of sail came to an end a new fast sailing vessel made its appearance. This was the clipper, that 19th-century model of speed and elegance. This merchant ship had a long, low hull, and the bow and stern had much the same form. The clipper marked a revolution in the construction of sailing vessels. These ships fought a losing battle after 1890, when they competed with steamships on the routes to California, Chile, and Australia, but there were moments when the outcome was in doubt. Among other things, the clipper was a more economical vessel to operate.

The last dramatic event of sailing days, the sinking of the *Pamir* in the Atlantic in 1957, is symbolic of a way of life at sea that has only survived in naval academy training ships and in sport racing, from the dinghy to the tall-masted ocean-racing yachts.

Type: **three-decked frigate**
Launching: **1813**
Length: **214 ft.**
Beam: **40 ft.**
Depth: **19 ft.**
Armament: **first battery, twenty-four 42-lb. carronades; second battery, eighteen 32-lb. carronades; smaller pieces, from 9 to 18 lbs.**
Crew: **678**

The last great naval battle between sailing ships took place in October 1827 in the Bay of Navarino on the Peloponnesian coast. The Greeks had risen against the Turks, who were supported by Mohammed Ali, viceroy of Egypt.

Public opinion in England, France, and Russia led those nations to try to mediate. Thus on October 20, 1827, ten men-of-war, ten frigates, and a dozen armed brigs and schooners arrived in the Bay of Navarino, where the Turkish and Egyptian fleets rode at anchor (65 vessels with a total of 1,960 guns). There had been no intention of combat, but the hostile movement of a Turkish fire ship and a careless rifle set off the battle. The Egyptian frigate *Irania* preferred to go down in flames rather than surrender to the French *Sirène*.

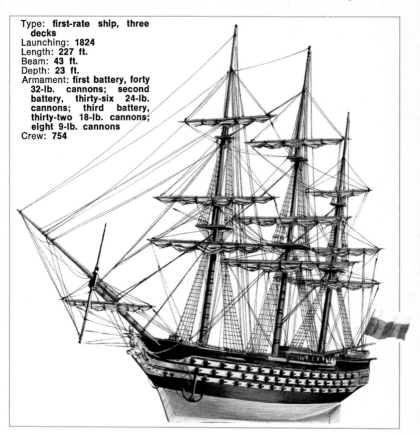

Type: **first-rate ship, three decks**
Launching: **1824**
Length: **227 ft.**
Beam: **43 ft.**
Depth: **23 ft.**
Armament: **first battery, forty 32-lb. cannons; second battery, thirty-six 24-lb. cannons; third battery, thirty-two 18-lb. cannons; eight 9-lb. cannons**
Crew: **754**

The Battle of Navarino was extremely confused, and it was never absolutely clear who opened fire first. Nevertheless the results of the battle had important historical consequences. After a century and a half of frequent hostilities, the French and English found themselves fighting side by side.

The Greeks, on whose behalf the battle was engaged, authorized their corsairs to halt European merchant ships. The Russians entered the Mediterranean for the first time as a naval power, and the *Alexander Nevsky,* Russia's largest man-of-war, took part in the battle. It damaged, then captured the frigate *Sultana,* the only Turkish ship to surrender. The Russians continued hostilities against the Turks until 1829, reducing Turkish power in the Mediterranean.

Belle Poule

The French navy named four ships *Belle Poule*. The first was a frigate in service from 1765 to 1781.

It was built in Bordeaux, and it made a long voyage to the Indies under the command of Viscount de Grenier. On June 17, 1778, the first *Belle Poule* officially opened hostilities between France and England. France had taken up the American cause in the revolutionary war. Under the command of Captain Chadeau de la Clocheterie, the *Belle Poule* engaged the 28-gun English frigate *Arethusa,* commanded by W. Marshall.

The second *Belle Poule* was built in Nantes to plans by Sané. It was more powerful than the first. It carried 44 instead of 30 guns, and a crew of 300 instead of 200. It saw active duty from 1801 to 1805, and won distinction in defending Linois' flagship during a long military campaign in the waters of the Indian Ocean.

The third *Belle Poule,* the one illustrated on the facing page, and in the line drawing below, was a magnificent frigate that was in service from 1834 to 1861. It was a typical French 19th-century frigate, a powerful, fast ship. This *Belle Poule* was a new and larger version of the plan drawn up by Sané for the earlier 44-gun *Belle Poule.* The new version, built for Louis Philip, was a veritable war machine with two gundecks. The bow resembled that of the great clipper ships and the last of the large sailing vessels.

In 1839 the *Belle Poule* and the Toulon squadron were assigned to naval operations along the Turkish coast. The following year, under the command of Prince Joinville, it was sent to St. Helena to bring back the

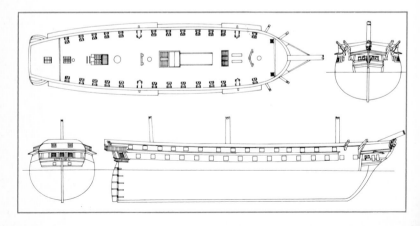

remains of Napoleon. Joinville left a detailed account of this operation in his *Vieux Souvenirs.* This handsome ship was decked out in mourning for the voyage.

The *Belle Poule* saw service in the Indian Ocean and took part in the Crimean War, one of the last military operations involving sailing ships. It was a masterpiece of naval construction and was once described as "a floating embassy that could be turned into a citadel in times of danger."

In 1859, during the Italian War of Independence, the *Belle Poule* was sent to Genoa to serve as a powder

Type: **two-decked frigate**
Launching: **1834**
Designer: **Danviel et Boucher (Cherbourg)**
Length: **178 ft.**
Beam: **50 ft.**
Depth: **19 ft.**
Displacement: **1,500 tons**
Armament: **sixty 30-lb. cannons; several 80-lb. howitzers**
Crew: **465**
Speed under sail: **average, 11 knots; maximum, 12.4 knots**

magazine! The armored battleship had already appeared on the scene, and the sailing ship finished its days in 1888 in the port of Toulon.

The fourth and last *Belle Poule* is a training schooner of the French navy. It was launched in 1932.

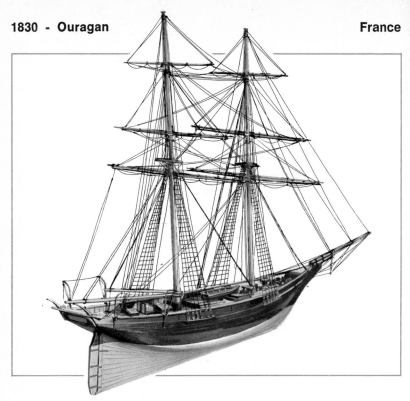

The *Ouragan* was a typical 19th-century brigantine slave ship and was famous for its speed. Slaving voyages had been extremely profitable, but the abolition of slavery in North and South America eventually drove the slavers out of business.

To escape capture by military vessels, the last slavers used heavily rigged ships of low displacement (150–300 tons) that could slip up the estuaries of African rivers. The *Ouragan* could carry almost 350 slaves in two compartments, one for men and one for women. These holds were barely four feet high. Along the walls were sleeping platforms, a little

Type: **slaving brigantine**
Launching: **1830 (Nantes)**
Length: **181 ft.**
Beam: **31 ft.**
Height of mainmast: **122 ft.**
Depth: **15 ft.**
Displacement: **300 tons**
Armament: **four 1-lb. cannons**
Crew: **96**

over five feet long for the men and less than five feet for the women. In bad weather the hatches were hermetically sealed, but in fine weather the slaves were allowed on deck for brief periods.

Needless to say, enormous numbers of slaves died during the crossings from Africa to America.

The *Marlborough* was one of the largest English merchant ships. It was built to the specifications of George Cockburn, Grand Lord of the Sea, who considered the slender, fast frigate the ideal ship both for combat and for commerce. The *Marlborough* was launched for the Blue Cross Line and was built of English oak and Malabar teak. The cost of the ship's construction was approximately 40 pounds sterling per ton. In addition to being outfitted for passenger service to the Far East, the *Marlborough* carried the armament of a military frigate.

The height of the decks was over

Type: Blackwall frigate, three masts
Launching: **1846**
Builder: **T. Green and W. Smith**
Owner: **Blue Cross Line**
Length: **183 ft.**
Beam: **40 ft.**
Depth: **22 ft.**
Displacement: **1,402 tons**
Passengers: **325**
Crew: **46**

six feet, and in the naval review of 1851 it was judged the finest ship in the merchant fleet. During its first voyages, under the command of Sir Allen Young, the *Marlborough* carried passengers and troops from England to Madras and Calcutta. Its first voyage from the Lizard to Port Phillip took 78 days.

At the time of its launching, the *Hogue* was considered the largest and most luxurious passenger ship ever built. Contemporary newspaper accounts described its appointments in glowing terms and pointed out that every cabin had oil lighting. An advanced commercial frigate, the *Hogue* was owned by Duncan Dunbar. Together with other companies, Dunbar had practically replaced the East India Company in Eastern trade. The *Hogue* plied the Eastern routes. It had one of the longest quarterdecks ever built, about 100 feet long. It was named, like most of Dunbar's ships,

Type: **Blackwall frigate**
Launching: **1855**
Builder: **Laing, Sunderland**
Owner: **Duncan Dunbar**
Length: **255 ft.**
Beam: **35 ft.**
Depth: **22 ft.**
Displacement: **1,331 tons**
Crew: **52**

for a famous battle.

For 30 years the *Hogue* sailed to Australia and once carried 443 immigrants to New Zealand. When Dunbar died, it was acquired by Devitt and Moore. In 1886 it was sold as a coal ship, and in 1897 was withdrawn from service.

Lloyd's Register of Ships lists three ships named *Star of India.* The most interesting of the three is the ship launched in 1861. It was superbly built and carried passengers first from England to Australia, then in 1873 to New Zealand. The hull had all the features of the famous Blackwall frigates and was constructed of wood that had been aged 20 to 25 years.

The *Star of India* was painted according to the Blackwall standards. The upper part was black with a broad white band, and the lower part was white, reminiscent of British

Type: **Blackwall frigate**
Launching: **1861**
Builder: **Stephen, Dundee**
Owner: **Joseph Soames, London**
Length: **188 ft.**
Beam: **34 ft.**
Depth: **22 ft.**
Displacement: **1,102 tons**
Crew: **42**

warships. The *Star of India* belonged to Joseph Soames, one of the most dynamic 19th-century shipping magnates.

The ship was later sold to the Norwegian Michelsen and assigned to Atlantic shipping. It had to be abandoned in mid-Atlantic in 1892, and later sank.

The *Antiope* was one of the longest-lived sailing vessels of the 19th century. It was launched in 1866 and demolished after 55 years of active duty. It was primarily a cargo ship but could also carry a few passengers. Originally part of the merchant fleet of J. Heap & Sons, it sailed the route to Australia. Superstitious sailors nicknamed the ship the "Anti-Hope," but it outlived the nickname. In 1883 the *Antiope* was acquired by Grace, Beazley & Co. and carried grain from San Francisco along Pacific routes. In 1897 it was acquired by Captain G. W. Murray, who took command of the ship. Captured by the Japanese

Type: **steel merchant vessel**
Launching: **1866**
Builder: **Reid, Glasgow**
Owner: **J. Heap & Sons**
Length: **238 ft.**
Beam: **38 ft.**
Depth: **23 ft.**
Displacement: **1,443 tons**
Crew: **38**

during the Russo-Japanese conflict (1904–1905), it was later acquired by Captain P. J. R. Mathieson.

When the ship was being towed into harbor in Tasmania (in its 50th year), it was driven on the reefs by bad weather. The ship was saved with all its crew.

Merchant Sailing Ships

Melbourne, iron hull,
England 1886

Blessard, iron hull,
France 1900

Country	Number of Ships	Total Tonnage
England	19,709	5,543,567
United States	7,312	2,387,876
Norway	4,718	1,360,663
Italy	4,469	1,222,832
Germany	3,477	853,290
France	3,877	751,854
Spain	2,888	551,201
Greece	2,092	418,689
Holland	1,471	403,788
Sweden	2,018	389,062
Russia	1,759	383,841
Austria	980	192,970
Denmark	1,291	176,941
Portugal	444	107,194

From the Bureau Veritas, 1875

Criccieth Castle, iron hull,
England 1901

Mneme, iron hull,
Germany 1904

Lateen Sails and Fore-and-Aft Sails

Lateen sails are triangular in shape. The longer edge is supported by a yard or directly by stays. Fore-and-aft sails are trapezoidal in shape and include the spanker, the gaff topsail, lugsails, and spritsails, depending on how they are attached to the masts.

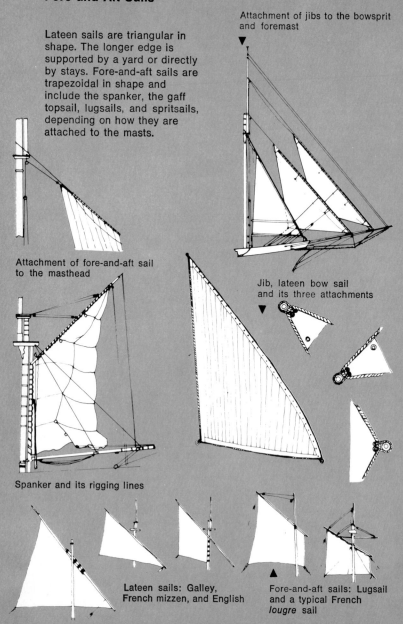

Attachment of jibs to the bowsprit and foremast

Attachment of fore-and-aft sail to the masthead

Jib, lateen bow sail and its three attachments

Spanker and its rigging lines

Lateen sails: Galley, French mizzen, and English

Fore-and-aft sails: Lugsail and a typical French *lougre* sail

The Schooner

Schooner, *golette, goletta, scuna, schoner, scoener, gweletten, schoener, skonert, ghouleta* are the names applied in various countries to two-masted ships with fore-and-aft sails. Centuries of experience had shown fore-and-aft sails to be highly suited for close hauling, that is, for sailing as close as possible to the wind.

The schooner was rigged with fore-and-aft sails supported by two yards. The gaff, the upper yard, had a fork-shaped element so that it could be hauled up and down the mast by a parrel. The lower yard was the boom, to which was attached the lower edge of the sail. The boom was attached to the mast and drew out the sail when the gaff was raised.

The schooner received its final shape in the United States in the first half of the 18th century. There were a number of variations on the rigging of the schooner. The hermaphrodite version had two square sails on the foremast as well as a square topsail on the mainmast, in addition to the fore-and-aft sails. Other variants carried only two square sails on the foremast. There was a three-masted model in which the foremast carried only square sails, and another version carried only triangular sails. Even six- and seven-masted schooners were built, but they proved unwieldly.

One of the most famous schooners was the *America*. In 1851 the American-built ship was the victor in a 53-mile race around the Isle of Wight against a large fleet of British ships. Prize for the victory was a magnificent cup, known since as the America's Cup and still one of the most coveted prizes in sail racing.

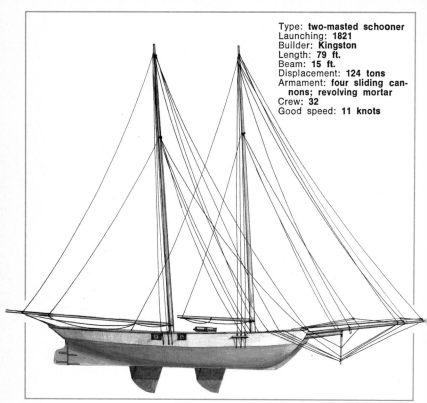

Type: **two-masted schooner**
Launching: **1821**
Builder: **Kingston**
Length: **79 ft.**
Beam: **15 ft.**
Displacement: **124 tons**
Armament: **four sliding cannons; revolving mortar**
Crew: **32**
Good speed: **11 knots**

Launched as the *City of Kingston,* this ship was rechristened the *Union* in 1827, when it was acquired by the U.S. Navy. This splendid long-lined schooner had two special features. First, it carried two moveable keel boards that could be hauled up by winch to reduce the ship's draft and make it possible for the ship to navigate shallow coastal waters. The sec-

ond feature was the schooner's armament. It carried four sliding cannons, two on each side, plus a mortar between the two masts that could be rotated 360°.

From 1827 to 1835, the *Union* was assigned to convoy escort along the routes to the East Indies, protecting ships from Arab, Chinese, and Malay pirates. It was disarmed in 1839.

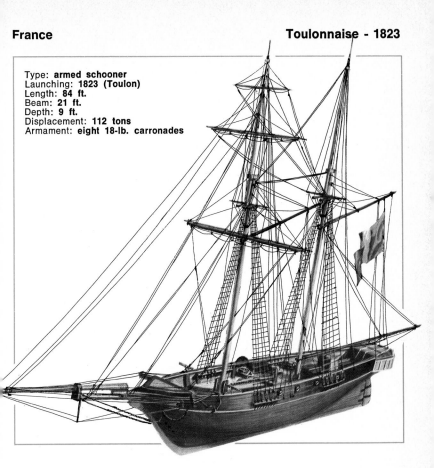

Type: **armed schooner**
Launching: **1823 (Toulon)**
Length: **84 ft.**
Beam: **21 ft.**
Depth: **9 ft.**
Displacement: **112 tons**
Armament: **eight 18-lb. carronades**

The *Toulonnaise* was one of the few schooners that was used as a fighting vessel. Generally this type of ship was assigned to scouting duty. But the schooner was extremely popular as a merchant ship because of its speed and maneuverability. Moreover, its simple rigging made it possible for a small crew to sail it.

The *Toulonnaise* saw action during the First Carlist War under Joursin. In Barcelona it garrisoned the city. Later it took part in the bombarding of Cadiz. It was overhauled in Brest in 1832. Four years later, on duty at Port Royal, Martinique, the hull and bulwarks were overhauled.

On December 18, 1834, the *Toulonnaise* was withdrawn from military service.

This schooner was given the nickname of the Nova Scotians. The history of the *Bluenose* is bound up with
the career of its owner and captain,
Walter Angus. Its history began in
1920 amid the keen rivalry between
the Canadian and American fishing
fleets operating on the Newfoundland banks. Lunenburg in Canada
and Gloucester, Massachusetts, each
claimed to have the finest ships and
the best crews. In 1920 Angus commissioned William Roue to build him
a fishing schooner that could match
any American schooner and win the

Type: **two-masted fishing schooner**
Launching: **1921, Halifax**
Designer: **William Roue**
Owner: **Walter Angus**
Length: **50 ft.**
Beam: **16 ft.**
Depth: **7 ft.**
Crew: **18**

International Cup, a veritable regatta
between the United States and Canada. The year the *Bluenose* was
launched it won the cup and kept it
for 17 years in a row. In the meantime it was a profitable codfisher. In
1933 it was shown at the Chicago
World's Fair.

Armed Schooner, late 18th century. Two-masted, rigged fore and aft.

Brigantine, 19th century. Two masts with square sails on the foremast.

In 17th-century Holland *jagts,* coastal sailing vessels, were the first ships to replace square sails with fore-and-aft sails. Thus they may be considered the ancestors of the schooner. The first schooner was launched at Gloucester, Massachusetts, in 1713.

Schooners played an important part in the American Revolution and during the War of 1812.

The barkentine was long used by fleets of the world because of the advantages offered by the combination of square sail at the foremast (excellent with wind from behind) and fore-and-aft sail on the other two masts (excellent with wind from the side or against the wind).

In the United States in the 19th century schooners were built with four or more masts. These ships grew larger and larger.

Barkentine, 19th century. Three masts with square sails on the foremast.

Barkentine, 19th century, with four masts.

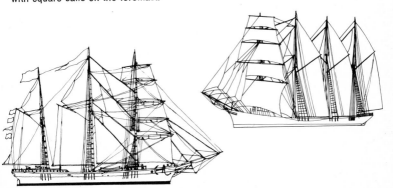

Figureheads

The practice of decorating a ship's bow with allegorical sculptures symbolizing the ship's name began in France in the early 16th century. Often the figurehead was designed by famous artists, and much of the ornament might be gilded. The use of these wooden sculptures declined with the appearance of the first steamships.

Half Moon, 1606

Terra Nova, 1736

Ajax, 1749

Victory, 1765

Seahorse, 1774

Queen Charlotte, 1780

Bellerophon, 1781

eander, 1786

Shannon, 1806

Edinbourg, 1812

St. Vincent, 1815

Formidable, 1825

Calcutta, 1831

Royal Albert, 1854

Black Prince, 1861

Warrior, 1863

Nautical Instruments

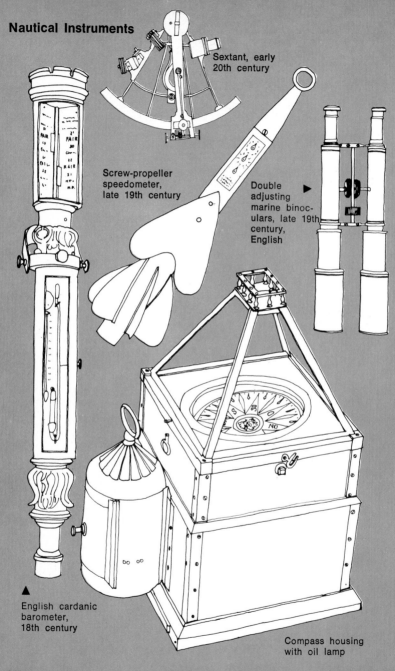

Sextant, early
20th century

Screw-propeller
speedometer,
late 19th century

Double
adjusting
marine binoc-
ulars, late 19th
century,
English

English cardanic
barometer,
18th century

Compass housing
with oil lamp

The Clipper

There is more than one explanation of how the clipper got its name. Certainly these sharp-bowed, narrow-beamed sailing vessels maintained a good clip at sea, and they clipped time off a lot of speed records. The clipper was the final development of the sailing vessel.

The clipper was born in America about 1820, when the merchant class was fully aware of the fact that the future of trade was on the seas. Over the following years American merchant ships were crossing the Atlantic and the Pacific, doubling Cape Horn, and plying the Indian Ocean. American shipbuilders constructed their vessels with a remarkable sense of independence, untrammeled by European tradition. They soon achieved results that had worldwide repercussions.

The two-masted brigantines built in Baltimore, with the low hull and sleek lines, may be considered predecessors of the clipper.

Its chief feature was that the beam was far toward the bow, which gave the vessel great stability at sea as well as its remarkable speed. It was a veritable greyhound of the sea.

The name clipper was later applied to a host of roughly similar vessels that were produced in shipyards in New England and New Orleans.

The clippers have a place all their own in the history of navigation. There were five types of clippers, and each one dominates a distinct period in the history of sailing and trade.

1830–1850 The Opium Clippers. The plains of Bengal, an English possession at the time, produced opium poppies in great number. The

East India Company had a monopoly of the opium trade, but once the opium had been bought from the company one could do with it what one chose, especially in the Chinese ports.

The clippers that carried opium were small, very well built, and extremely fast. Many belonged to English and American companies, while some were owned by individuals. They usually carried a few guns and light weapons, and their crews were rough and ready. The opium trade by clipper declined with the abolition of the East India Company monopoly and had all but disappeared by 1860.

1845–1860 The American Tea Clippers. The increasing demand for tea led to the construction of larger and faster clippers for carrying the tea from China to America and England. In January 1849 Owland & Aspinwall launched their *Rainbow,* a 750-ton clipper, the immediate predecessor of the great tea clippers. A host of others appeared in rapid succession, and the Americans led the field with such famous builders as Smith & Dimon, Well, and perhaps the most noted of all, Donald McKay. McKay launched some 137 sailing vessels in the golden age of the clipper for a total of 137,280 tons.

The wood used in the construction of the clippers was often only slightly aged and did not stand up well to the stress and strain of high-speed navigation.

After 1849 and the discovery of gold in California, the clippers car-

Careful stowage and good weight distribution were extremely important consider-
ations for maintaining optimum safety conditions aboard the clippers, which were
put under great strain to maintain their high speeds at sea.

ried immigrants and gold prospectors from the East Coast to San Francisco, before setting off to load tea from China. Laden with tea these ships would continue round the Cape of Good Hope and head for home. The first American tea clipper reached London with its cargo in 1850. This was the *Oriental,* which was the first to take advantage of the abrogation of the restrictive navigation regulations that had been in force since 1651. English shipbuilders took a long look at the ship that had sailed from Hong Kong to London in only 97 days.

The appearance of the first steamships and the sinking of several clippers by the Confederates during the Civil War ended the days of the American tea clipper. The remaining ships were sold to Portuguese traders in Macao and the shippers of Callao. These ships were used to carry Chinese immigrants to Peru.

1850–1875 The English Tea Clippers. The concept of English clippers is connected with the first tea clippers, which appeared in 1850. They were the 506-ton *Stornoway* and the 471-ton *Chrisolite,* as well as several ships that followed them. These vessels were built of solid, well-seasoned Burmese teak. The leading British clipper builders included Alexander Hall and Henry Hood of Aberdeen, Connell and Robert Steele of Greenock, Pyle of Sunderland, Challoner of Liverpool, Laurie of Glasgow, and finally Scott & Linton of Dumbarton, who built the celebrated *Cutty Sark.*

The lines of English tea clippers were longer and smoother than those of the American ships. There was a very small forecastle at the bow and an even smaller shelter deck at the stern. Lifeboats were stowed to the stern of the mainmast, and the captain and officers were lodged in the quarterdeck. The English clippers carried three square-rigged masts. Each mast carried five sails, and the lower topsail, the second from the bottom, was divided in two parts for ease of handling. Normally the clipper had 14 square sails, 6 staysails, and 6 jibs, as well as studding sails.

From 1863 on, the tea clippers were built in a mixture of iron and wood. The structure was metal with outer wood planking and wooden decks. The best clippers were built this way, and they marked the high point of rapid sea cargo transport.

1820–1865 Passenger Clippers. Although they were called packets, these ships were genuine clippers. Fast and comfortable, they carried passengers from the United States to northern Europe. They were square-rigged, three-masted vessels usually built of unseasoned wood and were relatively short-lived. The packets made their appearance about 1820 and continued to be built for another 45 years or so. They were the transatlantic liners of their time, carrying passengers rapidly across the ocean.

Commanded by experienced captains with highly-trained crews, these clippers offered comfortable, even luxurious accommodation for 40 first-class passengers, while immigrants were carried in second-class accommodations on the voyage to America. In general the Atlantic crossing took 15–20 days. A contemporary account of the retirement of a famous packet of the Black Ball Line noted that the ship was one of the fastest and most luxurious of its time. In 29 years it had made 116 round trip Atlantic crossings. It had never lost a man at sea and had never had particular mechanical difficulties. In its career it carried 30,000 passengers, 1,200 children had been born aboard, and 200 weddings had taken place on the ship. The ship was then transferred to coastal service. The packet was eventually replaced by the steamship.

1865–1890 The Colonial Clippers. This is chronologically the last category of clipper ships. The colonial clippers, or wool clippers as they were also known, were fast vessels built in England and the United States for transport service to Australia, New Zealand, and Tasmania. The first colonial clippers were built of wood, but after 1870 they were built of iron and wood. This new building technique made it possible to build sturdier and larger vessels. It was thanks to the introduction of iron in the construction that made it possible for the wool clippers to maintain their eminence on the Cape Horn and Australian routes until 1890.

The clipper was probably the high point of sailing ship construction. Later modifications and variations

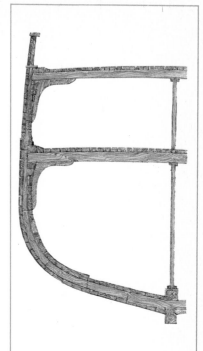

Cross section of the wooden hull of an English clipper ship. British clipper builders used more choice woods than did American shipwrights and let the wood age longer before being used.

did not fundamentally alter the superb vessel that the sailing ship became with the clipper, the long low ship with its complex of masts, its great sail surface, its great maneuverability, and its high speed even with light winds. The clipper was the finest expression of what sailing engineering could produce.

Composite Clippers

The distinctive feature of the tea clippers, especially those built in England, was speed. Several factors contributed to the speed of these vessels: the shape of the hull, the way the cargo was distributed in the holds, the skill of captain and crew, and the cleanliness of the submerged part of the hull.

A new kind of clipper appeared in England about the middle of the 19th century. This was the composite ship. It was developed by John Jordan, whose father had worked for one of the finest British shipbuilders, MacIntyre and Sons of Liverpool. The skeleton of the ship was built in iron, including the keel, ribs, and crossbeams, while the planking of the hull and the decks were in solid teak. These composite clippers were very popular in England, but only for a decade or so. This ship was certainly sturdier and therefore safer on the seas, but the construction technique represented only a transition

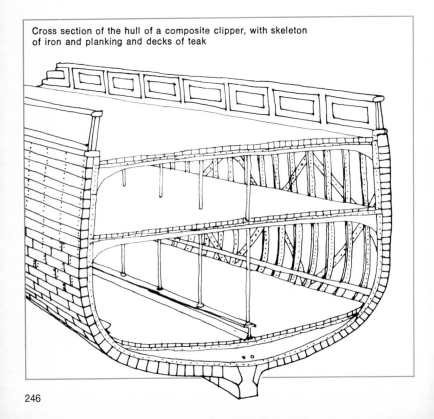

Cross section of the hull of a composite clipper, with skeleton of iron and planking and decks of teak

phase. For the age of the all-metal ship, first in iron and then in steel, had arrived. All-metal ships were also cheaper. The composite ship provided the advantages of metal construction, but it was argued that wooden hulls preserved the tea better during the voyage. Tea carried in wooden ships was believed to have kept more of its aroma.

The first composite ship to be built was the schooner *Excelsior,* which MacIntyre launched in 1850. The next composite ship appeared the next year. It was a three-master christened the *Marion MacIntyre.* The chief disadvantage of the mixed construction was the corrosive effect of wood and metal next to each other. This problem was solved by using sheet rubber between the wood and the iron, and by using stainless brass bolts.

The first composite clipper was launched in 1857. This was the *Red Robin Hood,* and this kind of clipper went into regular service in 1863. Some 35 clippers were built using the composite technique, and some of these were famous ships of their time: the *Taeping,* the *Pakwan,* the *Elsie Shaw,* the *Black Prince,* the sister-ships *Ariel* and *Sir Lancelot,* the *Leander,* and the *Norman Court.*

The composite clippers represented one of the final achievements of sailing ships and were highly prized on the tea routes.

Three of these ships, the *Ther-*

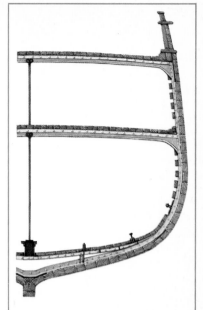

Cross section of a composite clipper; the metal skeleton is clearly visible

mopylae, the *Titania,* and the *Cutty Sark* (now anchored on the banks of the Thames), became world-famous.

The ships built after 1863 were the fastest and excelled in the last English tea races. In the 1863 race, 15 clippers took part; there were 23 in 1867; 18 in 1868; 23 in 1869; and 27 in 1870. About half of these were composite clippers. Most of the composite clippers were eventually lost at sea, although the *Titania* was sold in 1910 and demolished at Marseilles after 44 years on the seas.

The splendid clipper *Dreadnought* was famous for its speed, safety, and precision of construction. It was first assigned to Pacific routes and later transferred to the New York-Liverpool line under the banner of the St. George's Cross Line. Its first crossing from America to England took 24 days. On its return voyage it overtook the Cunard Line's steamship *Canada*, which had left port a day before the *Dreadnought*. The *Dreadnought* was so reliable that its captain could guarantee the hour and day of arrival. The shortest New York-Liverpool crossing was made in 1859. The ship sailed

Type: **American clipper**
Launching: **1853**
Builder: **Currier & Townsend, Newburyport, Mass.**
Owner: **St. George's Cross Line**
Length: **196 ft.**
Beam: **35 ft.**
Depth: **26 ft.**
Displacement: **1,400 tons**
Crew: **39**

3,018 nautical miles in 13 days and 8 hours. In 1864 the *Dreadnought* was transferred to Pacific routes again, joining the west and east coasts of the United States by way of Cape Horn. The *Dreadnought* went down off the coast of Tierra del Fuego in 1869.

The California Gold Rush gave an impetus to shipbuilding. The discovery of gold attracted hosts of immigrants, and the ocean route was one of the most popular to the West Coast. The *Great Republic* was built in the wake of this move west. The king of clippers, as it was called, was built by McKay in Boston for some Liverpool shippers. This four-master was seriously damaged by fire soon after its launching. It took two years to repair and overhaul it; this time it was built as a three-master. A total of 134,531 cubic feet of pine, 2,056 tons of white oak, 336 tons of iron,

Type: **four-masted clipper**
Launching: **1853**
Length: **324 ft.**
Beam: **53 ft.**
Depth: **25 ft.**
Displacement: **4,000 tons**
Crew: **130**

and 5.6 tons of copper went into her construction. It took 50,000 man-days to build the hull. The hull was not straight throughout its length but curved up for about 60 feet to the bow. The keel was lined with copper, and the stern part was elliptical in shape. The base of the mainmast was almost 4 feet high, and the total height was almost 250 feet.

This clipper was built specifically to outsail the *Fiery Cross,* the clipper that won the tea race in 1861 and 1862. The *Taeping* was famous for the purity of its lines, the perfection of its construction, and the excellence of its fittings. Its neck-and-neck finish with the *Ariel* in the 1866 tea race has gone down in history. The *Ariel* reached the British Downs (the roadstead at Deal, Kent) first, but the *Taeping* arrived in London first. In 1868 the *Taeping* set sail from China, competing against five other ships, including the *Ariel.* The *Ariel* won

Type: **tea clipper**
Launching: **1863**
Builder: **Robert Steele, Greenock**
Owner: **C. Rodger**
Length: **193 ft.**
Beam: **31 ft.**
Depth: **19 ft.**
Displacement: **767 tons**
Crew: **36**

this race with a 99-day crossing.

The *Taeping* was built of solid aged wood. There was a short forecastle and a small shelter deck at the stern, where the captain and officers were housed. Captain MacKinnon, whose name is indissolubly bound to the *Taeping,* went down with the ship.

Type: **composite clipper, three masts**
Launching: **1863**
Builder: **Bilbe, London**
Length: **162 ft.**
Beam: **28 ft.**
Depth: **23 ft.**
Displacement: **536 tons**
Crew: **34**

The *Coonatto* was one of the first passenger and cargo clippers to sail the Australian route around the Cape of Good Hope. The composite construction of this vessel increased its safety, but the metal elements tended to corrode.

Captain Begg commanded the *Coonatto* for some 20 years, a record in the annals of navigation. The *Coonatto*'s first crossing from London to Sydney was made in only 70 days, which gives some indication of the excellent speed this clipper was able to maintain.

This crossing was not without incident. High seas off the island of Saint Paul in the Indian Ocean carried away the helmsman and the rudder, but the ship nevertheless managed to reach its destination. The *Coonatto* was shipwrecked in 1872 off Beachy Head.

Type: **tea clipper**
Launching: **1865**
Builder: **Robert Steele, Greenock**
Owner: **Shaw, Maxton & Co.**
Length: **193 ft.**
Beam: **33 ft.**
Depth: **21 ft.**
Displacement: **1,058 tons**
Crew: **36**

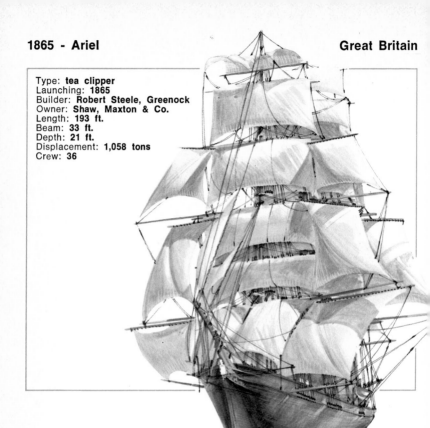

The tea races were a great sporting event of the 19th century. The finest clippers of the day, fully loaded with tea, raced from China to England. The 1866 race was won by the *Ariel,* whose captain considered her perfectly beautiful, with symmetrical grace in her proportions, sails, masts, and decks. She could cover 340 nautical miles in a single day at an average speed of 16 knots.

In the 1866 tea race the *Ariel* sailed from the Min River, near Fuchow, to the British Downs in 99 days.

This fast clipper continued to sail back and forth between China and England under the command of Captain Keay, but interest in the tea races declined.

In 1872, after a 114-day crossing from China, the *Ariel* set sail from England again, this time under the command of Captain Cachenaille. The ship was never seen again.

Type: **tea clipper**
Launching: **1868**
Designer: **Bernard Waymouth**
Owner: **White Star Line, Aberdeen**
Length: **210 ft.**
Beam: **32 ft.**
Depth: **21 ft.**
Displacement: **1,970 tons**
Crew: **35**

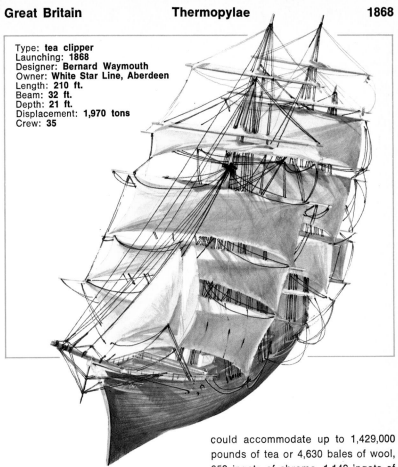

The *Thermopylae* was the great rival of the *Cutty Sark,* considered by many the fastest clipper in the world. The *Thermopylae* had a marvelous system of sails and achieved remarkable speeds in high winds, especially along the southern latitudes between the Cape of Good Hope and Australia. In fact, the ship was especially designed for this route. Its holds could accommodate up to 1,429,000 pounds of tea or 4,630 bales of wool, 650 ingots of chrome, 1,142 ingots of nickel, and 19 tons of iron rail.

The *Thermopylae* was sold in 1890 for 5,000 pounds sterling to the Rice Milling Company of Montreal, and then carried Burmese rice. Later it was sold to the Portuguese and became a naval training ship called the *Pedro Nuñez.* It was withdrawn from service in 1907 and sunk with cannon shot off the mouth of the Tagus.

Cutty Sark

The only surviving 19th-century clipper ship is docked in Greenwich, England, not far from the Royal Navy College. This ship, of course, is the *Cutty Sark*. The name of the ship ("the torn shirt") comes from the witch Nellie in Robert Burns' "Tam o' Shanter." The name was given to the ship by its owner, John Willis, who was nicknamed White Hat.

The *Cutty Sark* was built to outdo the *Thermopylae* in the famous tea races. The man who designed and built the ship, Hercules Linton, went bankrupt before the ship was launched. In any case, he had built an ideal ship. When the *Cutty Sark* was launched in November 1869, it was clear at once that its lines and balance were perfect. The outer planking was first-class wood, and

the decks were built of solid teak. The ribbing was in forged iron.

The ship was painted black with a double line of gold leaf emphasizing the elegant curve of the deck. At the bow was a figurehead carved by F. Hellier of Blackwall of Nellie the witch. The mainmast rose some 150 feet from the deck, and its sail surface was 31,979 square feet.

It made its first ocean crossing in late January 1870, under the command of Captain George Moddie. Its first return voyage from Shanghai to London, with a cargo of tea, took 110 days. Its rival, the *Thermopylae,* made the crossing in 105 days. On the *Cutty Sark*'s second crossing from China, it might have made record time, but it lost its rudder in a violent storm in the Indian Ocean. The ship

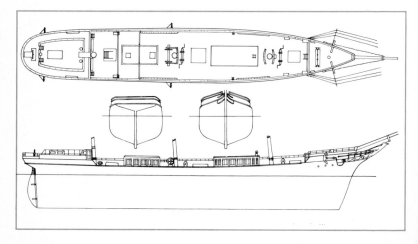

Type: **tea clipper**
Launching: **1869**
Designer: **Hercules Linton**
Owner: **John Willis**
Builder: **Scott & Linton, Dumbarton**
Length: **282 ft.**
Beam: **36 ft.**
Depth: **21 ft.**
Displacement: **2,133 tons**
Crew: **32**

made it back to London, sailing 8,000 miles with an improvised rudder. The *Cutty Sark* had several other captains, including W. Moore; W. E. Tiptaft, who died at the end of a fine crossing; F. S. Wallace, who killed himself because his second mate, who had involuntarily killed a sailor, had escaped; and the drunkard J. Bruce. Finally, Richard Woodget, a fine and honest sailor, became captain, and the *Cutty Sark* enjoyed a prosperous decade as a tea clipper and as a wool clipper on the Cape Horn route to Australia.

It was sold in 1895, because it was no longer economical to run. The buyer was the Portuguese shipper Ferreira of Lisbon, who used it on Atlantic runs. In 1922 the English captain Wilfred Dowman acquired the ship and restored it to its original form. It survived the bombing of London during World War II, and is now in dry dock as a memorial of the great days of sailing.

The *Sobraon* was the largest composite clipper built. The beams were steel; the rest was teak. It was extremely sturdy, and its passenger accommodations were so comfortable that sick people often voyaged on it to take the good sea air as a cure.

A fast ship, it could sail 16 knots per hour, and set several fine crossing records: 340 miles in one day and 2,000 miles in one week, far faster than contemporary steamships.

The *Sobraon* also carried live domestic animals and poultry aboard, to provide fresh milk, eggs, and meat.

Type: **composite clipper, three masts**
Launching: **1866**
Length: **317 ft.**
Beam: **40 ft.**
Depth: **26 ft.**
Displacement: **2,132 tons**
Sail surface: **86,080 sq. ft.**
Good speed: **16 knots**
Crew: **64**

Novelties for the period were the ship's freshwater condenser and the stowage of several tons of ice.

It was acquired by Australia in 1891 and transformed into a floating prison. Overhauled later, it served for many years as a training ship for the British navy.

This was the smallest three-masted clipper constructed in wood and iron. The rear deck, a little over 40 feet long, was covered with strips of New Zealand kauri pine. The four lifeboats were built of teak. The foremast was about 110 feet tall, the mainmast almost 115 feet, and the mizzenmast about 90 feet. This was an extremely safe sailing vessel. There was a famous race between the *Berean* and the *Thermopylae* from the English Channel to Tasmania. The *Berean* reached the Tasmanian coast only 17 hours after the *Thermopylae*. In 1896

Type: **composite clipper, three masts**
Launching: **1869**
Builder: **Pyle, Sunderland**
Length: **162 ft.**
Beam: **11 ft.**
Depth: **15 ft.**
Displacement: **526 tons**
Crew: **28**

the *Berean* was sold to a Norwegian company and was assigned to ice transport duty.

In 1910 it was struck by a steamship and damaged beyond repair. The *Berean* ended its days serving as a floating bridge in the port of Falmouth.

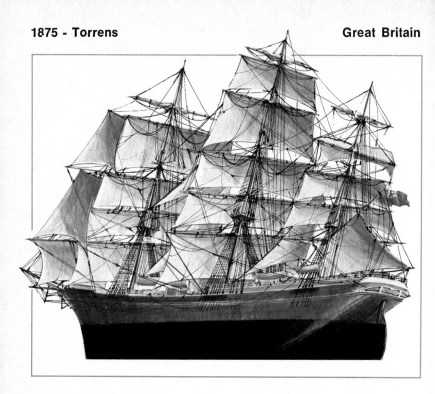

The *Torrens* was probably the most popular ship on the Australian run. Built of solid teak throughout, with a metal frame, the *Torrens* was a composite clipper. The ship boasted an extremely large sail surface. It was so well-balanced that its best performance did not require the high winds of the southern latitudes. In the calm equatorial waters it outstripped many equally famous clippers that were becalmed. The average daily speed was 300 nautical miles, and its top hourly speed was about 16–17 knots. It was rented by the British government in 1903 to carry a cargo of explosives from

Type: **composite clipper, three masts**
Launching: **1875**
Builder: **James Laing, Sunderland**
Owner: **Elder Line, London**
Length: **220 ft.**
Beam: **38 ft.**
Depth: **21 ft.**
Displacement: **1,335 tons**
Crew: **36**

Capetown to London. Sailing up the Thames, the *Torrens* collided with a steamship, which sank in three minutes. The *Torrens* was seriously damaged. The ship was sold to a Ligurian shipping company and remained in service until 1910, when it ran aground. It was decided to scuttle the ship.

Some Clipper Crossings

Honqua: New York to Hong Kong in 84 days

Natchez: Macao to New York in 78 days

Sea Witch: Canton to New York in 81 days

Surprise: Shanghai to New York in 81 days

Flying Cloud: New York to San Francisco in 89 days

Sea Serpent: Fuchow to Plymouth in 130 days

Thermopylae: Fuchow to Plymouth in 115 days

Titania: Fuchow to Plymouth in 116 days

Ariel: Fuchow to Dungeness in 99 days

Taeping: Fuchow to Dungeness in 99 days

Serica: Fuchow to Dungeness in 99 days

Fiery Cross: Fuchow to London in 101 days

Cutty Sark Crossings

As a tea clipper on the China route

1870	Shanghai to Beachy Head in 109 days
1871	Shanghai to North Foreland in 107 days
1872	Shanghai to Portland in 120 days
1873	Shanghai to Deal in 116 days
1874	Wusung to Deal in 118 days
1875	Wusung to Deal in 122 days
1876	Wusung to Start Point in 108 days
1877	Wusung to Scilly in 122 days

As a wool clipper on the Australia route

1883–84	Newcastle to Deal in 82 days
1884–85	Newcastle to London in 80 days
1885	Sydney to Quessant in 67 days
1887	Sydney to Lizard Point in 70 days
1887–88	Newcastle to Lizard Point in 69 days
1888–89	Sydney to London in 86 days
1889–90	Sydney to London in 75 days
1890–91	Sydney to London in 93 days
1891–92	Sydney to Lizard Point in 83 days
1893	Sydney to Antwerp in 98 days
1893–94	Sydney to Scilly in 87 days
1894–95	Brisbane to London in 84 days

High Sea Flyers

Baltimore clipper, 1820

Red Jacket, American clipper, 1854

The two-masted brigs and barkentines built in Baltimore shipyards in the 1820s may have been the immediate inspiration of the North American clipper ships. The largest section was far forward, the hull was slender and narrowing to the stern, and the ship rode low in the water.

The American clipper was the most elegant and best-fitted ship of its time, but living conditions for the crew left much to be desired. All the ordinary seaman had was a wooden bunk and a footlocker.

North Atlantic crossings, the opium trade, and tea transport stimulated the development of American merchant sailing ships. The discovery of gold in California added another impetus to shipbuilding. To meet these demands there was a need for fast transportation, and the American clipper ship became synonymous with speed.

At this time the United States did not have professional merchant seamen. Although there were experienced captains and officers, most clippers

Flying Cloud, American clipper, 1851

Paulista, French clipper, 1855

Marco Polo, English clipper, 1850

Norman Court, English tea clipper, 1869

were crewed by nonprofessional seamen who learned their trade aboard. This was no easy task. They had to learn how to handle the winches and climb the riggings from their colleagues.

The Englishman James Baines was one of the outstanding shipowners of his time, and he made a fortune from shipping on the Australian routes. In 1860 his fleet, under the Black Ball banner, consisted of 86 sailing vessels, 300 officers, and 3,000 seamen. His career with sailing ships lasted

only a decade before he launched his first steamship. But he was essentially a sailing man, and he soon lost his fortune in the era of steam.

The clippers built on the east coast of the United States for carrying California grain were known as Down Easters. The year 1862 was a remarkable harvest year, and barrels of grain and wheat were loaded in San Francisco and Tacoma by 154 American clippers and 405 vessels from England, Germany, France, Norway, and Italy.

James Baines, English clipper, 1850

Golden Gate, American clipper, 1853

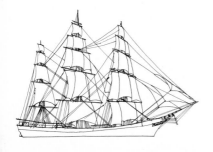

Rigging

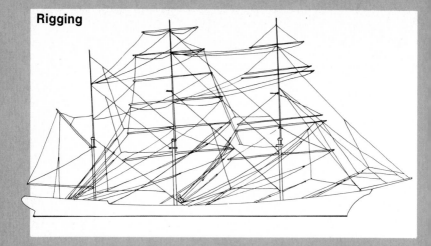

This is the main running rigging of a three-master. This includes all the lines and cables that are used to hoist sail and yards. The rigging consists of braces, halyards, sheets, tacks, bowlines, brails, and vangs.

The standing rigging of a three-master. These cables brace the masts. Every mast is braced by shrouds and stays.

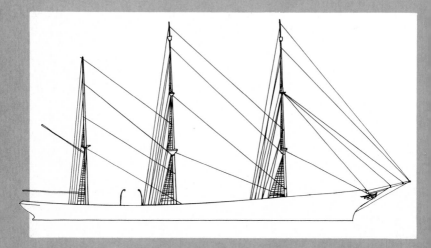

The Last Long-Distance Sailing Ships

The discovery of gold in California in the middle of the 19th century had repercussions on naval history. Anything that could float and stand up to the sea was marshalled by immigrants anxious to make their fortune in California, and every available ship headed for San Francisco. This was the period in which the Americans "invented" the clipper.

European ships doubled Cape Horn and raced west. It was a time of record-making crossings of the oceans. The Pacific Ocean attracted traders and shippers. Matthew Fontaine Maury charted the winds and the currents of the world's oceans, a monumental undertaking. Gold was discovered in Australia, and the large merchant sailing ships,

loaded with immigrants, continually crossed each other's paths on the Cape of Good Hope route. The gold eventually ran out, and so did the rush of immigrants. But South American guano, California grain, and immigrants to the vast territories of Australia kept the clippers in business. Indian cotton, English coal, Chilean nitrate (an excellent fertilizer), and New Zealand dried meat filled the holds of the large carriers, the last commercial sailing ships to resist the competition of the slower but more economical steamships. The age of the great wooden sailing vessels was drawing to a close, to be replaced first by iron and then by steel vessels. The opening of the Suez Canal in 1869 gave sailing ships a hard blow, and steamships on the shorter route became even more competitive. Steamers had taken over almost all passenger transport. Nevertheless the sailing ship still had some advantages to offer. It did not have to make frequent fueling stops, as the steamers did, and wind was available free of charge.

The French, Germans, and Scandinavians continued to build larger and larger sailing ships to accommodate ever-increasing cargoes. As the American merchant sailing fleet declined, the English fleet became the world leader. By the beginning of the 20th century France and Germany were the only countries that were still building sailing ships and manning them with experienced crews. But they, too, were soon to disappear.

In 1914 the Panáma Canal was opened, and the passage between the Atlantic and the Pacific was radically shortened. During World War I submarines blasted a host of sailing ships out of the water. By 1920 it was all but over.

The famous Bordes Company of Nantes still had an Australian grain transport service in 1921, but the company's ships were soon riding at

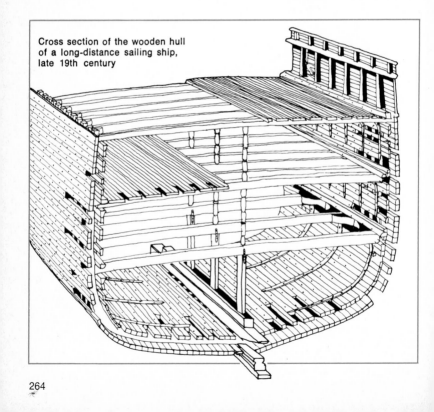

Cross section of the wooden hull of a long-distance sailing ship, late 19th century

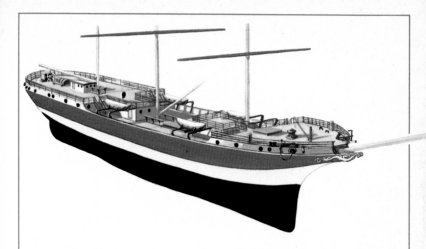

This three-masted oceangoing ship carries a superstructure deck, a holdover from the ancient sailing ships. The deck has a very low aft quarterdeck that includes, among other facilities, the captain's cabin. There is also a foredeck containing the kitchen and supply quarters.

anchor in the Martiniere Canal at Nantes. Until 1929 Stewart & Company of London had 28 sailing vessels in service, while the last ship of the Marine Corporation, the *Garthpool,* was lost in November 1929 on the reefs of Cape Verde. The last Danish, Swedish, and Norwegian sailing ships disappeared in World War I. The German Erich Ferdinand Laeisz rebuilt his sailing fleet and kept his Chilean saltpeter route going until 1931. The last outpost of the large sailing ships was the port of Mariehamn in the Aland Islands in the Gulf of Finland. Until 1940 Captain Gustav Erikson kept the last sailing fleet in the world there. Erikson's ships were saved from demolition and kept in functioning order, and he continued carrying

Australian grain until the outbreak of World War II. His crews consisted chiefly of young men who were in love with the sea.

The advance of technology gradually affected the fitting of sailing vessels. Wooden masts and yards were replaced by iron ones, fiber cables were replaced by metal ones, and the heavier riggings were replaced by chains. Around 1850 English ships replaced their tarred hemp cables with metal cables, and metal screws and fittings were added. Deadeyes for the lanyards became a thing of the past. Technical progress lightened the work of the sailors. In 1890 the Scotch captain J. C. B. Jarvis developed a steam winch that could be operated by two men, who could hoist the yards in bad weather all by themselves. The energy required in hoisting sail was reduced by the introduction of windlasses at the foot of the masts. Although sail surface increased, technical innovations made the sails easier to handle. The main topsail was divided in two, the upper and lower topsail. As the topsail had grown in size it had become extremely unwieldy. The first attempt to split the topsail had been made in 1841 by the American captain Robert Forbes, but it was another expert seaman, Commander Howes, who perfected the technique in 1854. Twenty years later the foresail was also split up, as was the topgallant sail, for ease of handling. Thus the typical rigging of the mainmast of a 20th-century sailing ship became the following: mainsail, upper main topsail, topgallant sail, and main royal sail. Naturally the number and arrangement of sails depended on the size of the ship.

With all these changes the crew was significantly reduced in size, and a large 19th-century sailing ship carried the same crew a much smaller vessel would have carried 20 years earlier.

It is no idle question to ask why people were still building sailing ships at the end of the 19th century, when the Industrial Revolution was in full swing and the world's economy was undergoing radical changes. The large sailing ship was obviously an anachronism in the age of steam. The apparent slowness and irregularity of its voyages and the difficulty of recruiting a well-trained crew would seem to be good enough reasons to discourage shippers. There was, however, on the part of shipbuilders, shippers, and seamen alike, a kind of mystic attachment to the sailing past. But more important, steamships still presented problems for shipping. There was the problem of finding convenient ports for loading coal, and there was the problem, given the distances involved, of repairing mechanical breakdowns, repairs that were extremely costly in any case.

The sailing ship, which often circumnavigated the world, was totally independent however long the voyage. Indeed, despite the fact that the ships looked anachronistic, there was work for them, and they still earned considerable sums for their owners. Ships sailed from Europe to America with various cargoes, then loaded barrels of coal oil in Philadelphia, doubled Cape Horn, reached Far Eastern ports and returned home after reloading in Australia. Other itineraries led straight to Australia with cargoes of machinery and various goods, loading wool and dried meat for the return voyage. Sometimes Australian coal was carried to Chile, and Chilean nitrate to Europe. European ships loaded nickel in New Caledonia and carried it to Glasgow or Le Havre. For some 40 years this maritime traffic around Cape Horn was the monopoly of the great Euro-

On this three-masted oceangoing sailing ship the deck is known as a "spar deck," one that is continuous from prow to stern, without quarterdeck or fore-deck. It is protected by a metal guardrail, instead of the wooden sides of the ship, and this rail is part of the hull structure.

pean sailing ships. The average speed of these vessels was about 14 or 15 knots per hour with maximums up to 18 knots per hour. The average over an entire voyage, including days of calm, was rather modest, between 4½ and 5½ knots per hour. The captain represented the commercial interests of the owners; he was the technical director of operations, the administrative authority, a judge in case of crime, and a justice of the peace for births and weddings. And when there was need, he might also serve as a doctor. The "old man" might only be 24 when he took command of a ship carrying four masts and valuable cargo.

The seaman on the large sailing ship might be the son of sailors or a newcomer to the sea. He worked 14 to 16 hours a day, and doubling Cape Horn he risked his life for low pay. Not uncommonly he was gone on voyages lasting a year or more. Going from cabin boy to able-bodied seaman, as he rose through the ranks he found himself often more at home on the sea than on the land. But that age is no more. The whole world of sailing ships and their men has disappeared in the modern world, and another rare harmony between man and nature has vanished.

There are still some survivors of that past age among the members of the Cap-Horniers Society in St. Malo, France.

Cosmos

With the unification of Italy, the single navies of Liguria, Venice, Sicily, and Naples were united in the Italian navy. It was a period of economic difficulty and social upheaval, and the new nation was slow to pass from sail to steam.

In 1862 the Italian navy's tonnage of sail amounted to 644,000 tons, while the tonnage of steam was only 10,000 tons.

The *Cosmos* was a fully-rigged three-master, a type of ship that reached its greatest splendor in the second half of the 19th century. Each mast carried six square sails: the mast sail (fore, main, or mizzen), a lower and upper topsail, a gallant sail, a royal sail, and a skysail. The fore-and-aft sails, triangular lateen sails, consisted of four jibs at the bow, six staysails between the masts, and a spanker at the mizzenmast.

The *Cosmos* was launched on December 10, 1865. The owners were the Frassinetti brothers of Genoa, and the builder was Cadenaccio of Sestri Levante. The oak hull was lined with copper, and the fittings were teak with copper nails. The ship was painted black with a white stripe running the full length of the hull. The *Cosmos* was the first Italian ship to have riggings of galvanized iron. The slender bow included the forecastle, where the crew was generally housed. Two shelter decks housed cabins and service areas. The total

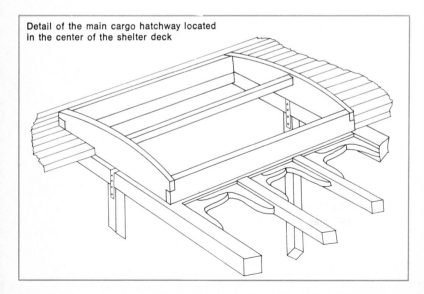

Detail of the main cargo hatchway located in the center of the shelter deck

cost of the ship was 735,000 lire.

The *Cosmos* carried cargo and passengers on the Genoa-Montevideo-Callao route, via Cape Horn. The central shelter deck had a large salon and 20 two-person cabins. Below decks were accommodations for up to 600 immigrants. The inaugural voyage on the Genoa-Montevideo route began on February 15, 1866, under the command of Filippo Frassinetti. There were 650 passengers aboard. The voyage from Genoa to Montevideo took 62 days; Montevideo-Callao, around Cape Horn, took 32 days. In December 1869 the *Cosmos* was seriously damaged in a storm that

Type: **full-rigged three-master**
Launching: **1865**
Builder: **Cadenaccio, Sestri Levante**
Owner: **Frassinetti, Genoa**
Length: **231 ft.**
Beam: **42 ft.**
Depth: **17 ft.**
Displacement: **4,200 tons**
Capacity: **2,800 tons**
Crew: **35**
Good speed: **14 knots**

blew up off Cape Horn. The crew managed to get the ship back to Montevideo. After repairs, the ship returned to Genoa. The owners transferred the ship to La Spezia for thorough overhauling. In 1879 a fire broke out on board, and the *Cosmos'* career came to an end.

Paul Rickmers

The *Paul Rickmers* was one of the last four-masters to be built of wood. It belonged to the Rickmers fleet of Bremen.

The North German Confederation, under Emperor William I, was much concerned with sea power. Indeed, the emperor had proclaimed at Stettin that the future of Germany was on the sea.

Between 1870 and 1890 Germany had 815 steamships, with a total of 617,911 tons. By 1905 the tonnage had increased to 1,774,072 tons. At the same time the 2,294 sailing ships accounted for 493,644 tons. Like the French and English merchant fleets, the German merchant fleet saw economic advantages still to be gained from sailing ships. The establishment of German shipyards made it possible for Germany to be independent of England and build its own ships.

The *Paul Rickmers,* which plied the Pacific on eastern voyages, was a single-decked ship. Unlike other contemporary vessels, it did not have a quarterdeck or forecastle. Instead there were shelter decks. One of them housed the boatswain, the ship's carpenter, and the sailmaker; another one housed the galley, the storeroom,

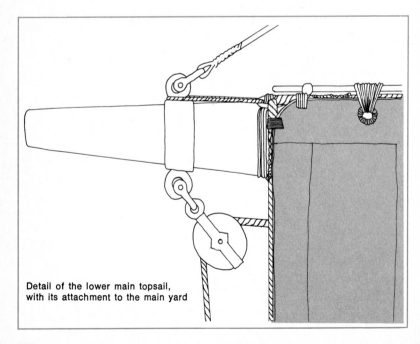

Detail of the lower main topsail, with its attachment to the main yard

and the engine room. (The engines powered the winches.) The 53,800 square feet of sail surface were broken up in several sails, which meant that a smaller crew could handle all the rigging. The long bowsprit carried four jibs, while the foremast, mainmast, and mizzenmast carried a total of 15 square sails. The fourth mast, at the stern, carried only a spanker. There were also six staysails. Under optimum conditions, the *Paul Rickmers* could reach 15 knots per hour.

The crew was all German, in accordance with that nation's tradition, and they were under strict discipline. The average age of the crew was 22, and the captain, "the old man," was certainly not one of the oldest aboard. The *Rickmers,* like almost all the

Type: **four-master, wooden hull**
Launching: **1896**
Length: **324 ft.**
Beam: **49 ft.**
Depth: **22 ft.**
Displacement: **1,020 tons**
Sail surface: **53,800 sq. ft.**
Crew: **32**

sailing ships of the German mercantile fleet, also provided men for the steam fleet. Sailing experience was considered the best training a seaman could have. Thus the *Rickmers* all but changed crews with every voyage. It was, in effect, a training ship.

The *Rickmers* sailed the Far Eastern route until 1906. It was out of service for a year and was then reassigned to the route to Chile. The ship was withdrawn from service on the eve of World War I.

France I

The French navy's *France I* was the first five-master ever built. The hull, masts, and yards were all made of steel. It was one of the best-constructed ships of the 19th century. Some of its dimensions bear mentioning. The height of the ship from the upper deck to the hold was about 34 feet; the bowsprit was cast in a single piece, with a maximum diameter of 2¼ feet and a length of about 45 feet. The foremast rose almost 130 feet and went down 26 feet inside the hull. The mizzenmast was over 45 feet tall. The boom, carrying the lateen sail at the stern, the spanker, was over 40 feet long. The spanker gaff was over 20 feet long. The mainmast was 195 feet high. It is worth noting that the average height of the mainmast on a fully rigged three-masted ship was at most 230 feet. The yards were also cast in a single

piece, and their length varied with their position on the mast, from about 75 feet to 45 feet, with a diameter from about 20 to 10 inches. The distance between masts was about 70 feet, and the height of the deck was over 6 feet.

The *France I* had a double water ballast and a watertight hold in the middle of the keel. The hold could carry up to 1,200 tons of water. When the ship was in port, water in the hold was enough to assure the vessel's balance, but when the ship was under sail and laden with cargo, the double ballasts were used.

The *France I* was launched in Scotland. It sailed the South American and California route by way of Cape Horn. In 1901 the *France I,* the largest sailing ship of its time, ran into a hurricane and sank off the mouth of the Rio de la Plata.

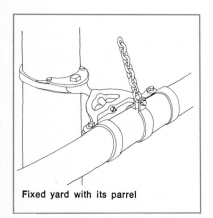

Fixed yard with its parrel

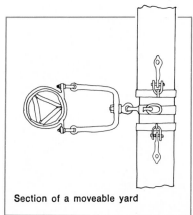

Section of a moveable yard

Type: **five-master, steel**
Launching: **1889, Parck,
    Glasgow**
Owner: **Bordes**
Length: **376 ft.**
Beam: **50 ft.**
Depth: **26 ft.**
Displacement: **6,160 tons**
Sail surface: **48,635 sq. ft.**
Crew: **46**

Nord

Launched in Scotland for the Bordes shipping company, the *Nord* was typical of the big four-masters that became so popular toward the end of the 19th century. The hull of the *Nord* was in wood, while the forecastle and quarterdeck, as well as two shelter decks, were built of steel. The forecastle was about 35 feet long and more than 6 feet high. It lodged the capstan, the crew's sanitary facilities, the boatswain's workshop, the carpentry shop, the paint room, and the lantern room. The central shelter deck accommodated the boiler that produced the steam for operating various winches. The doors of the boiler room were made of steel. The steam pipes were copper, lined with felt and galvanized sheeting. The steel boilers could provide steam for four winches simultaneously, and the condenser condensed about 680 quarts of water per hour. The two boiler water tanks could hold 13,620 quarts of water each and were cement-lined.

There were five hand winches for the rigging, in case the steam winches broke down. Masts, yards, and bowsprit were made of steel.

The double-wheeled helm had a clutch brake, so that the helmsman could handle the large wheel even with his feet. The *Nord* had six lifeboats, including four with sails. Moveable gangways made it possible to go back and forth between bow and stern without going along the main deck.

The double ballast was divided into three watertight compartments, and could hold 800 tons of water. There was also a watertight hold in the lower part of the keel that carried 1,100 tons of water.

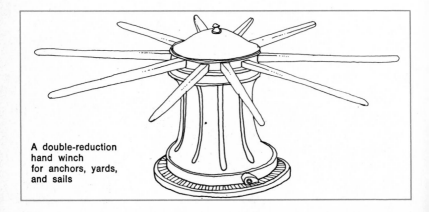

A double-reduction
hand winch
for anchors, yards,
and sails

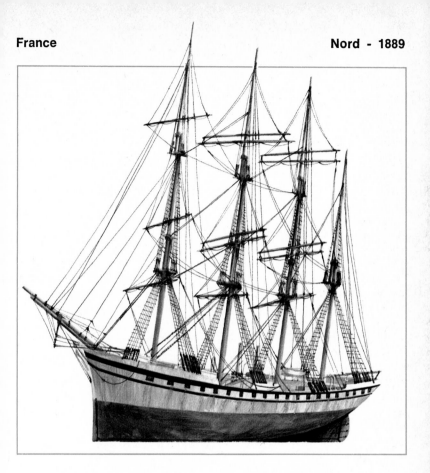

The quarterdeck was about 40 feet long and consisted of a salon, the captain's and officers' quarters, the bath, and the steward's office. The stern portholes had metal shutters in case the glass broke.

The ship was lighted by oil lamps, and the position lights were equipped with powerful lenses.

The *Nord* sailed American routes, carrying goods and immigrants from Europe to the California coast, by

Type: **four-master, wood**
Launching: **1889, Clyde**
Owner: **Bordes, Nantes**
Length: **333 ft.**
Beam: **47 ft.**
Depth: **26 ft.**
Displacement: **5,000 tons**
Crew: **54**

way of Cape Horn. In 1915, the ship was dismasted in a terrible storm off the cape. Captain Fourchon was able to rig up a temporary mast, and the ship made it to the coast of Chile.

Narcissus

The name *Narcissus* immediately evokes an image of dangerous sailing, courageous men, wild seas, and terrible calms. All this is due to the pen of Józef Teodor Konrad Nalecz Korzeniowski, better known as Joseph Conrad, one of the finest writers in the English language and perhaps the greatest narrator of tales of the sea. Conrad was born in Poland. At the age of 17 he went to sea. In 1886, at the age of 29, he earned his captain's papers.

Two years earlier he had sailed on the *Narcissus.* In 1894 he left the sea and spent the next 30 years writing novels, stories, and essays, including *The Nigger of the Narcissus,* which describes the ship and its crew during a crossing from Bombay to Dunkirk. Conrad describes the *Narcissus* as being born in clouds of black smoke, with hammers clanging on iron, on the banks of the Clyde. He rapturously describes the gray sky and the noisy river where creatures like the *Narcissus* came into being. And he describes the seaman's love of his ship.

The *Narcissus* was built in 1875 in Glasgow, where several Clyde-side shipyards turned out excellent sailing vessels. The ship had a forecastle at the bow, a shelter deck on the main deck, and a long quarterdeck running from the mizzenmast to the stern. The compass and the steering wheel were on the quarterdeck.

The *Narcissus* was fully rigged, with five sails on each of the three masts: the mast sail (fore, main, and mizzen), the lower and upper topsail, the gallant sail, and the royal sail. The bowsprit carried four jibs. There were staysails between the masts, and the mizzenmast carried a spanker and a gaff topsail.

After sailing the eastern routes, the *Narcissus* was purchased by the

The binnacle is reinforced inside and out with soft iron and magnets.

Italian shipowner Vittorio Bertolotto of Camogli. On January 17, 1907, while sailing to Talcahuano on the Chilean coast, the *Narcissus* was damaged during a violent storm. It managed to reach Rio de Janeiro on May 19. Back in Italy, the masts were removed and it was used as a pontoon in Genoa. In 1917 the ship was overhauled and rechristened the *Iris.* Registered in Rio de Janeiro, it collided with another ship on January

Type: **full-rigged three-master**
Launching: **1875**
Builder: **Robert Duncan & Co., Port Glasgow**
Length: **241 ft.**
Beam: **43 ft.**
Depth: **17 ft.**
Displacement: **4,340 tons**
Crew: **46**
Good speed: **13.8 knots**

14, 1922, and sank. The ship's figurehead is preserved in the re-created waterfront community at Mystic Seaport, Connecticut.

Thomas W. Lawson

The *Thomas W. Lawson* was a fore-and-aft schooner with seven masts. This short-lived vessel was built as an attempt to get the maximum out of fore-and-aft rigging. This sort of rigging functions extremely well when it is proportioned to the ship itself. The *Lawson* was some 400 feet long, much larger than necessary for the sail area. Its masts were composite: the lower part was iron, and the upper part was wood. The masts were all almost 200 feet tall. They were the foremast, the mainmast, the mizzenmast, the spanker mast, the jigger mast, the drivermast, and the pushermast. Each mast carried a spanker and a topsail. There were five jibs at the bow and six staysails, between the masts. This rigging was typical of fore-and-aft schooners, although on a larger scale. For the typical schooner had only two masts with spankers and topsails, plus three jibs. America was the land of the schooner, because, unlike Europe, it did not lack for wood. Especially designed to take advantage of the hydrodynamic qualities of the hull, the schooner did not undergo significant modifications with the passing of time. But because the *Thomas W. Lawson* had far too small a sail area for the size of the hull, it was not an especially fast vessel. Indeed, the *Lawson* carried only 4,304 square feet of sail surface; this was barely a third of the sail surface carried by the clippers, which

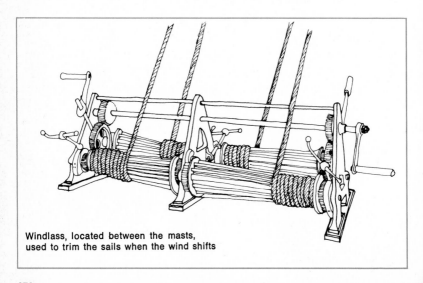

Windlass, located between the masts, used to trim the sails when the wind shifts

were three times as small.

A major advantage of the fore-and-aft rig was that it required few men to handle it. The *Lawson* was an extreme example, for only 15 men were assigned to the rigging. That is to say that 15 men, albeit aided by six steam winches, sailed a 400-foot ship. But it soon became evident that the ship was somewhat a white elephant. The crew themselves insisted that the ship was heavier than a 17th-century warship and just as hard to handle.

The steel-hulled vessel was designed by M. Crowninshield of Boston. It was intended as a coal ship. It was used for the transport of oil in barrels

Type: **seven-masted schooner**
Launching: **1902**
Designer: **M. Crowninshield**
Builder: **Fore River Shipbuilding Company, Quincy, Mass.**
Length: **433 ft.**
Beam: **55 ft.**
Depth: **27 ft.**
Displacement: **7,500 tons**
Sail surface: **4,304 sq. ft.**
Crew: **27**

from Texas to the east coast of the United States. The *Lawson* saw only six years of service. In 1907, after being transferred to European routes, it was caught in a violent storm on the English Channel and was shipwrecked off the coast of the Scilly Islands. Only two members of the crew managed to escape with their lives.

The Cape Horn Route

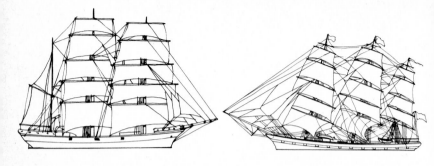

Persistant, wood hull. France, 1865

Stonehouse, wood hull. Great Britain, 1866

The voyage from the English Channel to the coast of Chile, by way of Cape Horn, was never free of worry. Once having got beyond the Bay of Biscay and Cape Finisterre, the ships made for the zone of the northeast trade winds, leaving Madeira 100 miles to the west and giving wide berth to the Canaries.

In the trade winds area the weather is mild, the nights are clear, the wind is regular, and the sea is smooth. The rigging was changed to accommodate the pleasant weather, and the old rigging was stored. A lot of work went into this, for some of the larger sails weighed up to a ton.

The crossing of the equator was no easy task. The winds died down and the sea was flat. Sudden rains would pour down, and the men were exhausted from trying to take advantage of even the slightest breath of wind. And the ship slowly rocked.

Then the ship would reach the southwest trade winds. The ship was rerigged, now with the sails for doubling Cape Horn. The sea grew colder and darker. The air temperature went down, and hatches were closed. The ship was ready to double the southern tip of South America.

The first gusts of the *pampero* would arrive, cold and harsh. By now

E. B. Sutton, iron hull. United States, 1881

County of Linlithgow, steel hull. Great Britain, 1887

Jeanne d'Arc, steel hull. France, 1893

Potosi, steel hull. Germany, 1895

the ship would be sailing along the Patagonian coast. The ocean swells would be enormous, and the wind blew from the west all year round.

It took at least six weeks to reach Cape Horn. The ship would be loaded with ice and snow, and hot water would be used to melt them. Soaked to the skin, the crew would man the pumps day and night. The microcosm of the ship would be in chaos because of the fury of the ocean around Cape Horn. Water got in everywhere, in the shelter decks, below decks, and in the boots of the seamen. In such a world of violence and danger, only method, order, and habit could pro-

vide defense against the elements.

It was a hard sail to reach the latitude of the tropics in the Pacific. Again the sun would shine and the air would be warm with gentle breezes; the nights would be warm and clear. And then one morning the Andes would appear a hundred miles away on the horizon.

According to the nautical guide of the Bordes shipping company of Nantes, the famous Cape Horn "has nothing of interest. It ends with black ragged rocks. From the west there are steps and descents down to the sea. The maximum height is 1,400 feet."

Duchesse Anne, iron hull. France, 1899

Laennec, steel hull. France, 1902

Kinds of Sailing Ships

The great development of navigation and merchant fleets made classification necessary. Ships were classed by function, construction, and state of repair. The most famous organization devoted to naval classification is Lloyd's Register of Shipping in England. The name comes from one Edward Lloyd, who owned a cafe in the 18th century where shipowners, captains, and insurers met. It was at Lloyd's that it was decided to compile two registers: the *Green Book* for insurers and the *Red Book* for shipowners. The data of each ship were registered. In 1834 Lloyd's Register of British and Foreign Shipping became an official society, responsible for classifying vessels. (Later, "British and Foreign" was dropped from the name.) Another famous institution is the *Bureau Veritas,* which was founded in Antwerp in 1728 and now has headquarters in Paris. On the basis of means of propulsion, sailing ships are those which are propelled by "the natural force of the wind acting on a system of sails which moves the vessel."

Fore-and-aft schooner

Topsail schooner

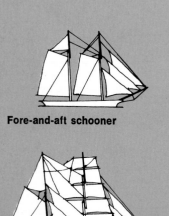
Hermaphrodite brig

Brig

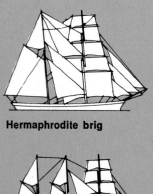
Barkentine

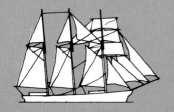
Barkentine-schooner

Bark

Full-rigged three-master

Four-masted bark

Four-masted ship

Five-masted bark

Five-masted ship

Metal-Hulled Sailing Vessels

The metal-hulled sailing ship first appeared at the end of the 1860s, and it was the logical development of the composite ship. By this time the steamship had come to monopolize passenger traffic, offering comfort and sometimes even luxury. The sailing vessel was almost exclusively a cargo ship, and in this area it was competitive with the steamer. In an attempt to keep up to date with the technological progress being made, the British undertook the construction of a new type of sailing ship to provide rapid and economical cargo transport. A series of medium-sized vessels, weighing approximately 1,200 tons to 1,600 tons, were built in shipyards in Scotland. They had smooth and fast lines and highly perfected sails and rigging.

These ships were veritable racers and were earmarked chiefly for the Australian routes. They carried different cargoes on the outward and inward voyages: They went to Australia loaded with a variety of goods and occasional passengers, and they made the return voyage loaded with wool, a commodity which was in great demand in England at the time.

This was the birth of the colonial or wool clipper, a short-lived ship. It remained in service until about 1895, despite the competition of steamships using the screw propeller. The wool clipper was finally withdrawn from service because its limited cargo capacity coupled with the cost of maintaining the large crew required by a sailing vessel made the ship uneconomical to operate.

But it was not only wool clippers that had metal hulls. Metal-hull construction had become standard procedure, and the last great merchant ships, the long-distance sailing ships, were also built with metal hulls. First iron and then steel were used in the construction of hulls; both had many advantages over wooden structures. The overall weight of the ship was reduced, and the hull was more durable and waterproof. The dangers of fire and flooding were also reduced. And metal-hulled ships were quicker to build, repair, and maintain. The developing steel industry was able to provide sheet metal, flat or curved. The nails that joined the various elements were heated to 1000°. Then they were inserted in the holes and hammered home in such a way that a second nailhead was formed before the nail cooled. As the nail cooled, it tended to tighten the seams it bound. Thus the hull was strong and elastic. The early iron hulls were fairly faithful copies of wooden hulls, but toward the end of the 19th century, a more rational procedure was developed, and the structural elements were applied lengthwise to strengthen the ship. With the introduction of steel, even larger and longer vessels became a reality.

The *France II,* the largest sailing ship ever built, was constructed this

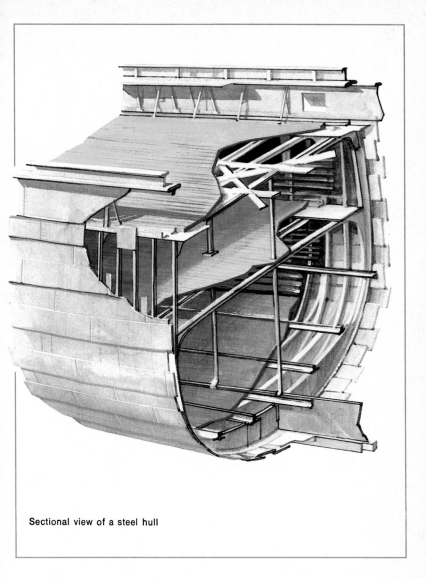

Sectional view of a steel hull

way. Launched in 1911, this five-masted vessel was over 400 feet long and weighed more than 5,000 tons.

Nevertheless the introduction of metal construction did not prove to be the salvation of the sailing ship. Rather, it merely postponed its inevitable demise.

Patriarch

The famous clipper ship *Patriarch* appeared late in the day on February 9, 1870, off Sydney, Australia. It had sailed from London on December 2, 1869, with 40 passengers and various cargo for the Australian markets. The nonstop voyage set a record: 67 days.

The *Patriarch* was built in Aberdeen, Scotland, to plans prepared by Walter Hood. It was the first iron clipper and for many years was known as the driest vessel afloat. The use of iron in ship construction still caused some worry, and traditionalists were somewhat skeptical of the possibilities of this material. They said an iron ship would leak at all its seams, that the iron would rust, and that

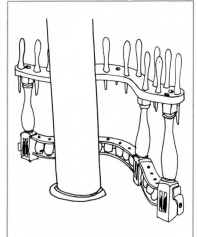

A belaying pin rack at the foot of the mainmast. The running rigging, including halyards, was attached to the single pins.

The foremast top with the main yard attached.

precious cargo, wool in particular, would be ruined. The obvious advantages of building in iron were larger ships and greater cargo capacity.

The *Patriarch* was ahead of its time. It was bigger than its contemporaries. The masts were cast in single pieces of iron, and the upper parts were collapsible in telescope fashion. The sail surface was split up among a great number of sails. Thus sail surface could be reduced gradually in high winds without losing speed. There were even lower stud-

ding sails that could be rigged on the sides of the ship to take advantage of even the slightest breath of wind.

The *Patriarch* never had mechanical difficulties or serious damages. During its first return voyage from Sydney to London, in 1870, it lowered the speed record it had established on the journey out, making the return in 64 days. Its performance was outstanding. It sailed 366 miles in 24 hours, for an average of 15.25 knots per hour. It sailed 2,060 miles in a single week, an average speed of 11 knots per hour.

Type: **iron clipper**
Launching: **1869**
Designer: **Walter Hood**
Owner: **White Star Line, Aberdeen**
Length: **250 ft.**
Beam: **40 ft.**
Depth: **23 ft.**
Displacement: **1,339 tons**
Crew: **58**

The *Patriarch* was extremely reliable and made all its crossings in 90 days or less.

On February 23, 1912, as it approached the Argentine coast from South Africa, the *Patriarch* went onto the reefs of Cabo Corrientes off Mar del Plata and was wrecked.

Mermerus

The *Mermerus* was built for transport. The clipper became famous for the regularity and reliability of its service between London and Melbourne. Each mast of this ship carried six square sails. The mainmast was 160 feet high, and the foremast was about 95 feet high. The *Mermerus* was smaller than the average clipper of its day. The ship could carry up to 10,000 bales of wool for a value of about 130,000 pounds sterling. The *Mermerus* made 20 crossings in the era of the wool clippers, and it always arrived on time for the opening of the English wool market. After service on the Australian route, the *Mermerus* was transferred to the San Francisco route, carrying coal from Newcastle. In good weather this crossing took 56 days. The *Mermerus* could make the round trip voyage around Cape Horn in 104 days, including loading and unloading time. When it was transferred back to the Australian route, the ship established its own record in 1876. It left London on June 25 and reached Melbourne on August 30, a voyage of 66 days.

This was the last crossing of Captain W. Fife, who had commanded the ship for several years. His successor, Captain J. B. Coles, remained in command until the ship was sold in 1897.

The ship was sold to Russia and continued service as a merchant ship between Europe and Australia to the end. At 3 o'clock on the afternoon of December 12, 1909, about 10 miles from Christiansand, it went onto a rock that split the keel. A tugboat threw out an anchor line, but to no avail. The ship was too badly dam-

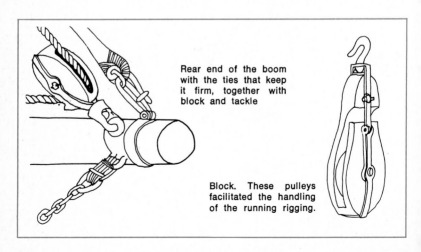

Rear end of the boom with the ties that keep it firm, together with block and tackle

Block. These pulleys facilitated the handling of the running rigging.

aged, and the commandant, Captain Gustafson, had to abandon the ship with all its cargo. The wreck was sold to Christiansand wreckers for a fraction of its worth. The *Mermerus* had seen 37 years of uninterrupted service.

The *Mermerus* was one of the finest of the wool clippers, with its elegant lines, slender masts, and excellent fittings. It was a distinguished member of that fraternity of ships that maintained connections between Europe and Australia for decades.

Type: **wool clipper**
Launching: **1872**
Builder: **Barclay, Curle & Co.**
Owner: **A. and J. H. Carmichael's Golden Fleece Line**
Length: **260 ft.**
Beam: **40 ft.**
Depth: **23 ft.**
Displacement: **1,671 tons**
Crew: **34**

The *Mermerus* may represent the apex of what a sailing ship of the 1870s could achieve in terms of speed and regularity.

Slieve Roe

The *Slieve Roe* was built to transport jute from India to England. It was the third of four sister clippers launched between 1877 and 1888 by W. P. Sinclair & Co. of Liverpool. The other three ships were the *Slieve More,* the *Slieve Bawn,* and the *G. W. Wolff.* The steel ship was considered one of the finest products of British ship construction of the period. The measurements of the masts give an idea of how much sail could be spread on the *Slieve Roe.* The bowsprit, including the jib boom, was 65 feet long. The mainmast was 155 feet high, the foremast 86 feet high, and the mizzenmast was 84 feet high. Some of the yards were 84 feet long.

The three masts carried square sails. Until 1858 the topsail of the large merchant clippers was a single sail, and each mast carried four sails. Later the topsail was split in two for easier handling. Thus there were the lower and the upper topsail. The *Slieve Roe* carried 14 square sails, a spanker, six triangular staysails between the masts, and three jibs at the bow. Studding sails could also be mounted.

Captain D. H. Ball commanded the ship for almost a decade. From his log we can learn something about the speed of this ship. On its second voyage it covered 1,500 miles in five days, an average speed of 300 miles per day. It sailed in this period at constant speed in optimum weather and sea, at a speed of 16 knots per hour. The speed increased to 16.5–17 knots off the Cape of Good Hope, raising the miles covered in one day

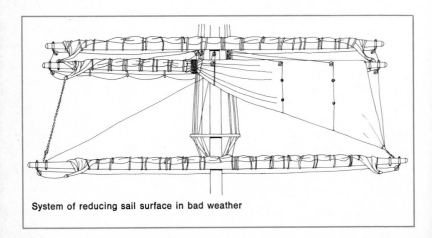

System of reducing sail surface in bad weather

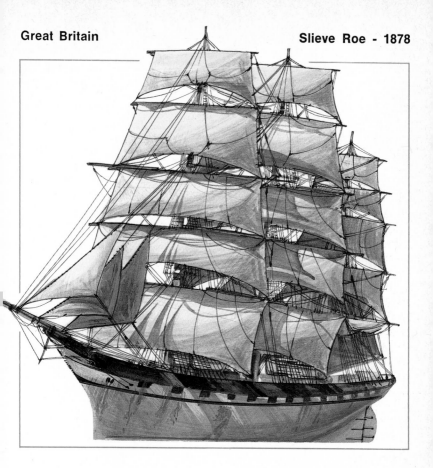

to 350. Thus the *Slieve Roe* was one of the fastest ships of its day. This is confirmed by the second officer, W. H. Clemens, who also described it as extremely comfortable and safe. Clemens, by the way, was the oldest member of the crew. At the time he kept his diary, he was 24.

In 1894 the *Slieve Roe* was sold to Simpson Brothers of Swansea and continued to sail the eastern routes.

Type: **steel clipper, three masts**
Launching: **1878**
Builder: **Harland & Wolff**
Owner: **W. P. Sinclair & Co., Liverpool**
Length: **253 ft.**
Beam: **38 ft.**
Depth: **23 ft.**
Displacement: **1,749 tons**
Crew: **32**

In 1910, after 32 years of service, it was sold to Norwegian scrappers, who realized a profit on the recoverable parts of the ship.

Balcutha

Beginning in 1870, when the first iron ships began to be produced by shipyards on the Clyde, the Mersey, the Tyne, and in Aberdeen, British merchant ships enjoyed some three decades of particular prosperity. Free trade gave a great impetus to transport, including shipping. Iron construction and then building in steel marked a great step forward in sailing ships. The era of the great clippers and the long-distance sailing ships that voyaged to Australia was over. Shipowners were no longer particularly interested in the exploits of such fast ships as the *Marco Polo,* which made the round trip between Liverpool and Sydney in 5 months and 21 days. The opening of the Suez Canal in 1869 made it possible for steamships to take over cargo transport to Australia and the Far East. Sailing ships were then generally limited to transport between America and Europe.

The *Balcutha* ("Mouth of the Clyde") was built in 1886 for transporting California grain to England. The ship was built of iron and therefore had more cargo space. Iron ships did not have all the ribbing and internal beams of wooden ships. British shipyards specialized in building metal-hulled ships and became the leading world suppliers of these vessels.

The *Balcutha* carried 25 sails and a relatively small crew, 26 men. For the first 13 years of its life the *Balcutha* sailed back and forth between California and British ports. It was sold in 1899 to a San Francisco shipowner and carried wood from Alaska until 1902. At that time it foundered in shallow water and was withdrawn from service for a while.

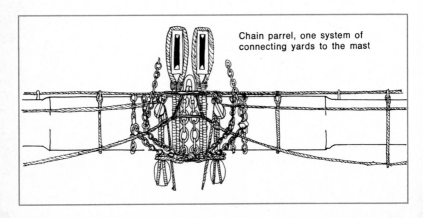

Chain parrel, one system of connecting yards to the mast

It was purchased by the Alaska Packers and overhauled. For about 10 years it carried passengers and cargo along the North American coast. In the meantime it had been rechristened the *Star of Alaska*. The iron ship was extremely sturdy and kept working even after sailing ships no longer proved economical. For some 20 years it sailed up and down the west coast of America as a show boat. In 1952 it was found abandoned on a sandbank near San Francisco. The San Francisco Maritime Museum has spent $100,000 and 13,000 man-hours restoring the vessel, and it can be visited at Pier 43 in the harbor.

Type: **three-master, iron hull**
Launching: **1886**
Length: **300 ft.**
Beam: **39 ft.**
Depth: **23 ft.**
Displacement: **2,660 tons**
Crew: **26**

Loire

In 1893 the French government passed a law giving an incentive to sailing ship construction. A premium of 1.70 francs was paid for every ton of displacement and every mile sailed. Shipbuilding boomed after a period in which total French tonnage had sunk to dangerously low levels. In a dozen years more than 200 new sailing ships were launched, all metal-hulled vessels. New shipping lines were established, and old ones flourished. One of the most important shipping lines was Bordes of Nantes. It had become quite successful in transporting sodium nitrate from Chile to France. By 1914, on the eve of World War I, the Bordes fleet comprised 44 large iron-hulled sailing ships with a total tonnage of 119,000 tons, as well as a 7,000-ton steamship.

Twenty-eight of the 44 sailing ships were four-masters. One of these was the *Loire,* which was built in Nantes and was considered a lucky ship.

The sail surface was 68,057 square feet, and the ship was extremely fast. It was one of the stars of the Bordes fleet. In 1897 it made the voyage from Portland to Iquique, Chile, in 66 days; in 1899 it made the voyage from Iquique to Dunkirk in 79 days; and in 1903 it made the trip from Iquique to Lizard in 80 days.

The ship never had serious damages or accidents.

In 1913, under the command of Captain Jaffré, the *Loire* demonstrated its mettle in a dramatic rescue at sea. On October 10 the *Loire* sighted the English three-master *Dalgonar* off the Peruvian coast at Callao. The English ship had been severely damaged during a storm and had been drifting for

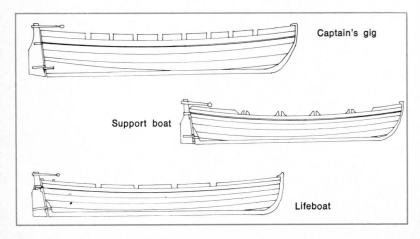

Captain's gig

Support boat

Lifeboat

two days. For three days the most that Captain Jaffré could do in the violent seas was to stay in the vicinity of the English ship. Finally, on the morning of the 13th, eight seamen under the command of the second officer, Cadic, set out in a launch to rescue the English crew. Cadic lost his life in the operation.

The *Dalgonar* drifted more than 5,000 miles before foundering on the reefs of Mopihaa in the Society Islands group. The *Loire* got back to Dunkirk on January 5, 1914. The *Loire* survived the German submarine attacks during World War I and was scrapped in 1924.

Type: **four-master, steel hull**
Launching: **1897**
Owner: **Bordes, Nantes**
Length: **335 ft.**
Beam: **45 ft.**
Depth: **24 ft.**
Displacement: **3,109 tons**
Crew: **54**

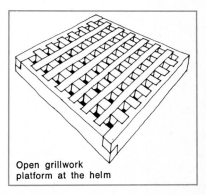

Open grillwork platform at the helm

Preussen

Early in the 20th century Germany ended its dependence on British and French shipbuilders and began to construct its own metal-hulled ships. This new German production was fully comparable to British and French work. One of the outstanding German companies, distinguished for its initiative as well as for the high quality of its vessels, was the F. Laeisz company. This company managed to keep pace with technical progress.

The history of the *Preussen,* one of the Laeisz company's finest vessels, is closely bound up with that of the company's owner, Ferdinand Laeisz. Laeisz was not born to the sea. He started out as a manufacturer and exporter of silk hats, chiefly to South America. His hats were so successful that he was soon exporting the raw materials—silk, leather, cardboard—and making up the hats on arrival. Soon he built his own ship, the *Carl,* and it was not long before he found himself in the shipping industry.

All the ships in Laeisz's company had names beginning with the letter P. About 1874 the company was the largest in Germany and one of the most important in the world.

The *Preussen* was a majestic five-masted ship carrying a total of 30 sails. The ship was built of steel. The masts, also in steel, had a base diameter of 30 inches, and the main-mast was 225 feet high. The total sail surface was 59,180 square feet. Needless to say, it was no easy task to handle this quantity of sail even with the help of steam winches powered by two large boilers amidships. Hoisting or lowering the sails, especially

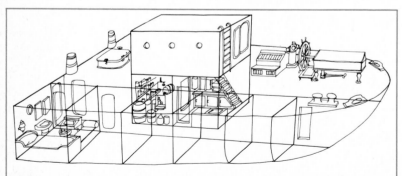

Cross section of the quarterdeck, including the second officer's cabin, the captain's mess, the pantry, and, at the stern, the helm

in high winds or at night, required a healthy dose of raw courage. Indeed, it was not unusual to see men climbing up the rigging to dizzying heights in rough seas.

The *Preussen* was designed by Robert Hilgendorf, and the year after its launching it set a record of 57 days for the crossing from Hamburg to Iquique, Chile. Throughout its career the ship sailed the South American routes around Cape Horn. On November 6, 1910, entering the En-

Type: **five-master, steel hull**
Launching: **1902**
Length: **436 ft.**
Beam: **54 ft.**
Depth: **29 ft.**
Displacement: **5,081 tons**
Crew: **46**

glish Channel in a thick fog, it was rammed by the British *Brighton*. The British ship struck it hard in the middle, and the *Preussen* was almost split in half. The once-beautiful vessel was towed to Dover and left to founder on the sandbanks around the harbor.

France II

The *France II,* the largest sailing ship ever built, was launched at Bordeaux for the Prentout shipping company of Rouen. It was the French merchant fleet's final attempt to meet the competition of steamships.

A look at the dimensions of this vessel will give some idea of the achievement of its builders. The figurehead at the bow was more than 44 feet above the waterline. The water ballast was 78,812 cubic feet, so that the ship could sail in perfect balance even without a cargo. The masts alone weighed 258 tons, while the cables of the standing and running rigging weighed 198 tons. The total length of the running rigging was about 30 miles, and there were 871 pulleys. The mainmast was about 210 feet high from the waterline. The 20 square and 12 lateen sails accounted for a total surface of 68,326 square feet. The ship was fully equipped with hand and steam winches for yards and sail. Thus it could be manned by a smaller crew.

Another novelty on the *France II* was the installation of four steam winches, one for each cargo hatch. Thus 2,000 tons of cargo could be loaded in a single day.

The *France II* also carried passengers, and the accommodations were remarkable for a sailing ship in that era. There were seven cabins each almost 40 feet square opening onto the main deck, as well as a large

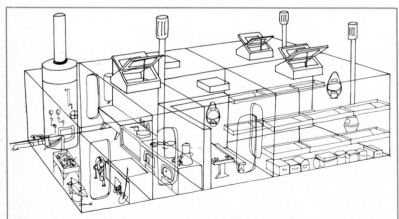

The central shelter deck accommodates the boiler that produces steam for the winches and also houses the kitchen, the crew's mess, and the quarters of the duty crew serving on the port side of the ship.

library-drawing room, several baths, a laundry, and an infirmary with an operating table.

The ship carried two auxiliary engines to facilitate maneuvers in port. They proved useful in 1919 when the *France II* carried a load of coal from England to America. A number of tugboats towed the *France II* down the Tyne to the open sea, where sail could be hoisted. All but one of the tugs turned back. Because of contrary winds and as a safety precaution, the large tugboat *Joffre* was still linked by cable to the *France II*. The wind rose higher and the cable snapped. The two vessels lost each

Type: **five-master, steel**
Launching: **1911**
Owner: **Prentout, Rouen**
Length: **420 ft.**
Beam: **53 ft.**
Depth: **27 ft.**
Displacement: **7,800 tons**
Sail surface: **68,326 sq. ft.**
Good speed: **16–17 knots**
Crew: **45**

other, and for several days there was no news of the *France II*. Its auxiliary engines enabled the *France II* to return to the Firth of Forth. When the damages were repaired, the ship set sail again. In 1922 the ship was wrecked on a coral reef. The wreck was sold for 300,000 francs.

Pamir

The *Pamir* was one of the last steel four-masters ever built. It was launched in 1921 for the German shipping company of F. Laeisz. The ship was heavy but had great cargo capacity. The *Pamir* remained in service for more than 30 years, making it one of the longest-lived ships of its class.

The steel mainmast was 2½ times the beam of the ship; the mizzenmast was 4/5 the height of the mainmast.

The *Pamir* was built in one of the finest German shipyards and was extremely functional in the arrangement of space and even in the smallest details of fittings. There was a large cabin at the stern for the cap-tain, which was lighted by oil lamps mounted on gimbals. The wheel at the stern was arranged in such a way that the helmsman enjoyed a maximum of comfort. He also had a small raised grillwork platform to stand on when water ran over the deck. For protection against the wind, the helmsman had a metal cubicle. The quarters of the boatswain, the carpenter, the cook, and the helmsman were between the mainmast and the foremast. Between the mainmast and the mizzenmast were the duty crew's quarters, the galley, and the boiler room. At the bow there was a pen with a cow or two, pigs, chickens, and other fowl. Four lifeboats were

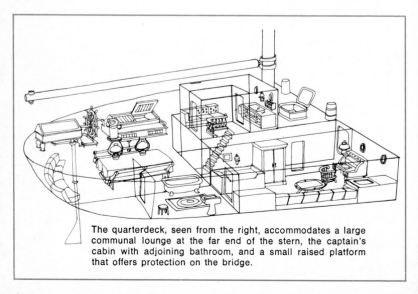

The quarterdeck, seen from the right, accommodates a large communal lounge at the far end of the stern, the captain's cabin with adjoining bathroom, and a small raised platform that offers protection on the bridge.

lined up along the stern. Amidships were the large cargo hatches, the only weak point in the whole ship, and they were reinforced with watertight metal plates.

For many years the *Pamir* was one of the few large sailing ships to sail the route to Chile, chiefly for nitrates. The ship was later sold to Captain Gustav Erikson of Mariehamn, one of the last men to use merchant sailing ships. Under the Erikson flag, the *Pamir* made several Australian voyages. In 1950 it was found abandoned at the docks of Antwerp.

Type: **four-master, steel**
Launching: **1921**
Length: **422 ft.**
Beam: **52 ft.**
Depth: **28 ft.**
Displacement: **4,670 tons**
Crew: **86**

The German government bought the ship, installed an auxiliary engine, and transformed it into a training ship. On September 24, 1957, while carrying a load of grain, it was struck by Hurricane Carrie in the Atlantic. The ship keeled over and went down with 80 crewmen.

Sails

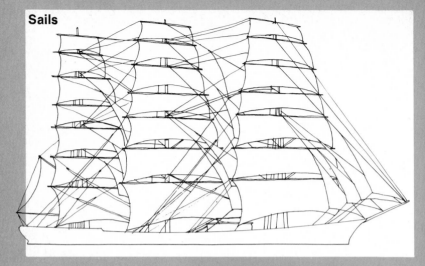

Square-rigged three-masted ship. This was the usual rigging of such a ship. There were 34 sails, comprising 21 square sails, 4 jibs, 8 staysails, and a spanker.

Three-masted bark. The mizzenmast does not carry square sails. The rigging consisted of 12 square sails, 4 jibs, 6 staysails, a spanker, and a gaff topsail, for a total of 24 sails.

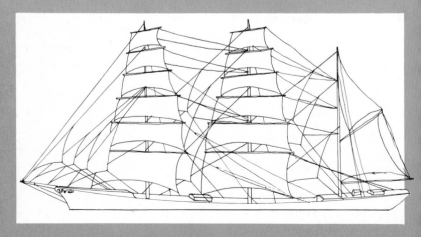

Sailing Ships Today

During the golden age of sail, officers and crew learned the trade aboard ship. Sailing, with all its dangers and sacrifice, was a trade that young men learned "on the job" with the help and guidance of older seamen. Aside from press gangs, which operated for centuries, young men ended up on sailing ships for a variety of reasons. Some had a yearning for the sea, others came from seafaring families, while others were tempted by the prospect of riches and booty.

In recent years the technical developments of weapons, engines, and navigation and electronic equipment have made some academic training indispensable for would-be sailors. But well-rounded naval training also requires practical experience at sea.

Thus sailing ships now function as trainers, maintaining part of an older tradition. Every year the large training ships make cruises all over the world. They carry professional crews as well as naval cadets. Almost all the navies of the world have sailing training ships: Argentina (the three-masted, square-sailed *Libertad*); Sweden (the schooners *Falken* and *Gladan,* 220 tons, 5,595 square feet of sail); the Soviet Union (the bark *Tovarisch,* 1,350 tons, 19,368 square feet of sail, as well as two square-rigged four-masters, the *Krusenstern* and the *Sedov*); East Germany; Yugoslavia; the Netherlands; Chile; Poland; and Spain, to name a few. There are also older sailing ships that have been preserved as monuments to the centuries-old traditions of the sea.

Type: **bark**
Launching: **1910**
Builder: **Blohm & Voss Shipyards, Hamburg**
Length: **300 ft.**
Beam: **41 ft.**
Depth: **19 ft.**
Displacement: **1,784 tons**
Sail surface: **20,444 sq. ft.**
Auxiliary engine: **430 h.p.**
Crew: **27 seamen and 12 officers**
Cadets: **150**

This ship was built in 1909 in Germany and was christened the *Prinz Eitel Friedrich*. The ship was ceded to France as part of war reparations after World War I. It was rechristened the *Colbert*. Poland then bought the ship with money collected from the citizens of Pomerania, and the ship acquired its present name, *Dar Pomorza* ("Gift of Pomerania"). It be-

longs to the Polish merchant navy and serves as a training ship, under the direction of the *Wyzsza Szkoła Morska* in Gdynia.

In 1972 the *Dar Pomorza* took part in festivities in honor of the Olympic yachting competition held in Kiel. It was a magnificent spectacle, with 67 other sailing vessels alongside the *Dar Pomorza*.

Type: **square-rigged three-master**
Launching: **1931**
Length: **272 ft.**
Beam: **51 ft.**
Depth: **21 ft.**
Displacement: **3,545 tons**
Sail surface: **33,356 sq. ft.**
Auxiliary engine: **1,900 h.p.**
Crew: **30 seamen and 7 officers**
Cadets: **98**

In 1861 the Genoa naval training school acquired one of the handsomest frigates of the period, the *San Michele.* In 1881 it acquired the *Vittorio Emanuele.* Italy's present training ship, the *Amerigo Vespucci,* has the same name as one of the first cruisers in the navy of united Italy. The modern *Vespucci* was built as a training ship in 1931 and incorporates the latest technical developments. Designed by Lt. Col. Francesco Rotundi, the *Vespucci* repeats the elegant proportions of a three-master of the golden age of sail. Its mainmast rises 180 feet from the deck. The rigging is handled by officer cadets during training cruises.

Type: **three-masted schooner**
Launching: **1934; remodeled in 1950**
Builder: **Nantes Shipyards**
Length: **227 ft.**
Beam: **33 ft.**
Depth: **16 ft.**
Displacement: **1,341 tons**
Sail surface: **9,662 sq. ft.**
Auxiliary engine: **375 h.p.**
Crew: **26 seamen and 5 officers**
Cadets: **54**

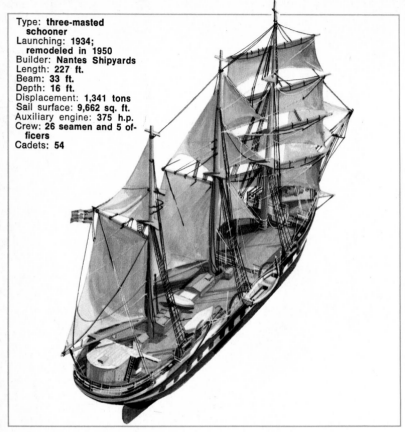

The Italian navy schooner *Palinuro* is the former French vessel the *Commandant Louis Richard,* which was launched at Nantes in 1934. Italy acquired the ship in 1950 and overhauled it to make it suitable for training purposes. It is now used for the training of harbor masters and helmsmen.

The *Palinuro* is a handsome three-masted ship. The foremast is 115 feet high and carries four square sails. The mainmast stands 114 feet tall, and the mizzenmast rises 100 feet from the deck. The mainmast and the mizzenmast carry a spanker and a gaff topsail. The ship also carries three jibs and three staysails. The *Palinuro* is able to sail at speeds of 10 knots per hour.

Type: **full-rigged three-master**
Launching: **1936**
Builder: **Blohm & Voss, Hamburg**
Length: **296 ft.**
Beam: **39 ft.**
Depth: **17 ft.**
Displacement: **1,561 tons**
Sail surface: **21,337 sq. ft.**
Auxiliary engine: **750 h.p.**
Crew: **50 seamen and 15 officers**
Cadets: **110**

This ship, part of the U.S. Coast Guard, is one of the last sailing ships to have survived the age of scientific progress. Before the United States acquired the ship it was the German trainer *Horst Wessel,* modeled on the *Gorch Fock,* which was built in 1933. The West German navy owns a replica of the original *Gorch Fock.*

The *Eagle* is rigged like a bark; the foremast and mainmast each carry five square sails, while the mizzenmast is rigged fore and aft. In 1972 the *Eagle* took part in the sailing regatta organized for the Olympics, a cruise of 650 nautical miles from the Solent to Cape Skegen. Commanded by Capt. E. D. Cassidy, the *Eagle* finished third, behind the *Dar Pomorza* and the *Gorch Fock.*

Type: **square-rigged three-master**
Launching: **1937**
Builder: **Framnaes Mek. Werkstad**
Length: **239 ft.**
Beam: **32 ft.**
Depth: **15 ft.**
Displacement: **773 tons**
Sail surface: **13,278 sq. ft.**
Auxiliary engine: **450 h.p.**
Crew: **15 seamen and 6 officers**
Cadets: **88**

This is one of the largest and most fascinating training ships in the world. It belongs to the *Oestlandres Skoleskib* of Oslo. The three masts carry a total of 15 square sails, as well as 5 jibs at the bow and 6 staysails. Every year the *Christian Radich* makes training cruises in the North Sea, the Atlantic, and the Mediterranean.

Every other year since 1956 England has organized Operation Sail, with competitions between the various major training ships. In 1972 the *Radich* took part in the Helsinki-Falsterbo regatta across the Baltic. The ship then proceeded to Kiel for the Olympics celebrations. The *Radich* participated in the celebration of America's Bicentennial in New York Harbor on July 4, 1976.

United States

A privately-owned vessel, the *Black Pearl* is one of the most beautiful and precise reconstructions of a late 19th-century American brig. The ship is the property of Barclay H. Warburton, and it makes annual training cruises with a complement of 13, five officers and eight trainees. For the most part these men are cadets of the American merchant marine. Cruising on the *Black Pearl* serves as an excellent introduction to sail navigation as well as illustrating some of the finer points. Since the ship is not equipped with the usual array of modern technical devices, sailing the *Black Pearl* can be a real test of a seaman's mettle.

Needless to say, sailing this ship, one of the smaller training ships, has nothing in common with cruising offshore for pleasure. Handling the rigging and sailing the ship require a great deal of self-discipline. Thus the crew develop a strong sense of co-operation and a high sense of duty, which make for an excellent esprit de corps.

The young men who sail on the *Black Pearl* acquire fundamental skills and get a taste of the romance of old sailing days.

Type: **brigantine**
Launching: **1951**
Builder: **C. Lincoln Vaughn, Wickford, R.I.**
Length: **66 ft.**
Beam: **15 ft.**
Depth: **6 ft.**
Displacement: **41 tons**
Sail surface: **1,990 sq. ft.**
Auxiliary engine: **150 h.p.**
Crew: **5 officers**
Students: **8**

1952 - Zawisza Czarny II Poland

Type: **three-masted schooner**
Launching: **1952**
Builder: **Stocznia Polnocna, Gdansk**
Length: **141 ft.**
Beam: **22 ft.**
Depth: **14 ft.**
Displacement: **197 tons**
Sail surface: **5,918 sq. ft.**
Auxiliary engine: **300 h.p.**
Crew: **20 seamen and 4 officers**
Cadets: **25**

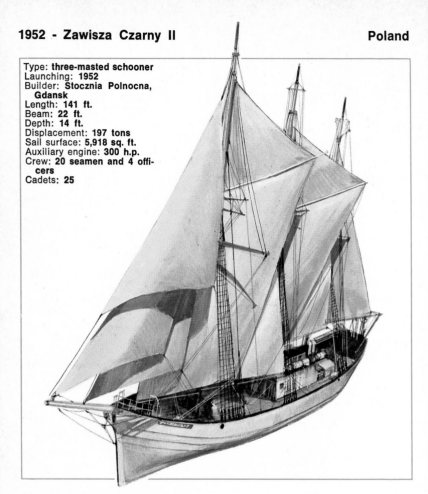

The *Zawisza Czarny II* is one of the finest schooners in the world. It belongs to the *Zwiazek Harcerstwa Poliskiego* of Kollberg and serves as a training ship for Polish merchant officers. It carries an impressive amount of sail. The three masts, which decrease in height from bow to stern, carry four jibs, three spankers, and three gaff topsails, the traditional arrangement of schooner sails. This amount of sail surface and its smooth lines make this ship a veritable flyer on the seas.

The schooner is a frequent choice for naval training, because of its sails. The Polish navy has two other fine ships with the same rigging. These vessels are the *Lew Morza* and the *Janek Krasicki.*

Type: **three-masted schooner**
Launching: **1965**
Builder: **Richard Dunston Ltd., Yorkshire**
Length: **150 ft.**
Beam: **27 ft.**
Depth: **16 ft.**
Displacement: **299 tons**
Sail surface: **8,790 sq. ft.**
Auxiliary engine: **240 h.p.**
Crew: **8 officers and 3 seamen**
Cadets: **44**

Great Britain, like the northern European countries, has maintained a tradition of sail. Per capita, it has more sailing ships than almost any other country in the world. Although sailing merchant ships have vanished, the Londoner Sail Training Association continues to hold high the practice of sailing as it was in previous centuries.

The *Sir Winston Churchill* and its sister-ship the *Malcolm Miller* are schooners. The *Churchill*'s crew usually consists of 11 men, together with 44 young people between the ages of 16 and 21. Once a year the ship also carries adults. The three masts are made of anodized aluminum and are totally resistant to corrosion. They are about 100 feet high.

School at Sea

The last large sailing ships in the world are training ships, schooners, three-masters, and brigantines that belong to naval academies.

In the age of nuclear propulsion, these last sailing ships may seem an anachronism, but the sailing ship remains the forge where courage, loyalty, and a spirit of sacrifice are formed.

Esmeralda, four-masted Chilean schooner, 1954

Juan Sebastiano de Alcamo, four-masted Spanish schooner, 1927

Danmark, Danish steel three-master, 1933

Sagres, Portuguese three-master, 1937

Gladan, wooden-hulled Swedish schooner, 1947

Index

315

316

Bibliography

BOOKS

Alphandery, Paul. *La Chrétienté et l'idée de la croisade*. Paris: Editions Albin Michel, 1971.

Anderson, Romola, and Anderson, R. C. *The Sailing-Ship, Six Thousand Years of History*. New York: W. W. Norton & Co. Inc., 1961.

Annovazzi, Giuseppe. *50 navi italiane famose*. Milan: U. Mursia & Co., 1971.

Anthony, K. *La Reine Elizabeth*. Paris: Payot, 1971.

Aubin, Georges. *Nous, les Cap-Horniers*. Paris: Flammarion, 1973.

Bass, George F. *Archaeology Under Water*. New York: Penguin Books Inc., 1972.

Bradford, Ernie. *The Wind Commands Me, A Life of Francis Drake*. New York: Harcourt, Brace, Jovanovich, 1973.

Brendon, John. *Great Navigators and Discoverers*. Garden City, N.Y.: Doubleday & Co. Inc., 1972.

Cartier, Jean Pierre. *L'aventure de la Marine*. Paris: Larousse, 1973.

Casson, Lionel. *Illustrated History of Ships and Boats*. Garden City, N.Y.: Doubleday & Co. Inc., 1966.

Clowes, Geoffrey. *Sailing Ships, Their History and Development*. London: Her Majesty's Stationery Office, 1948.

Curti, Orazio. *Modelli navali*. Milan: U. Mursia & Co., 1968.

Daniell, Albert Scott. *Explorers and Exploration*. London: B. T. Batsford Ltd., 1962.

Fisher, Herbert A. L. *History of Europe*. Boston: Houghton Mifflin, 1939.

Hackney, Noel C. *HMS Victory*. Newfoundland, N.J.: Haessner Publishing Inc., 1974.

Hackney, Noel C. *The Mayflower*. Newfoundland, N.J.: Haessner Publishing Inc., 1974.

Hawthorne, Daniel. *Ships of the Seven Seas, The Clipper Ship*. New York: Dodd, Mead and Co., 1969.

Hough, Richard A. *A History of Fighting Ships*. London: Octopus Books Ltd., 1975.

Lacroix, *Les derniers voiliers*. Editions Maritimes et d'Outre-mer, 1970.

Le Scal, Yves. *La grande epopée des Cap-Horniers*. Paris: André Bonne Editeur, 1973.

Lewis, Michael. *L' "Invincible Armada"*. Paris: Payot, 1973.

Lloyd, Christopher. *Batailles navales au temps de la Marine à voile*. Paris: Flammarion, 1973.

Lloyd, Christopher. *Sir Francis Drake*. Mystic, Conn.: Verry, Lawrence Inc., 1957.

Longridge, Charles Nepean. *The Anatomy of Nelson's Ships*. New York: International Publications Service, 1973.

Macaulay, Thomas B. *History of England*. New York: Dutton & Co.

Macintyre, Donald, and Bathe, W. Basil. *Man-of-War*. Portland, Maine: Castle Publishing Co., 1974.

Il Mare, Grande enciclopedia illustrata, 10 vols. Novara: Istituto Geografico De Agostini, 1970.

Martin-Allanic, Jean Etienne. *Bougainville navigateur et les decouvertes de son temps*, 2 vols. Paris: Presses Universitaires de France, 1971.

Masefield, John. *Sea Life in Nelson's Time*. London: Sphere Books Ltd., 1973.

Mordal, Jacques. *Venticinque secoli di guerra sul mare*. Milan: U. Mursia & Co., 1973.

Penrose, Boies. *Travel and Discovery in the Renaissance, 1420–1620*. Cambridge, Mass.: Harvard University Press, 1955.

Phillips-Birt, Douglas. *Storia della marineria*. Milan: U. Mursia & Co., 1972.

Randier, Jean. *Hommes et navires ai Cap Horn*. Paris: Hachette, 1974.

Randier, Jean. *Marine Antiques*. Princeton, N.J.: Pyne Press, 1974.

Santoro, Luciano. *Orizzonte Mare*. Rome: Edizioni Bizzarri, 1970.

Warner, Oliver. *Great Sea Battles*. London: Weidenfeld and Nicolson, 1963.

Warner, Oliver. *The Seas and the Sailors' World*. New York: American Heritage Publishing Co., 1958.

Wilcox, Leslie Arthur. *My Pepys' Navy*. London: G. Bell & Sons Ltd., 1966.

Winter, Heinrich. *Le navi di Colombo*. Milan: U. Mursia & Co., 1974.

PERIODICAL

The Economic History Review. Welwyn Garden City, Eng.: Broadwater Press Ltd.

Printed in Italy